Hobgoblin Apollo

BOOKS BY DONALD SIDNEY-FRYER

Books Written

Songs and Sonnets Atlantean, The First Series (1971)
The Last of the Great Romantic Poets (1973)
Emperor of Dreams: A Clark Ashton Smith Bibliography (1978)
Songs and Sonnets Atlantean: The Second Series (2003)
Songs and Sonnets Atlantean: The Third Series (2005)
The Atlantis Fragments, omnibus collection (2008, 2009)
The Golden State Phanstasticks: The California Romantics & Related Subjects, Collected Essays and Reviews (edited by Leo Grin and Alan Gullette) (2011)
The Atlantis Fragments, the Existing Chronicle: A Vision of the Final Days (2011)
West of Wherevermore: The Wedding Voyage of the Princess Aïs and the Prince Atlantarion (unpublished novella, part of the novel, 2011)
Hobgoblin Apollo: Hobgoblin Run Away with the Wreath of Apollo: A Life of My Own: The Autobiography Of Donald Sidney-Fryer (2016)
The Case of the Light Fantastic Toe, The Romantic Ballet and Signor Maestro Cesare Pugni, A Chronicle and Source Book (forthcoming)

Books Edited

Clark Ashton Smith, *Poems in Prose* (1965)
Robert E. Howard, *Etchings in Ivory* (1968)
Clark Ashton Smith, *Other Dimensions* (1970)
Clark Ashton Smith, *Selected Poems* (1971)
Clark Ashton Smith, *The Black Book of Clark Ashton Smith* (1979)
Ambrose Bierce, *A Vision of Doom* (1980)
Clark Ashton Smith, *The City of the Singing Flame* (1981)
Clark Ashton Smith, *The Last Incantation* (1982)
Clark Ashton Smith, *The Monster of the Prophecy* (1983)
Clark Ashton Smith, *Strange Shadows: The Uncollected Fiction and Essays of Clark Ashton Smith* (with Steve Behrends and Rah Hoffman) (1989)
Clark Ashton Smith, *The Hashish-Eater*, 1922 edition (1990; with CD by D. Sidney-Fryer, 2008)
Margo Skinner, *As Green as Emeraude: The Collected Poems of Margo Skinner* (1990)
Clark Ashton Smith, *The Devil's Notebook* (with Don Herron) (1990)
Nora May French, *The Outer Gate: The Collected Poems of Nora May French* (2009)
Clark Ashton Smith, *The Averoigne Chronicles* (with Ronald Scott Hilger) (forthcoming from Centipede Press)

Books Translated

Aloysius Bertrand, *Gaspard de la Nuit* (2004)

Hobgoblin Apollo

Hobgoblin Run Away with the
Wreath of Apollo

A Life of My Own

The Autobiography of
Donald Sidney-Fryer

Hippocampus Press

New York

Copyright © 2016 by Donald Sidney-Fryer

All rights reserved. Except for review purposes, no part of this book may be reproduced or transmitted in any form or by any means, electronic or mechanical, including photocopying, recording or by any information storage and retrieval system, without permission in writing from the publisher.

Published by Hippocampus Press
P.O. Box 641, New York, NY 10156
www.hippocampuspress.com

Cover artwork and design by Jared Boggess, incorporating a line drawing by Norman Lindsay (1879–1969). Four interior line drawings are also by Norman Lindsay. Norman Lindsay's drawings are © H. C. & A. Glad and are used by permission.
Photo on p. 10 provided by Robert W. Thompson.
Hippocampus Press logo designed by Anastasia Damianakos.

First Edition
1 3 5 7 9 8 6 4 2

ISBN 978-1-61498-167-1

Contents

Hobgoblin Apollo 7
    Induction 11
        I   I Enter a New Dimension 15
        II   Childhood and Family Background 20
        III Schooling and Adolescence 32
        IV Early Sexual Experience 45
        V   Further Schooling and Adolescence 56
        VI Military Service and Young Adulthood 82
        VII U.C.L.A. and Odd Jobs 108
        VIII Later Life and Sexual Experience 127
        IX Northern California: Auburn and San Francisco 154
        X   Sacramento and Beyond 195
        XI Westchester and Back 215
        XII Catching Up 237
    Afterword 271
Odds and Ends 277
About the Poet 381

HOBGOBLIN APOLLO

"HOBGOBLIN RUNNE AWAY WITH THE
GARLAND FROM APOLLO."
(Gabriel Harvey in a letter to Edmund Spenser, 1580.)

Dedicated to the memory of Constance Loftus,
my first Latin teacher at New Bedford High School
(for the first two of the four years of Latin).

Donald Sidney-Fryer at 26

Induction

In the first of his three autobiographical volumes—*Far Off Things*, *Things Near and Far*, and *The London Adventure*—Arthur Machen forthrightly recognizes and states his indebtedness as a man of letters (not just as a profession but as a vocation in the same fashion as a poet) to the strategic role played in his life by his exceptional, if not in fact unique, place of birth.

> I shall always esteem it as the greatest piece of fortune that has fallen to me, that I was born in that noble, fallen Caerleon-on-Usk, in the heart of Gwent.

Thus in the same way, following Machen in the same vein, do I realize and state my own indebtedness to my own place of birth, New Bedford, Massachusetts, as a solid part of New England, no less than of the eastern seaboard of the United States of America.

If Caerleon-on-Usk began life as the Isca Silurum established by the Second Augustan Legion of the Imperial Roman Army, and accordantly claimed a glorious past, thus in a parallel way did New Bedford begin as a Quaker village established sometime in the seventeenth century, as a seaport located on the western shores of the tidal and very deep Acushnet River across from the eponymous Fairhaven immediately to the east. In time New Bedford easily surpassed its maritime neighbor as a major port and commercial center. Eventually it became the greatest whaling port in the U.S. and in the world, no less than the wealthiest city on the entire East Coast at the start of the Civil War.

The city held this distinction only for about a year, that of 1861, before other East Coast cities eclipsed it. That one year marked the apogee, if not the apotheosis, of the whaling industry but not quite of the virtual decimation of the different species of the whales themselves worldwide. That phenomenon would happen later, during the later nineteenth century and the first quarter of the twentieth, when the very last whaling voyage out of New Bedford took place around 1924. Although this ocean city did in fact become the preeminent whaling port in the world, other towns and cities took part in this maritime industry, or wholesale butchery, which it also was, if the reader might prefer that latter phrase. These communities included Sag Harbor, Fall River, Martha's Vineyard, Nantucket, and Gloucester.

Before whaling began close by in the offshore waters of the Northeast, the oceans abounded with all manner of cetaceans, these being for the most part gentle and peaceful creatures. It was the rare whale that attacked whaling ships and their crews, even if as recorded it did happen at least once. It requires nowadays a real effort to imagine the sheer abundance of all these whales throughout the oceans of our planet Earth, never mind the sheer abundance of all marine life. The whales teeter still on the brink of extinction, and we the human species have almost exhausted the major stocks of fish by means of our inexhaustible and insatiable hunger. This remarkable feat has taken us not quite a hundred years.

If historical whaling in retrospect might have a certain glamour, in terms of the wealth accrued therefrom, we cannot say the same thing for the actual whaling process itself, which constituted a dirty, dangerous, if not filthy business, as practiced before the emergence of the modern factory-style whaling ship. No real danger, at least from the whales themselves, threatens that type of vessel!

Just as American whaling was reaching its peak, as well as the wealth accruing therefrom, a new type of oil, petroleum, was discovered in 1859 in Pennsylvania, which would eventually make whaling oil, if not obsolete, much less in demand. But other factors led to American whaling's decline. First, during the Civil War, many of the whaling and other ships were commandeered by the Union as part of its naval blockade of Confederate ports. Filled with stone as ballast, they were sunk at the entrance of the chief harbors in the South. Second, and much worse, on one occasion many of the remaining whalers overstayed their hunting season in the Arctic, becoming frozen, abandoned, and ultimately destroyed in the hyperboreal ice of winter.

Meanwhile the whaling merchants and captains put their riches to work by establishing textile mills (for making cotton) in New Bedford and Fall River, and providing employment for the French-Canadian emigrants and their families from Québec, Trois-Rivières, and other parts of the original French Canada lying mostly in the east. By the 1930s, in the midst of the Great Depression, the textile industry was itself declining, and the textile mills emigrated to the South, where cheaper labor made it more profitable for them to function. Despite the setback, New Bedford managed to maintain itself as the great city that it remains, presently accounted as the greatest fishing port in the Northeast, if not indeed on the entire eastern littoral of the U.S.

My family on both maternal and paternal sides took part in both the maritime and fabric-making industries. On the Fryer and Fisher side, the Yankee or English line of descent, the family worked as farmers, sailors, fishers, and in the textile mills. On the Teillière and Dufresne side, the French and French-Canadian line of descent, the family worked as farmers and in the textile mills. No record exists of artists, writers, poets, etc., on either side until my own generation. For the most part both sides of the combined overall family preoccupied themselves with raising families and working to support them, the usual story of most families. However, the Dufresne side of the family did give rise to a number of priests, some of whom advanced upward in the ecclesiastical hierarchy, especially one ancestor or (more accurately) predecessor who played a prominent role among the White Fathers in Central Africa, that is, the Congo.

I was born on 8 September 1934 and resided in New Bedford from the mid-1930s until the mid-1950s (around October 1953), and the historical aspects and nuances of my birthplace have exerted a major and continuing influence on my life and my perspective on life in general, even if I have not lived there on any kind of regular basis except briefly and sporadically since 1953. Growing up, I partook of the general so-called classical culture that still prevails there for many cultivated people not just in New England (centered more or less in Boston) but in the Northeast overall. Language and languages; literature in those languages; painting and sculpture; institutions in various civic places, like the theatre, the opera, the musical, the ballet, the symphony, etc., whether native or imported from outside the region, all played their important part in my own formation and education.

This then is the background in which I first appeared (at least in this particular incarnation), in which I grew up and evolved, before settling in California, where I have mostly resided since September 1955. This then is the story of my life. I have tried to tell it as succinctly as possible. Still, I have tried to tell it with enough detail to flesh out more than the bare bones of autobiography.

—Donald Sidney-Fryer

Auburn, California,
17 August 2014

Chapter I. I Enter a New Dimension

What does one remember of one's earliest childhood? I remember quite a bit because over the years since my birth I have often revisited my memories. They remain perfectly vivid. Lest the reader think that I embroider or create out of somewhat vague fantasy—without imagination and fantasy our species cannot function in a mere practical and physical way!—let me define here what fantasy means in its most basic received sense. Fantasy derives from the Greek verb *phantazein*, meaning to make visible or tangible, to realize, in its most fundamental meaning: to make real.

What follows is what I can remember from the perspective of almost eighty years old, minus fifteen days or so, as I begin these memoirs. For all practical purposes I have gone around the sun on our planet Earth eighty times. Measured time remains important: we live in it and by it. Or as I express it elsewhere, "the local non-infinity." I make these memoirs as truthful as I can, as my accumulated years allow me to do, since my birth on 8 September 1934.

Years later I recalled for my mother the immediate circumstances of my birth in time and space—she had largely forgotten them—and as she remembered things with my help, she verified my recollections. What then do I recall of my birth, both before and after? I can't say that I recall my past lives, but I do recall the long sojourn in my mother's womb, a very comfortable time drifting in and out of consciousness, a period that seemed to last forever.

One has no real sense of time until one is born in, or into, a specific dimension, which apparently has existed for an incalculably long period, a dimension receiving as it does the wandering souls from yet further dimensions. No wonder we aspire instinctively back to the womb!—a time of secure and effortless existence. As one deep thinker has expressed it—Ashley Montague, if memory serves—during my life so far (1934–2014), what we really want as adults is a womb with a view. Very well said!

Be that as it may, I can only recall, and vouch for, my very own experience. With a certain dramatic portentousness, I remember my moment of birth, indeed a momentous point in time and space, at least for me. For convenience, whether scientific or not in terminology, we shall refer henceforth to the other state of consciousness, whether in the womb or before the womb, as the other dimension or as the other side, or (let us capitalize it) the Other Side, evidently governed by a different set of rules from those dictated by our common dimension. Some entity of light (an angel?) counseled me, but not in words, the sentiment being unmistakably, "Don't be afraid." Thus love and fear, our two chief emotions, have dominated my own life ever since, love in the womb and afterward, no less than fear in varying doses ever since!

Apart from the older or oldest housing stock inherited from the whaling days, most people resided in usually wooden houses of two or three stories (with modified A-frame roofs), plus an attic for storage and a basement or cellar with furnace and coal supply, a space also usable for storage. For the people who did not own their own homes, and who rented, each floor served for the given family as an individual flat, or as we then termed it, a tenement. My family lived in a six-flat building, three on the north and three on the south. We inhabited the middle flat on the north side.

Our flat resembled all the others: a front chamber, the living room, in our case, with a sofa in the window bay; a middle chamber, which was the kitchen with gas stove and an icebox (served with new ice once a week) in those days before the widespread use of the newfangled refrigerators; and a kitchen that opened into a further space that my parents used as their bedroom. The family usually ate in the kitchen at the kitchen table. Front room, kitchen, and improvised bedroom made up one continuous, more or less open space.

Beyond this lay a regular separate bedroom containing the cribs or beds of my brother and myself, and to one side a bathroom (toilet, wash basin, and bathtub). Whereas the living room overlooked Pleasant Street (running north and south), continuing from the downtown further south, our bedroom looked east out over the multiple railroad tracks and other industrial areas that spread between the apartment buildings and the harbor. However, the big ships usually dropped anchor in the deeper river further south.

My mother gave me birth on the sturdy kitchen table as she did in the case of my brother the year before. While in the throes of giving birth either to my brother or myself, she broke off the edge of one of the flyleaves extended for the occasion, later repaired and glued back on. The same table continued in use for many years after that. If I caused this breakage, I never found out about it until much later. But as for being born, hmm.

There seems to exist a kind of consciousness that can see but without eyes, that can function outside the body. Thus one cradles in the womb, a special place of comfort and protection, for an extended period, and (moreover) drifting in and out of consciousness. I don't recall, nor can I recall, any previous incarnations, but I do remember cradling inside my mother, and also, simultaneously, existing outside her body in some kind of spiritual form, as if I were watching over her, and myself inside her, and as if from the astral plane, to use a New Age term.

This became most pronounced at the time of my birth. Just before emerging from the womb into the outer air, some entity on the Other Side but with me somehow inside my mother, an entity of light (an angel?), spoke to me, but not in words, and the message meant the same as "Do not be afraid." I have never forgotten this, because contrariwise and ironically I have always felt a certain vague fear or even panic. Of course, I have learned to live with this, and it has rarely disturbed me directly. Now I understand this admonition as good general advice.

Once I emerged into the kitchen, following the cutting of the umbilical cord and so forth, my in-body and extra-body states of consciousness united. At first the dimension in which I found myself appeared alien and bizarre. My vision at the very first did not conform to things as I generally see them now. Almost at once the two layers of sight or consciousness, inner and outer, like tracing papers with the same design laid one on top of the other, became as one. Then from that time forward I saw things in the usual three or four dimensions. I was born, I was in a body, I was a baby! The long, laborious process of growing, learning, and "inculturation" in this new space had begun, and occupied my being and attention in full. I had commenced another and utterly novel existence.

On a factual basis I was born to a human male and female on 8 September 1934, to Donald Sidney Fryer (Senior) and Annette Eva Marie Teillière (Fryer). In this case I was the second child, the second son, born on the exact same date as the first birthday of my brother Ronald Jean Fryer. My brother and I both slept in the one regular bedroom, both ensconced in our respective cribs, vaguely aware of the overview accessible to us from the rear apartment windows looking out eastward over those railroad tracks (mostly running north and south), out over and onto the harbor, the Acushnet River, a Wampanoag (Amerindian) name whose meaning I have never ascertained.

Our mother later told us that we functioned as exemplary babies. We lay quiet most of the time, we made little fuss, and we caused no great bother. That could only have happened because Annette took exemplary care of us, changing our diapers and feeding us regularly, but each with a bottle. She had no milk of her own to nourish us. Nevertheless, she functioned as a magnificent mother to us both. That explains it all, even when she had to work outside the house, whether part-time or full-time, usually in one of the textile mills. Her own family had long worked in those same mills, or factories, both her mother and especially her father Jean Teillière. He worked as a so-called mule spinner, supervising the manufacture of especially fine cotton cloth, similar to the bedsheets made available commercially under the name of Wamsutta.

Once a baby has emerged, getting its drink and food and oxygen from and in the Outer World, whether from its mother or from some other person, it can continue to drift in and out of consciousness as it had been doing while cradling inside the mother's womb. My first year or so of existence in that crib in that back bedroom, along with my brother, I drifted pleasantly along the current of domestic life, with no particular intellectuality, nor missing it, since I had not yet discovered it. That would come eventually but only when I learned to read around the age of five or six.

I recall how I gradually learned to focus attention on the course of the day (and somewhat of the night) by watching the patterns of light and shade across the ceiling above and around me. The progression went from the black of late night to the gray before dawn to the first light from the east (coming in through the bedroom window or windows), slowly banishing the darkness. But the shadows remained as they manifested themselves always upon the aboveness of the ceiling. I found all this very easy to do because I seemed to be usually lying on my back.

As the day progressed, the patterns were constantly changing their traceries. Around noon they fell quiet for a while. Then, as the afternoon moved forward, the patterns continued to metamorphose, but their character had changed, since the light now came from the west, only not directly, given the interior arrangement of the rest of the flat. With the advent of night, darkness began to reign, bringing calm and sleep and oblivion, until across the selfsame ceiling a new cycle of light and shade would commence the following day. I never grew tired of this progression, finding it always new and fascinating.

Chapter II. Childhood and Family Background

Sometime during or just after my first year lying on my back in the crib alongside that of my brother, I expanded my territorial surveillance from the restricted but safe region of the crib to another restricted but slightly larger area of the playpen laid out on the floor of the bedroom, and shared (of course) with brother Ron. Soon these protected areas became those of serious play. We did not seem to remain in them very long. We were soon enough playing directly on the floor whether in the bedroom, or then in the main room (or rooms) to the west, where it was easier for the adults to keep an eye on us.

I recall my fascination and strong predilection for building blocks, which allowed me to construct elaborate structures at will and for hours. This established early on in this existence my lifelong preference for architecture. For long hours I would play with the building blocks, creating miniature labyrinths, regular little houses, if not whole towns. I thus tasted early in life the joy of creating my very own world à la Edmund Spenser in *The Faerie Queene* or J. R. R. Tolkien in *The Lord of the Rings*. But then, just as easily, I would conclude the epic of creating a whole world, a whole city, by knocking the entire elaborate structure down in a trice. And then, contrarywise, I would burst into tears over my wanton but enjoyable destruction like that of the Great Cataclysm fabled by Plato for his Atlantis.

No later than when I was two or three years of age, I was already struggling, manfully, to stand, to keep myself erect, and to walk. Because of his modest advance in age over me, my brother always preceded me in these childhood activities, and usually gave me a helping hand whether in word or in deed. I now gratefully acknowledge as a fact that my brother always acted in an exemplary way to make me his buddy and to assist me whenever and wherever he could. I recall one instance of his kindness. Unless this has changed, in Massachusetts, unlike California, pedestrians had to walk defensively against the traffic.

Our mother had carefully taught us to cross the streets only at the corners, and with caution, always heeding the traffic. The drivers in their vehicles did not look after you per se, even if they might have paused before running you down. Ron and I must have been around four and five, respectively. We were crossing Pleasant Street going west not far from home. My brother waited patiently for the vehicles to pass, and then, firmly holding my left hand in his right one, he hustled us to the other side, safe and sound. A small gesture, quite necessary, but reassuring and significant

In fact, I remember one later incident, when we were again crossing the same street in the same direction but in the forbidden middle of the block while a few cars were passing. Did a car hit us, actually hit us? No, but caught off guard by our unexpected movement, the driver of the vehicle put on his brakes in the nick of time and merely gently bumped us. No harm done. We may have gotten a good scare, but we suffered no real damage, shed no tears, and just carried on, like the tough little kids we had become.

During the long process of our growing up, Ronald and I manifested very little sibling rivalry, and that much later, in our teens, and as we approached our teens. But our rivalry proved superficial for the most part, except when it came to certain aspects of drink and food. We insisted on receiving absolutely equal portions, not always easy to arrange. It drove my mother almost crazy at times, but she soon regained her balance as she instructed us firmly not to act like that. Shamefaced, we would reluctantly heed her admonition. I don't want the reader to get the wrong impression. We did not imitate the title character in *The History of Little Goody Two-Shoes* (that nursery tale published in 1765, and perhaps authored by Oliver Goldsmith), that insufferable self-righteous "perfect child" . . . no, we were not two *Little Goody Two-Shoes*, not by any means. We functioned as regular healthy kids, who also tried not to get into any kind of serious trouble out of respect and consideration for our parents, who were always working to feed, clothe, and care for us.

The New Bedford where I grew up, and where I no longer live, has remained more or less the same, with some development and expansion but largely on the edges or outside of the older city. When I was growing up (1934-53), the city had some 100,000 people. Fishing, but no longer whaling, lingered on as a principal industry. Various factories, some of them still textile, made various products, and freight trains duly took them to other cities. The city itself, long and narrow, lay north and south along the Acushnet River, and big ships could enter and dock in the deep-water harbor or channel more or less located where the central part of town lay. The big ships could travel at least that far, and maybe farther.

Built along an extended low ridge (surmounted by County Street) running parallel to the river, New Bedford has three main parts. First and foremost, the central or older core (the city of the whaling days) began at the docks and warehouses, and marched up the hill (the ridge) to the whaling mansions along County Street with its formerly frequent and picturesque elm trees, as they existed before the Dutch elm disease and several hurricanes. The south end was where many Portuguese, mostly immigrants from the Azores, lived. The north end was where many French-Canadians lived and worked. Both in the south end and the north end, once-isolated houses and other buildings from the whaling days had managed to survive intact and in good shape, some of them impressive and easily recognizable.

As I grew up, I mostly circulated in the central and northern parts of town, and rarely in the south end that always appeared more remote and less accessible to me, who walked or took the bus everywhere. Continuing from the older core and going past County Street, the city had also a west end with Buttonwood Park and with many attractive family homes but built later than the whaling mansions. I had relatives living in a detached house in the west end, and because of that I also got to know that part of town somewhat, and better than the south end. This then was and is the old historic city of my youth and youngest adulthood, where I resided from birth until at eighteen I graduated from high school. Instead of going on to college (necessarily on a scholarship), I went into the Marine Corps, to fulfill my military obligation. As I continue to relate my own story, I shall continue to describe New Bedford here and there as I come to wherever the scene takes place.

Outside of our neighborhood I first came to know the city at large as I became acquainted with our family at large, the two sides, the paternal and the maternal, dominated by the two sets of grandparents, each representing a different language and a different culture. Grandfather Fryer and Grandmother Fryer, née Fisher, had produced a large family of five sons, all of whom married and produced yet further offspring. These five sons with one exception lived in and around New Bedford. Sidney Fryer had come to New England as a young man of twenty-one, embarking from Liverpool, England, but his original family home lay to the north, somewhere in Lancashire or even Cumberland, or Cumbria. By the time I came to know him, Sidney had lost all trace of a British accent. Grandmother Fryer came from an old Yankee family, the Fishers (established c. 1650?), centered in Sandwich on Cape Cod. The Fryer-Fishers had survived as farmers, mill-workers, and sailors whether in Old or New England.

Although they spoke English, of course, because of sheer necessity, the other grandparents, the Teillière-Dufresnes had immigrated into New England to work in the textile mills there. As children my brother and I had called them Pépère and Mémère, probably the first words that we learned in French. When he was five or six, Jean Teillière, Pépère, had come with his farming family from Lyon in the south of France, the port of embarcation most likely Marseille. They settled in East Taunton, a farming community north of New Bedford. They had thus emigrated from the former province of Lyonnais, that part west of the Saône and Rhône rivers, whose capital Lyon had flourished as a major city since Roman times (originally Lugdunum), and no less as a celebrated gastronomic center.

Clarice Dufresne, Mémère, had emigrated with her family from Trois-

Rivières (Three Rivers), southeast of Québec, the capital of French Canada. Long established in North America (since 1650?), the Dufresnes had also survived as farmers, but came into New England to work in the textile mills, as did many French-Canadians. Jean and Clarice produced two children, Roland and Annette, and they all resided in the north end of New Bedford. Jean lived a fairly long life, dying in the early 1950s at the age of seventy-two during my junior year in high school (by an odd coincidence Grandfather Fryer died in his mid-nineties but sometime after my senior year). Pépère and I bonded early on, and he remained my favorite grandparent. Although she died when I was about five, I remember Clarice very well, an especially warm and gracious lady. During the several years that I knew her, she impressed me profoundly.

For a variety of reasons, not just because of the "exotic" French language, I always preferred the French side of the family, the Dufresnes being dispersed throughout French Canada and the Northeast (U.S.A.). Our Yankee relatives were decent and hardworking people, but not especially tactile or affectionate, whereas the French side of our family, Pépère and Mémère above all, always demonstrated great warmth and affection for Ronald and myself, with hearty embraces and juicy kisses. It was that physicality which decided me to favor the French side of our extended family. (Also, they were better cooks!)

The Fryer grandparents resided to the south of our flat, not far away (half a mile?), on a quiet street running parallel to the Common (which runs from east to west, where the early settlers grazed their animals in common), now a park broken into a few major sections by several streets going north and south. The Common marches up from Pleasant Street all the way to County Street, on the gradual and easy slope ascending to the top of the city's north-south ridge. Midway of the park an imposing monument with a spire stands in commemoration of the local troops who had taken part in the Civil War. This park had, possibly still has, an immense and imposing beech tree, even if the park itself has far less trees overall than Buttonwood Park in the west end (part of that is a real forest).

Such as they were, the trees in the Common fit in perfectly with the then abundant trees that graced many of the city's boulevards and byways, trees that made the town pleasant and attractive to inhabit. It took only a short walk to go from our flat to visit the Fryer grandparents, who rented and lived in an old but sturdy wooden house from the whaling days. Guided thereto by our mother, Grandmother Fryer often treated us kids to a "tonic" (now called soda pop, and in this case the brand called Moxie), or hot dogs and beans, or doughnuts that she made herself. These last remained a special treat. Another attraction for visiting them: their flat, the first home where we knew them, which consisted of the second story and the finished attic divided into bedroom spaces, otherwise a continuous open area.

The Teillière grandparents lived in the north end, a real distance that we traversed by the then local trolley cars. We mostly visited them on Sundays, arriving in the late morning and staying until the late afternoon, or early evening. Helped by my mother, Mémère served us dinner, not lunch, around noon. Sometimes we stayed for supper. I recall their flat vividly, the second floor of a two-tenement building, oriented south and north. On the southern side we ascended the back stairs (the usual entrance), to enter the kitchen with large pantry (containing stove and icebox), and beyond that the dining and sitting room, and then, behind sliding glazed doors, the fancy, off-limits parlor with fancy furniture and big potted plants, a place used only on holidays or for special events. The front stairs (little used) led down to the front porch. On the western side of their flat and just off the kitchen lay the regular bathroom (toilet, wash basin, and big tub), and beyond that in the corner Uncle Roland's bedroom, and the two separate bedrooms first for Clarice, and then for Jean. Another incentive for visiting them: Clarice, quite a good cook, made better, tastier, and more varied meals, including the usual Sunday-dinner roast meats.

An added attraction for my mother and us kids: Clarice had a sister, also living in the north end, but some distance from their flat, a widow if memory serves (I don't recall ever meeting her husband),

Tante Marie (Aunt Mary). We did not get to know her better until the late 1930s and the 1940s when we moved into a government-sponsored housing project a mile or more from her cute little flat. She later played, but posthumously, an important role in our lives when Ron and I were attending high school.

About halfway through that high-school career, dear sweet Aunt Marie went into the decline that signaled that her death approached. Even while our mother had to work at her regular job at the Capital Theatre, she managed to take care of her aunt (and our great-aunt). Marie's decline and death proved rapid, and in gratitude for her care she left our mother Annette her estate, such as it was—furniture, domestic (mostly kitchen) stuff, personal clothing and jewelry, and several thousand dollars in a savings account. Annette paid off her own debts (around a thousand dollars), and with a major chunk of the remainder she had my brother and myself go to an excellent dentist in Fairhaven across the river. He gave our teeth some proper care, which they needed badly. He then extracted some of our back teeth that had decayed beyond redemption. He also put in new fillings where the dentist could save the teeth. Thank you, dear Tante Marie, for your inadvertent posthumous benefaction!

Clarice and Jean gave Roland the opportunity to attend high school, then the equivalent of college, but he turned it down, going to work at once after grammar school. Annette very much wanted to attend, and expressed that wish, but her parents did not offer her the same chance, and so she too went to work soon after grammar school.

Every Sunday after dinner at noon Jean and Clarice would enact a mildly dissonant ritual but with positive results. To one side of the dining table they each had their own leather (rocking) armchair, facing each other. Here they would sit and confront each other over the activities of the past week. Sometimes this led to a shouting match, which served as a genuine safety valve for both of them. Then they would reconcile, quiet down, and each retire to their separate bedrooms for a Sunday afternoon nap. Sometimes we would nap with them.

A special note on Uncle Roland, who would later live with us off and on. His mother doted on him, his father not so much. I first knew Roland as a handsome, well-formed young man, the size of the average Frenchman of today, say, five foot eight inches. He did not resemble the tall, big-boned French-Canadians, an ethnic reminder of the similar French warriors going back to the Germanic Franks, whose Napoleonic descendants mostly perished on the winter retreat from Moscow out of Russia.

Roland early on became involved with a French-Canadian family headed by a Dr. Pacquin, a family that made their own gin in the cellar of their big house set in a big yard, a handsome and impressive property. Roland first married Jeanne, one of the Pacquin daughters. When she divorced him during or just after World War II, he later married another daughter, Beatrice, best known as Fifi. A third daughter married James Goggin (a postman), and lived in a nice big flat not far away from the Pacquin mansion, in the same city block.

The marriage celebration of Roland and Jeanne turned out to be quite a fancy event, a big catered affair with many guests held in the Pacquins' back yard. One of the bartenders kept giving me, then about five or six, little glasses of alleged orange juice. When Annette found out their mixture to be of homemade gin and orange juice, she put a stop to it and had the bartender give me only orange juice to drink. Later, when we had moved not far from the Pacquin mansion, I would often visit them, especially after beginning to study French in high school, so I could practice the language outside class.

Some random aspects of our life on Pleasant Street still recur to mind, such as when Annette would take an afternoon nap on one of her days off while reclining on the sofa in the window bay (in the living room) facing west. She would sleep away from the light with her back to the back of the sofa, and would have my brother or myself cuddled up next to her, thus facing east and looking through the unencumbered space of the two or three rooms opening into each other. This nearness to Mommy gave me great comfort, a feeling that I can easily still summon today. And yet how long ago that seems, seventy-five years in the past.

Three special events from that early childhood period stand out particularly. First, the great hurricane of 1937, a real shocker. No hurricanes of any real force had evidently happened for quite a little while. The reader might like to look at a map of North America to note how New England (including Long Island) and extreme eastern Canada (Nova Scotia, Newfoundland, and Labrador) jut way out into the Atlantic Ocean. The hurricanes originating in or near the West Indies travel along off the eastern seaboard of the U.S. and often strike New England with full force. Thus it happened the late summer of 1937, totally unexpected except right at the moment the storm arrived.

Damage proved extensive and expensive to repair. The big family cottages made of wood at Horseneck Beach, southwest of New Bedford, suffered near total destruction, tossed around almost like toys. Ancient elms all over the city had fallen, the root systems leaving big holes wherever they were dislodged. The older people in particular throughout the town bemoaned the loss of these and other older trees. The perfect Gothic arches that the elms had made for so long on County Street had now gone forever.

For the night of the storm we had gone over to the home of our paternal grandparents, where we found genuine shelter. We slept in the bedroom spaces up in the finished attic. I can still see Grandma Fryer in her old-fashioned nightgown and mobcap lighting us in our pajamas into bed while literally holding an old-fashioned kerosene-fed hurricane lamp with glass chimney. Carried on the ubiquitous telephone poles, the electric power had failed earlier, late in the afternoon, when Annette had shepherded us over to the parental Fryer household. Despite the howling winds and the torrential rains we felt perfectly safe and slept soundly, thus cozily ensconced very much in an older New England (the house itself), as indeed we were.

The adults had feared that we ran a greater risk of harm if we had stayed at the flat on Pleasant Street, which as it happened we did not.

But better safe than sorry. By the time the storm had passed the next morning, we returned home to find no damage. We did find a lot of water covering the many railroad tracks between our row of tenements and the edge of the harbor to the east. The hurricane received full and ongoing coverage in the local newspapers, above all in New Bedford's own long-established *Standard Times*. Annette dutifully cut out the articles and photos from the latter and made an excellent scrapbook out of them, which may still exist someplace. This great storm remained the first phenomenon to demonstrate to me the puniness of humanity vis-à-vis Mother Nature's inherent and outrageous force. Luckily, overall, we reside on a relatively gentle planet. Otherwise we would not survive.

The second of the three major events from that early childhood period that still stands out: the death of Mémère around 1939, when she must have been in her later fifties or around sixty. (Pépère would outlive her significantly by twelve or fourteen years.) Her funeral took place at a local funeral parlor in the north end of the city. Our mother took us boys to the place, where we saw her ensconced in her fancy coffin. She looked rather nice and at rest. Annette did not tell us that she was dead but only asleep. Later Ron and I figured out that she had actually deceased. I would soon learn to miss her charm and graciousness.

I don't know if I can say that Mémère doted on us, but she certainly loved us vibrantly. I still feel that vibrancy from across the years. She had a warmth of personality that always appeared so different from the Yankee reserve of Grandma Fryer. I recall when my mother bought Ron and me some delightful matching cowboy outfits. One of my parents took snapshots of us outside arrayed in those outfits. With our hair neatly parted and combed, while we held the cowboy hats in hand, I must say that we looked like a couple of cute little boys. Thanks to our mother's admonitions we also behaved quite well in private and public, which caused adults to regard us as "darling." Mémère loved how the two of us looked in those cute outfits. We wore them several times on the Sundays that we spent with Mémère and Pépère. Bless you, dear Mémère, wherever your spirit may have emigrated!

The third special event that I recall vividly turned out to mark the very end of that first phase of childhood, but not necessarily the end of childhood innocence. I was four or five, and Ron five or six. My mother and father separated, and when we were seven and eight, respectively, they divorced. My father moved rather dramatically out of the flat. My parents had had a series of quarrels that led to the final one. Donald Senior (I was the Junior) in his frustration kicked the metal kitchen trash container (the type with a lid controlled by a pedal at the bottom) so hard that he actually dented it with the tip of the hard leather shoe on his right foot. I should mention that, before Ron and I arrived on the scene, my parents for a brief time resided with my mother's parents. There my father, I think, felt outclassed in a household that spoke French as much as, if not more than, English. My father spoke little French or none at all, nor as an Anglophone New Englander would he have felt obliged to do so.

Although people did not then use terms like First World, Second World, etc., they can apply retroactively just as well to describe some aspects of life in the 1930s, 1940s, and 1950s. The difference between the old established New Englanders (such as Grandma Fryer's Fisher family), the real Yankees, and the "foreign" French-Canadian immigrants working in the textile mills in New Bedford and Fall River could not have made a greater contrast. That the Yankees might on occasion manifest a certain superiority in regard to this then minority should come as no surprise. It still happens, or something like it, as in the case of non-Hispanic natives in the U.S. in regard to Hispanic immigrants today.

Even if my paternal grandparents had patronized Ron and me to some slight extent (because of our "foreign" mother), it went unnoticed, but I may have felt it ever so subtly, and Ron felt it more than I. We both liked hot dogs and beans quite a bit, but my brother pointed out to me many years later that Grandma Fryer almost always fed us that combination when we visited her and Grandpa, as if they represented the First World, and we the Second, or even Third, World. If they did, they intended nothing malicious or malevolent: no, not at all. If the Yankee side looked askance at us, Annette and the boys, I remained blithely ignorant of it, since the uncles, aunts, and cousins on my father's side usually treated us with warmth and respect. A minor point at best and not to be blown out of proportion. Something would arise much later, during the time I was coincidentally in the fourth grade, but I shall deal with it at that time.

Chapter III. Schooling and Adolescence

During my childhood and early schooling—after my birth, after entering this dimension, after starting yet another incarnation—the memory of the moment when I was born, just before and after it, would return every now and then to haunt me and cause me to wonder profoundly, and not just the "Don't be afraid" communicated to me by the entity of light. I recall especially with what intense, yearning eagerness I had wanted to be born, such burning eagerness as to exist beyond words, in utter literalness, "ineffable." This recollection made me pause every time it visited me, even if it was comparatively rare. I kept these particular memories to myself. Meanwhile my day-to-day life continued as usual.

Sometime after the break-up of my father and mother, Annette and we two boys moved away from Pleasant Street near the waterfront, some real distance westward, inland, and a little upland into a marginally better neighborhood. There we occupied the upper flat of a rather nice tenement building on the northwest corner where two streets crossed each other at right angles. The new flat had fairly ample space, definitely more than that on Pleasant Street. Before we moved, we may have stayed briefly with Aurilla Branchard, a great good friend of my mother's. Aurilla had two boys herself about our age and plenty of room in her flat to accommodate the three of us. She remained our steadfast friend through thick and thin. Of course, we attended a new school, the one on Kempton Street.

Our first school stood (probably still stands) some distance away from our flat on Pleasant Street, and near the home of the Fryer-Fisher grandparents. The school and grounds occupied a whole city block, a small square one. A sturdy brick structure, it rose up in the middle of an asphalt-covered schoolyard, with a full basement (with the windows plainly visible), a first story, and a second story, all covered by a mansard roof (probably with dormers), thus a fourth story containing usable space for school supplies and so forth. We did not attend this school for very long, kindergarten for me, and first grade for my brother, before we moved into the new flat.

With Mémère gone, Uncle Roland did not wish to continue living with his father in their old flat. Thus he came to live with us, paid for room and board, and helped his sister out with the rent and household expenses. This happened before he married Jeanne Pacquin. My mother occupied one bedroom, we boys another, and Uncle Roland yet another. The apartment had the usual complement of kitchen (where we usually ate) with pantry, a regular bathroom, and both a front room and a middle room that opened into the front one. Uncle Roland would continue living with us, off and on, over a period of many years, and was generally (emotionally and morally) supportive of Annette and us kids. Often on Sundays, no matter where we lived, Pépère would come over and eat noontime dinner with us.

The Kempton Street School, another brick building, had greater space whether in regard to the structure or the schoolyard. In the main Ronald and I functioned as good but not great students, attentive and obedient and respectful toward our teachers. We generally liked school and did well by the instruction given us from the dedicated staff. At some point for some reason Ron became dissatisfied with the school routine and became truant. After the first day of such (at first unbeknownst by me) he enlisted me in his truancy. However, after two days of absence from the school (we hid out in the cellar of our tenement building), the authorities informed our mother. She duly punished and sternly admonished us not to play truant again, but to make sure that we went to school, or else! Quite frankly I preferred the regular school routine (we both got along well with the other kids) to hiding out in a cellar, waiting for the daytime to pass!

I recall another special memory before we moved from Pleasant Street. Schooling includes, of course, much more than just attending a series of schools, but involves education in general, which can include almost anything else, if not everything: excursions, socializing with the family at large as well as outside the home, and so forth. The following experience falls under the heading of education at large. The last episode of Ken Burns's excellent landmark series *The Civil War* reminded me of it years ago, when it first aired on television. The last episode shows the veterans (already at an advanced age) of both the Union and the Confederacy by then convening in friendship and camaraderie, as they had already done at similar conventions. Only now, the latter 1930s, it marked the very last such occasion, or some such.

I remember Annette taking Ron and me during the latter 1930s to the Civil War monument in the Common during a celebration in honor of New Bedford's local Civil War veterans, that is, what remained of them. At the age of four or five I had no real concept of history, apart from the whaling days, certainly none of the Civil War. But to this day I recall with poignancy how tenderly the people in attendance at the event in general treated these venerable men, as they moved slowly and with difficulty, assisted by their own families or by other people, some with canes, some leaning on walkers, some in wheelchairs. By the early 1940s, only a few years later, the ancient veterans had all disappeared.

To avoid endless repetition, let me reiterate here: my brother was exactly one year older than I, and one year ahead of me in school. If I don't always mention him (except, for example, as in the case of his truancy), it is because I have no need to stress the slight difference in age and school class: our lives became quite integrated early on.

I should mention that, as part of my Yankee cultural education away from my formal schooling, I heard from very early on, when I was around Grandpa and Grandma Fryer (especially the latter), much older English speech surviving from the early colonial period, except dialectical in the British Isles. I heard not just rather odd idiomatic phrases (like "Put plug in hole" for "Close the door") but also uncommon words, usages, and so forth. Some of these older words occur on occasion in my poetry, but they should not jar the reader's linguistic sensibility unduly. I have carefully integrated them into the overall web of sound and style. The point here that I wish to make: I have acquired all such words legitimately as part of the process of growing up in Massachusetts, that is, in New England, first settled in the early seventeenth century.

As soon as I learned to read (at the age of five in kindergarten), I began going to the main library in downtown New Bedford in the civic center (at first almost exclusively utilizing the large juvenile room, until I went into high school, at which time I could begin using the adult section or sections, that is, all the remainder, the major part, of the library). The main library is a solid and magnificent structure with two Doric columns inside the recessed portico in front, all constructed out of granite like several other buildings dispersed throughout the city. I shall describe some of these later, all impressive.

In front of the library on the right hand side (as you face the structure) there stands a striking and celebrated monument in honor of the whaling days, realized in cast metal. A handsome and muscular man stripped to the waist is about to launch a hefty harpoon into some unsuspecting cetacean (not shown). He stands in the prow of a whaling rowboat, only shown in its front half, and in front of an upright rectangle of stone with the well-known inscription: "A dead whale or a stove boat." (Indeed!) I continued using, and borrowing from, the main library until I went into military service at the age of eighteen after graduating from high school.

My mother was Catholic, but although my father was not (he was a Christian, of course), he permitted my mother to have us baptised and raised as Catholics. We never attended parochial school, only public school on a regular basis. Quite early on as well, we began attending catechism class (as part of being Catholic) on Saturday mornings at a parochial "academy"–Sacred Heart School, where both nuns and priests taught. However, because of my early reading, I soon became aware of a major discrepancy between religion and the world at large. I gradually developed a distaste for Catholicism, even while I continued to go to church per my mother's preferences.

Despite my early and enduring antipathy toward my childhood "religion," and aesthetically the instinctive revulsion that it created in me—even if I did enjoy the churches themselves, the priestly robes, and the whole paraphernalia of the mass along with the church rites and rituals—a wonderful volume came to my rescue, a copy of which I discovered in the fourth grade but at home, a volume filled with many photos of Greek and Roman sculpture—*The Age of Fable* by Thomas Bulfinch (sometimes titled *Bulfinch's Mythology*). I found the stories in that volume far more interesting and satisfying than the meager and sanctimonious myths propagated in catechism class. Well now, I thought to myself, the Graeco-Roman mythology sounds a lot more like genuine religion than the ugly fairy tales narrated by the Catholic priests and nuns about Jesus Christ and his crew.

Although school by necessity loomed large in the life of Ron and myself, if not indeed paramount; and although the individual teachers who taught us in grammar school performed an essential part in that life; my teachers overall did not play an important *personal* role for me until I entered high school, when I developed special friendships with certain selected instructors. Those early years coincided with a remarkable political development. The first eleven years of my own life I spent under the federal administration of Franklin Delano Roosevelt. His presidency lasted from 1933 until 1945, when he died in April at some resort in Georgia, and thus the only presidency that I knew from childhood onward, until Harry S Truman, elected as vice president, succeeded him in due course. Elected for an unprecedented four consecutive terms, FDR "presided" as the head of our government for not quite the duration of those four terms.

FDR created certain sustained innovations and conditions that greatly benefited the working classes, no less than the working poor, and their families, including myself, in terms of long-lasting health. During the 1930s and later, the public schools received many benefits thanks to FDR's enlightened administration. The federal government subsidized X-ray examinations (to detect tuberculosis) for schoolchildren everywhere. The kids also received free whole milk in school (in pint-sized cartons), along with Graham crackers, which went down well with the milk. As children of the working poor, Ron and I considered the milk and Graham crackers a real treat, and one that really gave us some nutrition.

We did not remain in that new neighborhood, nor at the Kempton Street School, for very long—no more than one or two years. We did get to know rather well our neighbors right next door on the north, who resided in their own detached house, the McGinnis family. We became real friends with them. Before we moved to a brand-new housing project in the north end of New Bedford, I somehow became enamored of the idea of running away from home, or less dramatically, simply of leaving it. Why, I can't remember. I had no complaints, and I did well in school and at home. A strange fancy, I guess, possibly influenced by my reading children's fiction borrowed from the juvenile room at the downtown public library.

For some reason Jeanne Pacquin (not yet my Uncle Roland's wife) had walked south from her home, the family mansion on Coggeshall Street, and then walked back. (Jeanne was a beautiful and classy woman, always kind to us kids.) I had already declared my intention to run away from home. No one demurred, but bided their time to see what would happen. Holding her hand and a few of my possessions (including my toothbrush), I accompanied Jeanne on what I assumed would turn out to be the first step or phase of my running away. I had a vague idea that I would first sojourn with the Pacquins, but Jeanne seemed rather dubious about that when I mentioned my plan. She would need to discuss it with her parents and family. This made me think. We had only gone a few blocks north toward the Pacquin mansion when I became beset with some serious doubts and misgivings. I started to weep, asking her if I could please change my mind. The reality of my situation had hit me: was I leaving my home with mother and brother forever? With a kind but knowing expression Jeanne smiled and guided me back home. My mother greeted me warmly, embraced and kissed me. I began weeping and sobbing all over again.

Once my little emotional tempest had blown over, I firmly declared that I never wanted to leave home again (that is, on a permanent basis) in order to live elsewhere, at least for a then undetermined period of time. And I didn't leave until I entered military service at the age of eighteen in October 1953, having graduated from high school the preceding June.

Pépère! I have already touched upon Jean Teillière, but here I shall devote a whole section to him. Of all my relatives, apart from my mother—beyond my brother, my father, and my stepmother—Pépère became and remained my favorite. Otherwise Mémère would have fulfilled that role, but her early death when I was five prevented that. Among all my adult relatives Pépère certainly stood out. Although not vulgar, nor yet using vulgar language, he always expressed himself in a forthright manner, perhaps not always discreetly but genuinely, mentioning topics and subjects in such an honest way that it remained unparalleled among my experience of older people, the all-powerful adults (or so I thought), including my teachers.

Jean did not concern himself with what we call today political correctness. He projected a definite glee whenever taking an unpopular viewpoint or position. He rarely or never spoke with malevolence or maliciousness, but delighted in pricking the balloons of overweening ego or of sheerly ridiculous persons or things that took themselves too seriously or presented themselves as gospel truth—that is, whenever he discovered them, which happened often enough to call conspicuous attention to them. Although we did not see him all the time, we saw Pépère often enough that we could easily follow his particular career. After Mémère died, Jean moved out of their flat and paid room and board in the flat of a neighbor lady a few tenements away. Pépère probably retired sometime during the middle or later 1940s when he turned sixty-five or somewhat later, and was to die in the autumn of 1951.

Surely a solid part of our education in the broadest sense, Pépère played an important role in the life of my brother and myself. Jean relished his position as grandpère, and often on Saturdays, Sundays, or holidays he took us to places throughout New Bedford or outside of it via the trolley cars. Dressed in our Sunday or holiday best, we went to various amusement parks in our region, starting before we began attending school. First he took us to Acushnet Park way down in the south end of town just off the waterfront. The great hurricane of 1937 destroyed it and, if memory serves, the owners did not rebuild it. My favorite ride there remained the merry-go-round, a gorgeous, glittering affair full of little mirrors and other reflecting devices, not to mention the several circles within circles of the sculptured wooden horses brilliantly painted and often moving up and down.

Next he took us to the biggest amusement park in our over-all area, Lincoln Park, halfway between New Bedford and Fall River to the west. It required a fairly long but fun ride to get there via trolley car, going up and down a series of low hills, a ride that I thoroughly enjoyed. The park itself had every kind of ride or amusement happening at that time in such parks, plus the usual eats as hot dogs, hamburgers, popcorn, cotton candy, soda pop, candied apples, and so forth. But the real thrill for me was to ride the trolley car there and back, the only time that the vehicle truly managed to build up some relative speed while traveling inside its own special series of "islands" fixed in the middle of the highway between the two major textile cities. Once at the end of the line, marked by the amusement center itself, the conductor would push the backs of all the seats in the opposite direction. As I recall, the seats (inside metal boundaries) were made out of narrow strips of bamboo, plaited closely together: not especially comfortable, but endurable enough for the passengers, and long-lasting. As kids we felt no discomfort sitting in such straight seats.

Once we entered high school, our studies and grades claimed priority, but on one occasion at least Pépère took me out of school (with my mother's permission) for a special excursion. First we bussed to Taunton, the seat of Plymouth County, and from there to East Taunton. There the Teillière family had first settled when they emigrated from Lyon or from near that city. But now, en route on the bus, Pépère regaled me with the glories of East Taunton, projecting it as a city as great as, or greater than, the capital of Massachusetts, to wit, Boston. Of course, I suspected that he was joking, and I realized for a fact that he was when we finally arrived at our destination. It turned out to be a small, unpretentious, but still picturesque rural community, a farming village. We sat on a park bench, and after Jean entertained me for a while commenting on the town and the townspeople going by, we found a restaurant, ate a late lunch, and bussed back home. The excursion had occupied the major part of the daytime hours, to go there and then return. It probably happened in the spring of 1951.

I recall one especial moment from the excursion, and this typified one of the reasons why I loved my grandpère—his honesty. While we were sitting on that park bench in East Taunton, a cute, chic, and very attractive young woman went by at a little distance from us. Jean turned to me and quietly asked me if I could see this lovely apparition. I said yes, and then he said, "That young woman thinks that she has the world by the ass, but the truth is, it's the world that has got her by the ass." Although she could not have heard us, I still tried to suppress my laughter, but not with any great success.

Wherever we ended up moving, Pépère continued coming to Sunday or holiday dinner (usually around noon), especially after we moved to Presidential Heights, the housing project, thus closer to his home in the north end of town. And whenever he visited us, Jean always provided a sense of clandestine amusement, tied in as it was with a certain unpredictability, albeit proper in a civilized manner.

Movies and radio programs at that period provided not just the chief entertainment but often considerable education in their own peculiar way. The movies in general, especially with their usually first-rate artistic direction (at least as demonstrated in the best films), provided a rich and abundant education in aesthetics, above all in the historical movies, often endowed with excellent music expressly composed or adapted from the symphonic repertoire of classical music, from Haydn and Mozart through Tchaikovsky and Rachmaninoff. My brother and I saw many movies, good, bad, and indifferent, while we grew up. When we moved into the housing project, Annette got a job working at the Capitol Theatre in the north end, sometimes at the candy counter, but more often as a cashier selling tickets inside a small contained chamber the size of a very big box at the front of the lobby under the movie marquee, hot in the summertime and very cool in the winter.

Father worked in a first-run house with one change of feature and co-feature per week; mother in a second-run house with two changes of feature and co-feature per week. Father's house, the Olympia Theatre (which occupied almost an entire city block in the downtown area), specialized in movies made by MGM and Paramount (including the De Mille epics). My mother's movie house specialized in movies made by 20th Century–Fox and Warner Brothers, but also showed many undistinguished films, formulaic and artistically dismal. I saw my first movie at the age of three. I shall discuss the movies in greater detail, including my favorite films, but later, primarily during my last years in high school.

During the 1930s and 1940s the Roosevelt administration subsidized the construction of low-rent housing projects across the country. Our city, no exception, had at least several of these, one in the south end, and one in the north, the latter west of the older settled part. They provided excellent but not spacious living quarters, well heated (often too much so) in winter. The project into which we moved, Presidential Heights, a large long rectangular space longer than wide, extended up and across an easy slope from a low flat area to the east all the way up and west to Mt. Pleasant Street.

Beyond the street lay quite a sizeable cemetery extending west in two parts, one on the south, one on the north. Later the graveyard also served as an impromptu playground, even if we had several regular playgrounds inside the housing project. To the north and south of Presidential Heights lay mostly undeveloped big city blocks, semi-parklike areas with few or no houses but with trees and bushes. The block on the north had several baseball and softball diamonds. The undeveloped areas also served as impromptu playgrounds.

The individual apartments ran to ten per one big housing block, mostly two stories, made out of brick and cement, each block set amid front and back yards furnished with lawns (which the tenants cut themselves), but with few trees. However, the ambient areas around the project had plenty of trees and bushes. The housing blocks, each one about one hundred feet long, extended three across in rows that marched up the easy slope from low to high, from east to west, all the way to Mt. Pleasant Street.

To the east, low-lying and occupying a roughly rectangular but immense city block, lay the ruins, the foundations, of an old textile mill, whose owners had apparently moved to the South during the 1930s, where the labor cost less. Wonderfully evocative—I could fancy them as from antiquity—the ruins had become utterly overgrown with trees, bushes, and vines; and flooded by our occasional rains over a long period of time, they had metamorphosed into swamps filled with bulrushes, cattails, and (in the warmer weather) gigantic garden spiders that spun beautiful webs. The authorities had allowed part of the immense city block to become a municipal dump that quite gradually took over almost the entire space of the former mill. Of course, we kids also took it over as yet another playground, but all the better for its wildness.

Within easy reach of the western, upper end of the housing project, and south of the cemetery, occupying a full two acres, stood Mt. Pleasant Grammar School, a very large two-story rectangular structure with a full basement, made out of brick, wood, and cement. This very well-constructed building also had a large auditorium (with space in front of the stage for a small or medium-sized orchestra). Mt. Pleasant, thus a complete grammar school, offered all the classes from kindergarten through the seventh and eighth grades. This then was the principal school that my brother and I would attend, I during grades two through eight, Ron during grades three through eight. It possessed a big beautiful lawn in front to the east and on the sides, and an enormous playground in the back to the west. Beyond the street bounding the playground on the west there lay more undeveloped land whose trees and bushes and open areas also served as impromptu playgrounds.

Our mother applied for one of the new apartments, and had no trouble obtaining it, No. 155, located in the middle of the second row of the big housing blocks that marched up the slope, where in the middle stood the office building where Annette paid the nominal rent of $7.00 per week. The apartment had two rooms downstairs, kitchen and large storage closet on the east with back door, living room and staircase on the west with front door. Upstairs it had two bedrooms, each with its own closet, mother's room on the east, and that of us boys on the west. The regular bathroom in the corner lay next to Annette's bedroom.

We would live there for quite a long stretch of time, from when we moved in, the early 1940s, until one by one we each moved out. I did so when I entered the military in the autumn of 1955. Ronald moved out after he graduated from New Bedford Textile Institute or sometime during his last years there. He attended the college during the years 1952-56. Annette herself did not move out until the last years of her life; her second husband found a new rental home for them out in the lovely countryside, the duplex in rural Mattapoisett en route to Cape Cod.

The big move to Presidential Heights as well as to Mt. Pleasant Grammar School effectively signaled the end of our childhood and the start of our adolescence. The move remained a major landmark in the family life of Annette and her two boys. We now lived closer to Grandpère, to the Pacquins, and to the Capitol Theatre, where our mother presently obtained the job that lasted for her until she went to work for her brother, our Uncle Roland, and as the chief "clerk" for the dry-cleaning business in Fairhaven that her brother had started or had bought. Later during high school both Ron and myself would work at this dry-cleaning shop. Working and sometimes overnighting across the Acushnet River turned into a real treat for all of us. (Roland continued living with us while we resided in the housing project until he married his second wife and lived in his own residence not far from his business.) Fairhaven to this day remains an especially lovely town, but minimally changed since the whaling days.

Chapter IV. Early Sexual Experience

My earliest sexual experience of any kind happened when I was four (mother and brother had gone elsewhere). An eight-year-old girl was babysitting me. She had me take off my clothes. She had already uttered the sacred mantra in regard to the private parts of the body: "If I show you mine, then you show me yours." I would hear this often from boys and girls throughout my childhood, but mostly in adolescence. I noted the anatomical difference, but there was little to notice in or on her body, at least to my untutored eye. She attempted some sexual play but at that early age I could not respond. I had no physical sexual sensitivity. The sexual nerve endings had not yet developed. This first affair simply remained a curious episode that I never mentioned to anyone. Life was odd and mysterious, and this was just another odd mystery.

As to my earliest *meaningful* sexual experience, let me reminisce. I was eight and in the second grade, and we had already moved to the housing project, around which I often walked, wandering in different directions when I was not attending school. To the south and north there lay big undeveloped city blocks with woods and open spaces. Beyond the big block on the north (largely given over to baseball diamonds) there lay a much larger undeveloped territory, especially beyond the railroad running east and west, a space dominated by a continuous woodland, which early attracted my wanderlust as a favorite destination, as it did that of other guys—and with good reason, as I would soon discover.

On this occasion I had walked halfway through it, going north, when I turned west, coming out into a clearing before entering out on the sidewalk next to the street. I noticed a handsome young man, somewhere between fifteen and eighteen, and hardly had I turned west when I paused. The young man had come up silently behind me and grabbed me but not roughly. He covered my mouth with his left hand and put his hand over my crotch with his right. As he did this, he said, "Jerk me off." I became sexually excited rather than scared, even if I did not yet know much or anything about masturbation. I was already big for my age, especially my penis, but after this experience I worked at enlarging it. The young man probably thought that I was in my early teens.

Later I learned that the woodland served as a place where guys picked each other up for immediate homosexual activity, and thus the young man assumed that I had gone there for the same purpose, a safe assumption on his part. We had sheltered behind some bushes. He pulled down my pants, and from behind me he had me hold his big, already adult cock. I noted how much bigger he was than I. He had me feel his, and even if I felt a little scared, this mutual feeling-up turned me on, although I had not quite yet discovered solo sex, or masturbation. But I did soon, and did I ever! The cute guy kept playing with me, to get me a hard-on, while he was pressing his cock-head against my asshole. He inserted a couple of fingers to help loosen me up.

It worked. Finally he inserted the big head of his big fat cock, and the anus opened up for him, as he slowly slid his member on into my gut, doggie-style. He had spread his jacket on the grass, where I lay flat on my stomach. It did not feel uncomfortable, although I mistook it for a fecal-rectal sensation. This intimacy greatly excited me, and thus I received my very first feeling of something uniquely sexual. The fucking did not last long, only five or ten minutes. At last he withdrew and let me get up. He had reached his climax, but quietly. I pulled my pants back up, and buckled my belt. He smiled and nodded, and said that I could go. Although he had continued to play with me, I did not quite develop a full hard-on. I did have a big dick for a kid of eight, no kidding and no boasting.

Confused, I left him. Should I tell my mother what had occurred, or just keep it quiet? I chose the better part to keep it quiet. I chose the better part, to keep it all to myself as it had happened. After I left him, I became sexually excited and ran back to find him for more sexual fun, but he had gone. Many times after that I would return to seek him out, but I never found that beautiful older teenager again. The wilderness coupling had made me horny for more clandestine sex-play with guys—which did happen, and with marvelous ease. No one talked about sex—you knew that it was all weird the way people actually carried on—but most everyone was having sex in some form or fashion, especially the younger people.

Although I never had anal sex (receptor) again until my middle or early twenties, this early episode in time became a treasure for me, because I knew that I as a male could pleasure another guy in a deep and intimate way. Years had to pass before I found out directly how much sex-play was happening at that time in my own backyard, as it were. Guys married and unmarried were having sex with other guys on into middle age and later. One special episode took place when I was in the fourth grade, and when, as the spring was warming up, I did something original for my time and age. I had turned eleven in September 1944. A full moon was approaching, and when I went out alone that certain evening, it coincided with the full moon. This happened in the big undeveloped lot to the south of the housing project, in a glade amid the trees and bushes, and unobserved.

I had removed my clothing apart from my briefs, which I had rolled up to look like a loincloth. I kept my socks and shoes on, and necessarily, as I had realized via a fast experiment without them. I had a painfully hard erection. I took it out and gamboled a little over the immediate area while I handled myself. I went back to my clothes and masturbated until I attained that eternally shattering climax. I dressed and went home to bed. I have never forgotten that real-life episode, because it gave me assurance of sexual adventure in the years to come. That full moon became for me a sexual eucharist, a manifestation as of the monstrance presented on rare occasions during the Roman Catholic mass.

At a certain point (otherwise involved with my serious studies in late grammar school and all of high school), I moved away from Presidential Heights as a regular place to hang out with kids my own age, finding such in other neighborhoods. As in the Cub Scouts and Boy Scouts, new sexual adventures opened up for me as I went home from the scout meetings while en route.

Thanks to our father's generosity to get us out of the city, qua city, my brother and I went to various summer camps from our early teens onward. Phantastisch!—thanks, Dad! First, Camp Clark, solidly located in the western part of Cape Cod, and inland. We had gone from Cub Scouts to Boy Scouts, and I at thirteen and Ron at fourteen would spend our first and quite extended sojourn at the Boy Scout camp, aptly named Camp Cachalot (the sperm whale!), situated in that little southeast corner of Massachusetts not far from the southern entrance into the great Cape Cod Canal with its two magnifick official bridges that spanned it at the north and south ends.

The camp had five residential units, each containing big and small tents raised up atop sturdy wooden platforms. On the eastern side of the lake, units one through three, going from south to north. On the western side, units four and five, going also from south to north. South of unit four there lay the mess hall or tent (on a platform, of course) with adjoining kitchen (a regular wooden structure). Each unit had its own unit leader and assistant unit leader. First assigned to, and living at, Unit No. Two, along with my brother nearby, I soon "graduated" to Unit No. Four, as supervised by unit leader and assistant. (I change the names just a little in case these people are still alive.) In this case, Marshall Brown and Sonny Griffith, both fifteen and close to Eagle Scouts, both being what I would now term beautiful guys, in a physical sense. Marshall seemed to go away a lot, and so Sonny ran the unit by default, as it were.

Sonny was part Yankee and part Portuguese, tall but sturdy, masculine but slender and elegant, with unusually long legs, which he attributed correctly to his riding horses (something he did on his own time quite a bit). Inside the unit he seemed to wear much of the time a white T-shirt and some kind of regular briefs, maybe Hanes with the extra big pouch. You could not help but notice that the pouch bulge appeared full, or more than full. I realize now that Sonny wore his member pointed down, deep into the pouch, thus curving comfortably back toward his body under his balls. Adding to his youthful glamour, he had olive skin.

I had been looking at cocks for a long time, ten years from three to thirteen, starting when male genitalia literally hung at my eye level. So I automatically always checked guys out in that way. No big thing in general, but Sonny's enormous bulge intrigued me. I had advanced by now to a special level of appreciation, following almost six years of sexual experimentation—a rather intense pursuit, given my passionate nature.

Before we went to Camp Cachalot, my father had us examined (as required) by a private doctor in the same way as before our stay at Camp Clark. Only now I had myself grown quite a bit in the pouch of my own briefs. In fact, so much so that my father made a point of letting me know his alarmed perception and minor disapproval of my large member—that is, for thirteen. When we left the doctor's office, he asked me if I played with myself. I asked him in turn, pretending innocence, what did he mean? He warned me not to play with myself lest I develop my private into something of gigantic size. My ears pricked up! Such a possibility existed? I kept the thought to myself.

Thereupon my father told me a cock-and-bull story of what might happen if I played with myself too much. The warning came too late: the stallion had already long since left the stable! He described a man so large genitally that he had to carry his member in a special cart in front of him wherever he went, but covered up with a suitable cloth. I had already noticed how big my dick had become since the anal assault when I was eight, by dint of manual experimentation. In this way I found out that I was big, so to speak. The future thus prophesied, with such a member, a potential sexual playground. But I kept it all to myself, apart from experimentation with others, always there, always easy.

I started mentioning to a few simpático friends in Unit No. Four, whether they had not noticed Sonny's huge endowment in his aptly sized briefs. Yeah, so what? Being younger and smaller peniswise, we all noticed the members on older guys, especially among us teenagers. I was bold but determined. So then I mentioned or rather asked, what Sonny's member might look like when it was hard. The conclusion that they affirmed by experience and intuition: BIG OR VERY BIG!

We were hanging out in one of the unit tents, half in and half out, in the later A.M. One of the scouts, to whom I mentioned the possible size of Sonny's erect penis, brought up the subject with mention of my name as the person broaching the topic. I felt a leetle embarrassed, but some other guys readily seconded my curiosity. Sonny acknowledged casually the obviously large size of his member, and as it turned out, much in demand among a variety of boys and girls about our own age, or so he lightly noted. He declared his willingness to satisfy our curiosity. He invited us all in the unit to enter the so-called Big Tent around bedtime, when he would verify our suspicions.

Everyone appeared excited by the revelation to come! The time passed. The moment came. We were all gathered inside the Big Tent, also known as the Big Top. No flashlight or Coleman lantern on the scene, tactility only permitted. Sonny had hoisted himself up on a top bunk, metal like all our bunks, double or single. But the Big Top had a lot of these double bunks. We began. One by one, all of us felt, or felt up, Sonny's really big and (I must add) beautiful penis. My hands have not changed in size since my early teens, remaining medium-sized. I could not put my hand or hands all the way around it on the shaft. Sonny allowed me in particular extra time to feel him up, including his balls, and as it turned out, only regular-sized.

The dimensions? Either of my hands could only encompass about six of the eight or nine inches that made up its thickness, quite large by any common measure. As for the length, it must have measured about eleven or twelve inches as taken from the ventral or interior side of the shaft (not from the dorsal or exterior side), that is, from the inside bottom at the lower abdomen. Circumcised like most members at that time, it seemed well proportioned overall, somewhat thicker at the base. A large ridge dominated the backside of the penis.

It stuck out and up to full extension, not at any angle to right or left. As time elapsed, later that summer, Sonny permitted me to measure it by hand. Minus the thumb, I could put both hands on it, one above the other, two times, that is, four hands high. I never again encountered any other penis quite like Sonny's.

To what can I compare it? Looking back in time, I can only compare it to an idealized Art Deco sculpture of a very large penis, or a rubber dildo of the same size. The full appreciation came to me only days or weeks later, after mild intimacies between us as a group and Sonny himself, as one after another, night after night, he invited us into and out of his bunk bed. Gradually he permitted me more and more time with him, and sometimes I slept over in his tent, same bunk or the unit leader's bunk on the other side of the tent across from Sonny's bed. Although the unit leader per se, Marshall Brown, came to know about these erotic exchanges, it made no real difference to him; he rarely fooled around with other guys, campers or staff, but he did not prove hostile to what had evolved.

In this way Sonny's Art Deco masterpiece of living flesh became my own gold standard for penises in general, which it remains to this day. By now I have seen many guys naked and excited, but I have never seen anyone quite so large, or long or thick, even compared to the ultimate standard (somewhere between the men in the Congo, that is, the Negroes, and the natives of Papua New Guinea), the Afro-dong or Afro-dildo-dong. Anent the Afro-dong, I speak from a long experience of anthropological research that I have conducted among many males, and intimately, including many American Negroes. No boast, but I do know the subject extending over many years. I have become, since eight or ten years old, a convert to the religion of the phallus, all at once, and forever! Amen!

I went back to summer camp at Camp Cachalot for two more summers. I worked for my keep my last summer there, at fifteen, by which time I had become pretty wise in sex-play guy to guy. Cocksucking remained the pleasure of choice, whether receiving or giving.

Some of the other guys gave great head, but at the age of eleven or twelve I had become the regular cocksucker of a young sexy guy, Johnny, an usher at the movie theatre where my mother worked in the north end of New Bedford. I soon learned what my role included around Johnny, i.e., intimate oral appreciation of his ever-ready hard-on. He became a whole sexual education for me, because through him I learned a lot about males in general. The sexual aspect certainly made boys and men more interesting, and eminently practical because of easier access. This off-and-on relationship with Johnny continued until I joined the U.S. Marine Corps at the age of eighteen, after which I rarely saw him again.

As one of the consequences of the anal assault when I was eight, indeed almost immediately after it, I discovered masturbation, and on my own. I recalled how the older teenager had manipulated my cock, moving the foreskin back and forth. I repeated the gesture over and over and over. An incredible sensation overtook me and came into existence for me. It happened on the very next day. Hidden from casual view, I was alone in an empty lot, where none could easily come near me, as I played with myself, and for the first extended time. My first climax, relatively subdued, produced no semen. The second time, bonanza! Both times I thought that I had vacated my body temporarily! What an unprecedented sensation! I got so excited about masturbation that I soon started initiating other kids my own age and older into doing it, and then finding out at the same time that a lot of kids were discovering it. Yes, simultaneously!

By that final summer at Lake Cachalot and Camp Cachalot when I was fifteen, my own member had enlarged so much that I had every confidence that I was in fact a male, and right up there with other big boys in their mid-adolescence. As before, no matter my own solo progress, I always found other guys during my high-school years with whom I could play sexually, some of them very sophisticated in their manual and oral techniques. A big and pleasant surprise!

By that last summer at camp, I worked for my keep in the kitchen and eating area, south of units four and five; the kitchen and mess hall together had their own dock on the lake, as did all the units. On the south margin of the lake lay the regular beach with docks or piers making a big U onto the sands with the two stems of the U extending from the beach, and with the tie-bar out in the water. I recall a couple of times (everyone generally swam in the nude) when a buddy and I half swam and half waded in the shallows near the shore all the way from the kitchen dock to the regular beach, taking turns sucking each other's cocks, and thus hiding our activity by doing it just underwater. How simple all this activity turned out, whereas union with a woman could change one's life, and permanently: expenses, complications, complexities, and so forth. Who wanted that at an early age? I remained with what I had learned on my own, safe and sound.

Father and stepmother were quite enlightened for that period; and when Ron and myself had reached our early teens, they had us each read a slender book, or part of it, that explained in brief and simple terms how human sexuality functioned, how the penis entered the vagina, how human females became pregnant, and so forth. The entire explanation proceeded in a quite non-erotic way, but it still gave me an erection where I sat in an armchair. Because I was sitting down and could use the book to hide the erection, nobody became any the wiser as to my condition. Later I went into the bathroom, closed the door, and relieved myself while sitting on the toilet.

To show how passionately sensitive I was, instinctively, I should recount another and strategic episode. On one occasion, when Ron and I were staying in the flat somewhere in the west end of New Bedford, where our father and stepmother Ernestine resided, Dad took it upon himself to make sure that we cleaned our genitals properly. Because Donald Senior and his four brothers (Everett, Kenneth, Malcolm, and Melvin) were all uncircumcised, as were Ron and myself, it became imperative to keep the foreskin clean and free of smegma.

Father, brother, and I had all gathered in the bathroom, while Donald Senior at the wash basin demonstrated upon himself the way to keep clean, using water, a little bit of mild hand soap, and a dampened face cloth to do so. He rolled back his foreskin way down, exposing the head of his penis all the way to the glans below the slightly projecting corona of the penis head itself. Having demonstrated the method he then had us take turns emulating his example, rinsing out the face cloth when finished, and so forth.

The whole procedure seemed patently non-erotic, but it made me, despite myself, somewhat sexually aroused. To my embarrassment I began to get an erection. Neither father nor brother became similarly excited. Without comment from anyone else, concentrating my attention, I managed to go through the entire procedure despite my half-erection, putting my cleansed penis back within my shorts inside my pants. Phew! I had just avoided having a full erection and causing myself a major embarrassment.

It might seem strange today, but back during my childhood and adolescence most parents not only did not encourage their teenagers and younger children to fuck, but rarely talked about sex in any form. Some parents practiced a certain realism about it; some had their daughters fitted with a diaphragm and advised their sons to use a condom if and when they fucked. If they did speak on the subject, the parents advised abstinence. Most people seemed to understand that kids discovered sex on their own, had sex with other kids of the same gender, or practiced abstinence between male and female. For the most part it worked out okay, this undiscussed subject and/or system. As for my brother and myself, we practiced abstinence (well, somewhat) until we could complete our education (or whatever), get a job or profession, then have sex with a woman, get married, etc.

Deliberate avoidance of young women on intimate terms, due to the real possibility of pregnancy, became the norm, at least for me. My first experience of fucking with women would not happen until my early thirties. I purposely evaded heavy petting, the embracing and kissing before sex, with girls while in high school. I witnessed kids hardly become adults (from middle teens to middle twenties) when the girls became pregnant, the couples married, took any dead-end jobs that they could find, and thus became fixed more or less for life, thus effectively terminating other possibilities in their existence. I decided early on in my own life that I did not want such a fate. I would wait and see. This policy served me well, very well, and saved me much frustration, expense, and complication, as I have expressed it earlier in this chapter.

This résumé effectively covers my early sexual experience from preschool on into early high school. Of course, much else was happening in my life, not to mention in the world at large, the often dreaded "topical events," such as the war that was raging in much of the northern hemisphere, most of which (fortunately for me) impinged on my immediate life but lightly. Years later, during my early adulthood, I discovered what sheer hell much of Europe and the Far East had been undergoing while I was leading my carefree and innocent existence far from gulags, concentration camps, and the ghastly death camps. I give thanks that I had not come into this world in Central or Eastern Europe!

Chapter V. Further Schooling and Adolescence

The big move to Presidential Heights meant not only a different and somewhat better domestic milieu (at least in terms of cost for our mother) but an entire novel environment overall. For me this meant a whole new region to explore, in which I could play on the west (at the top of the housing project), the double cemetery; the big and mostly undeveloped city blocks on the south; the same on the north (the latter continuing on into the woodland beyond the railroad tracks running east and west); the gigantic parcel of land once dominated by the enormous textile mill one story tall—and now the more or less flooded swamp, our new playground, left by the mill's equally large basement area when the owners deconstructed the factory during the early 1930s. To the east of the latter another and more important railroad ran south and north, whose train horns (melodious and evocative) we often heard in the near distance, about a quarter of a mile away. Although school naturally preoccupied us, Ron at nine, me at eight, a complete other world thus came into existence for our discovery and exploration.

Soon after we moved, our mother got her a job at the Capitol Theatre, a movie house, as box-office cashier and attendant at the candy counter, first located just past the lobby, and later moved out onto the north side of the lobby (still within a wall of glass doors). To these meager earnings of hers our father contributed a small but vital weekly amount: $10.00, $5.00 for each of us. (Yes, money was worth more then, but people did not earn much in routine jobs.) The rent for our unit, No. 155, cost $7.00 per week, and we just managed to survive thanks to my mother's disciplined management of money for food and other necessities, the absolute needs in truth.

She would get all dressed up on Saturday to go shopping (in the downtown, the geographic center of New Bedford) with us in tow. The meat (chicken, pork, beef) that she bought for, and roasted on,

Sunday (dinner always happened at noon, as she went to work during the afternoon and evening), lasted us most of the school or work week, often prepared in varied ways as the days went by toward the next weekend. Luckily, good to great health blessed all three of us. We had an excellent doctor, Jeffries by name, whose office lay about a mile to the east en route to the movie house; but he also made house calls at no extra charge at a time when doctors routinely made house calls. We had our own telephone (as another modern necessity), of course, one of the ubiquitous landlines.

We came home from school for lunch. Annette went to work in the early afternoon: the movies were exhibited in the afternoon, and then repeated in the evening, thus at least twice, with feature and co-feature. Our mother often talked to us in a serious mode about our general behavior. Although she knew that we were kids, she always let us know how fortunate we were in terms of the basics: to eat, to have a roof over our heads, to have good health, and to go to school. She admonished Ron and me to make the most of our situation. Although she expected us to play when not in school, she let us know many times that, while she loved us and kept us alive as best she could, she expected us to act as good kids, responsibly, and not to make trouble for her in terms of the police—that is, not to act as the feared juvenile delinquents who lived in the really big cities like Boston, New York, and Chicago.

Meanwhile, when Ron and I were not playing (usually outside), school totally preoccupied us. Socially our mother had prepared us quite well as early as we could talk and get around, whether at the kindergarten level or later. She gave us good manners and other social skills: politeness, courtesy, and respect shown to older people, not just to young or middle-aged adults, but above all others, to the aged and infirm. Relatives and strangers often complimented her on how good, how polite, our speech and behavior appeared in public and private. We got along well with our neighbors, especially in the same big two-story block where we had our own apartment, and where we soon developed longterm childhood friends, the Lachapelles, and Mrs. Clark with her family, on the south, and somewhat later, Mrs. Baker and her three kids on the north. Most of these women, the mothers, seemed to have no husbands (either dead, separated, or divorced), but they all had rather large families. Like us, again, they just seemed to survive, and not so badly, thanks to the low rents possible in our government-sponsored housing project.

This became the pattern of our days from 1942 to 1953 (or slightly later), grammar school for the seven school years 1942-43 to 1948-49, high school for the four school years from 1949-50 to 1952-53. Because my brother and I had such excellent health, we could participate in all exercise programs in school, particularly when we got into high school with its elaborate exercise program involving organized sports, regular gym and running, and extracurricular athletics.

For entertainment we had radio programs, movie houses (the Golden Age of Hollywood turned out to be the 1930s and 1940s), and above all else for Ron and me, we had wonderful and variegated books for endless reading from the downtown public library. Of course, both radio and movies also provided education and instruction, as well as entertainment. I became a voracious reader as soon as I could read (yes, reading transported me to other worlds remote in time and space); and this reading stood me in good stead, not just in grammar school, but even more in high school, where I really blossomed as a student, with emphasis on the arts and humanities. I did okay in the few sciences that I had to take, but I never pursued them on their own at that time.

In grammar school Ron and I did all right even if not spectacularly, at least until we got into the seventh and eighth grades, where we changed classes from one room to another (moving among four class rooms), in preparation for changing classrooms in high school. Otherwise the children in kindergarten and the lower grades usually remained in one given classroom during much of the school day. Our grammar school boasted a remarkable roster of teachers, very well trained and educated, mostly unmarried, as well as dedicated to their vocations, their professions, and hence on a much higher level than just discharging the duties of a mere job. They also exhibited a cultivated sense of culture in a classical sense. I remember them as rather strict but certainly not unkind in any way. They regarded and handled their professions with all due seriousness. Yes, how fortunate we were to have such marvelous teachers, something I vaguely realized then, and all the more today!

First comes the tall and slender person of Miss Cole, under whose instruction I finished the second half of the second grade. A complete musician, she played the violin and led the little orchestra (including student violinists, who made an "interesting" sound with their whining instruments) that gathered in the large auditorium. This chamber could easily hold all the students and staff, plus guests and parents (if need be, but that rarely happened), all at the same time. The regular weekly assembly took place on Friday morning. We would all march into the auditorium in due procession while Miss Cole and ensemble would play this odd little, rather jiglike march. (I can still play it at will inside me at any time!) I should add that this dedicated professional also functioned as an excellent instructor, who prepared us well for the third grade under Miss Ayers, older than Miss Cole, but just as patient and professional.

Under Miss Ayers the humanities received an even bigger push. With her guidance we read, and read literally aloud, several narrative masterpieces in verse by Longfellow: first, *The Courtship of Miles Standish* (my least favorite, if at all); and, second and sublime, *Evangeline*. I wish that we had read *Hiawatha* instead (which I did read later on my own), but *Evangeline* made up for the deficiencies (too anthropocentric) of *Miles Standish* ("Speak for yourself, John," indeed). Miss Ayres would begin by reading aloud a short connected passage, and then she would have us each read a similar passage in due sequence. This provided us all with the direct experience and appreciation of literature, qua literature, in a way much better than reading the text initially by ourselves alone without articulating the text.

I recall distinctly how by the time that we reached the end of *Evangeline*, with the poignant reiteration (more or less) of the poem's opening lines, we were all weeping openly and unashamedly. The ending represents much more than mere sentimentality; it means something profound, at once human and humane. After such an emotional epiphany I can recall almost nothing of grades five and six, but I can remember the fourth grade under Miss O'Malley with distinct clarity. Under her enlightened instruction we studied, among other subjects, geography for the first time. It was winter, the school year of 1944–45, and the Second World War still raged in many parts of the northern hemisphere, and in parts of the South Pacific. It was then that I understood the considerable distances between Europe and the U.S. on the one hand (the Atlantic Ocean) and the U.S. and the Far East on the other (the Pacific Ocean), and the role that these oceanic distances had played in keeping the U.S. mostly safe and sound from direct attack by the Germans and the Japanese. Thank you, dear Miss O'Malley, for my grasp of physical and geographical reality!

Another special event occurred as the war in Europe was coming to an end, an event that shook our nation to its core. In April 1945 our president Franklin Delano Roosevelt died at some hot-springs resort in Georgia, he who had guided the U.S. out of the Great Depression of the 1930s, and then through the first half of the 1940s, as we navigated our way in the dangerous and murky waters of World War II. I myself as a child had benefited from all the health and social programs that he had put in place for working people and their families. But more than that, I had also benefited from the sense of hope and inspiration that he and his fireside chats had instilled in us all. Although I was only in the fourth grade, I knew enough to grasp what he as president had accomplished, to mourn his loss.

My brother and I were walking uphill to school along the access road on the south of the housing project, and had almost reached

Mt. Pleasant Street, ready to turn toward the school on our left, when we encountered a mass of students coming toward us, a phenomenon rather unprecedented. A variety of voices advised us, "Go back home. There's no school today. The president died." Parents and other adults had lined up not only along the access road but also along Mt. Pleasant Street near the cemetery. Many if not most of the kids and adults were weeping and sobbing openly, and Ron and myself joined in this universal expression of grief.

We returned home to tell our mother and the neighbors what had happened. They already knew and were weeping as well. The grief and sense of loss were universal. I never again experienced anything like it until the assassination of another president, John F. Kennedy, in 1963, in Dallas. However, whereas Kennedy had acted as president for only a little more than half of his one term, and had moreover died as a relatively young man in his middle forties—a real tragedy—Roosevelt had passed on in his early sixties and had already begun his fourth term, worn out as an old man from the strain and stress of his elected position. Comparatively few people seemed to have realized just how frail and weakened he had become, and how crippled from polio, conditions that the government carefully screened from the general public.

To return to the microcosmic from the macrocosmic, I recall very little of grades four and five. I did not really come into my own as a student before high school until grades seven and eight. From the latter I particularly remember the gracious and beautiful Miss Lyman, who taught English, and—that rare phenomenon in elementary school at that period, a male teacher—Mr. Parsons, who taught civics and history, if memory serves. It was during these last two grades that I developed a sense of purpose and seriousness in regard to school, which I would carry over into high school. I now desired to excel scholastically, and this boded well for my learning aptitude in high school.

One final character in our grammar school I must limn: the principal, whose name escapes me. Dressed always in tie, shirt, and complete suit (including a vest), he resembled Pépère facially, but was taller. A no-nonsense person, he radiated strength and purpose. A student, especially a male, did not want a teacher to send him to the principal's office for "correction," which might involve corporeal punishment by means of a good strapping with a large leather belt, or the worst (if rumor had it right), a good slugging, if the student put up any physical challenge to the big man in charge. On one occasion, when in grades five and/or six, a teacher sent me to his office (located on the first floor at the northern end of the main floor, or hallway) for some minor infraction. He realized that he did not need to hit me, and that a mere reprimand would suffice. It did, and I never appeared before him again as a student requiring "correction." Again, as I never could forget, I had to behave properly so as to cause my mother no problem. She had enough difficulty in her life without my adding more.

Nobody could have been more content than I when I graduated at last from grammar school in June 1949 at the age of fourteen, and at the end of the school year of 1948-49. In everyday terms nothing could have beckoned me more powerfully than the prospect of high school for four years ahead. Our graduating class turned out to be the next to the last to graduate from our grammar school. After the last graduation all students, if they continued in school, went to the junior high school in the north end of New Bedford, grades seven through eight or nine. As I had advanced through grammar school during the last few years, teachers had featured me in the auditorium to give brief recitations learned by heart, my first experience of performing, and performing solo. Apparently I recited to their satisfaction, and to the applause of my fellow students, especially those near my own age.

I have a special memory from those early years, but from outside of school whether grammar or high. On Saturdays, whenever we went shopping with our mother, if we did not eat with our father in the little luncheon shop (with booths) in the Olympia Theatre building (north of the wide lobby); instead, we ate at a special cafeteria-restaurant called Lorraine's, also located on Pleasant Street, but just a few blocks to the south, and as usual as my father's treat. The only booths available lay at the back, where the four of us usually sat. Otherwise the customers sat down on large wooden chairs and placed the trays holding their food upon a large special flat wing that they moved up over the chair's right arm from its position at the side of the chair.

This eatery boasted the most mouth-watering smells, compounded from the sawdust on the floor, the strong brewed coffee, and above all else the eatery's specialty, the beef meat pies (ground beef, potatoes, and onions) served with a rich brown gravy, the latter sheerly irresistible. (Lorraine's also served other types of food, of course.) The customer took a large tray from a pile near the door and on it placed the hot or cold food (already prepared), as he ordered and received it, along the serving line, in the usual cafeteria style, a long wide shelf in front of the glassed-in large metal trays holding the hot food, kept heated by the hot water underneath these warming trays. Ah, how those delicious beef pies linger in memory!—not to mention another specialty, their strawberry shortcake smothered in real whipped cream!

At fourteen, rather than the usual thirteen, I graduated from grammar school, which meant that I would graduate from high school at eighteen, rather than the usual seventeen. When I entered high school in the late summer of 1949–50, at almost exactly the same time as I turned fifteen on 8 September 1949, I had my first intimations of becoming an adult. The idyllic freedom of summer camp had ended. My mother, as the chief clerk dealing with the customers, had already started working for her brother, our Uncle Roland, at his dry-cleaning business in downtown Fairhaven to the east across the Acushnet River—a better job for her with better earnings and better conditions. Uncle knew that he had a hard-working clerk in his own sister. Now my brother and I would be working for him as well, on weekends, vacations, and summers, Ron delivering the dry-cleaned and carefully pressed clothes to the homes of the customers, and I doing the same job as my mother during her days off, generally Saturdays.

Still a fishing port, Fairhaven truly lived up to its name, indeed a fair haven with distinctive civic structures and beautiful old homes, especially the high school just east of the New Bedford-Fairhaven bridge, and in the town center further south (but just east of uncle's business and other shops), the town hall with a theatre where summer troupes came to act, the Millicent Library (a small but elegant public building), and so forth. Nearby stood handsome and even unique homes from the whaling days, including the Howland mansion made out of wood painted gray, set back a little on its own corner, inside its modest wooden fence. Raised up on a low, grassed-over earthen mound (it had a cellar, of course), it was only one story tall but with high ceilings, the structure essentially a low-roofed square, and surrounded by a wide colonnaded porch, which I particularly noticed because the handsome fluted pillars have Ionic capitals. I had just learned about the standard Graeco-Roman column orders.

Between high school and our part-time jobs my brother and I kept busy but stayed happy. Compared to the high school in Fairhaven, conceived in a sumptuous Jacobean style, our own high school, a huge three-story rectangular block stretching from east to west, seemed relatively restrained with simple classical decoration applied flat onto the walls. The front façade, enlivened with four engaged Ionic columns, faced east and looked down William Street all the way to the old and magnificent Customs House made out of granite that faced west, looking up to the high school. A Greek Revival structure, the Custom House boasted a superb pedimented portico with eight large fluted columns with Ionic capitals, thus making a neat symmetry with the Ionic pillars on the high school up at the other end of William Street.

While Ron took business and science courses, I pursued the humanities, technically the college classical preparatory curriculum, including English, French, and Latin; algebra (I performed only moderately) and geometry (much better because I could visualize); and biology (my one science, at which I did very well). Inspired by my outstanding teachers, I worked hard at my studies in high school and got high grades. The languages became my favorite courses, especially Latin, which provided me with a direct connection to the ancient Mediterranean world. For the first two years I studied with Miss Loftus (Caesar's commentaries on the Gallic Wars and Cicero's easier orations); and for the last two with Miss Ryan (Cicero's longer and more elaborate orations and the first six books of the twelve making up Virgil's magisterial epic, the *Aeneid*). I studied my three languages for four years each.

In English I had a different instructor for almost every year, but the one that I had for two years, my best one, turned out to be Miss (Gladys) Blackmer. In French I had Miss Bégin for all four years. She, too, became a favorite, and I did so well my first year that she took me with other outstanding students (toward the end of the school year) to a meeting with the cultivated members of the French cultural society, the Alliance Française—a complete revelation for me and the other students, chiefly accustomed as we were to the Franco-Canadian workers in the textile mills, not conversant with the higher levels of art and literature for the most part.

Meanwhile I continued reading voraciously on my own, and while in high school I devoured all the fifteen novels by Edgar Rice Burroughs that Uncle Roland had once read and collected (all published by Grosset & Dunlap), all miscellaneous titles except for the first five Mars novels. Also at this period I read an exceptional short novel that became a great favorite with me—a work of speculative fiction, and saturated with theosophical thinking and feeling—and that I have reread many times over the years since then: *The Veil: A Fantasy*, by Mary Harriott Norris (Boston: Richard C. Badger, 1907). It is well worth seeking out in used bookstores.

More than just inspired by my high school teachers—in all my courses the wide reading I had already accomplished now came into play—I developed special friendships with several of them, rather unusually for this period in school history, when custom, if not regulations, tended to discourage or directly rule out such relationships. Although I never had a special friendship with him, I did have a special relationship, by default, with Mr. Whitmarsh, who taught Ancient History. Language and history have always fascinated me. I managed to get good grades from him, but I failed to fulfill a basic requirement, about which (as I found out) he was adamant. At the start of every class Mr. Whitmarsh dictated to us an outline of what he would cover. At year's end we would each surrender to him a handwritten copy of his overall outline. I failed to do so, and I failed the course, and had to repeat it all over again the next year. The next time I did indeed hand in my own handwritten outline, and I passed the course. I had in fact learned my lesson(s) in more ways than one.

I write about this class and instructor in detail first because Ancient History came first in my daily schedule for that first high school year. Mr. Whitmarsh usually stood in front of the class but before his desk, holding the little cards (rather like business cards) with the names of the students arranged alphabetically. A thin man with good features, superficially he seemed like a martinet. An excellent instructor, he was actually a kind man, but did not wish to advertise this kindness. He could get better results by appearing a little severe, when his dry wit did not betray him. I cite the following example.

When we would return from some week-long school vacation, he understood our restlessness, our difficulty in adjusting once more to the classroom rhythm. Accordingly he would surprise us by not reading from his prepared outline but from some book of short stories, some tale that would just fit the length of the class hour, and allowing some slack to deal succinctly with practical school matters, usually at the class end. The first story that he read aloud? Rudyard Kipling's tale about the mongoose, "Rikki-Tikki-Tavi." He read it very well, a little drily, which only increased its humor and its impact. He made it a delight.

Late in the morning a small group of us (a few of the same students from Ancient History) would enter the classroom over which presided

Miss Loftus, who taught us basic and then gradually more complicated Latin. With its grammar and syntax, with its declensions and conjugations, the disciplined quality of the language entranced me. Such a different rhetoric from our vernacular English! Gradually, as we advanced, I came to realize how much Latin had helped to form and inform the Anglo-Saxon that became the modern English that we know from Chaucer and Spenser, then later from Shakespeare and Milton.

At the time that I passed through high school, Miss Loftus must have attained her early sixties, getting closer to retirement at sixty-five. A serious and very cultivated woman, she had a broad and profound appreciation of the arts, including music both classical and popular, and surprisingly in the latter category a real grasp of Bing Crosby's crooner artistry, among other singers. In addition to opera (the Saturday afternoon Metropolitan Opera radio broadcasts with Milton Cross, which I also followed when I could), she knew and enjoyed the popular music of other Western countries and had followed it since her younger days.

She also soon appreciated that I had literary and musical tastes much like hers, only minus a liking for much of the popular music of the 1940s and 1950s, particularly the latter, the nadir of Tin Pan Alley. She had taught most of her life up to that point, and lived with her well-off parents (then in their nineties) in a comfortable house in the west end of New Bedford, a fancier part of town with nice family homes. She had endured years of ill health, which did not prevent her from pursuing her teaching career. When she walked, her legs made odd snapping sounds, which some of the non-classical-curriculum students would sometimes mock rather cruelly, but out of her hearing, mercifully. She had fostered over the year the careers, academic and/or artistic, of a good number of her best students, including Joseph Perry Ponte III, well on his way to a career as an exceptional concert pianist. He graduated from Harvard University *summa cum laude*, a distinctive achievement. However, after all those years of extensive and expensive schooling and musical training (supported by his father Joseph Perry Ponte II, one of the chief surgeons at our local big hospital, Saint Luke's), he became a priest!

Once per annum, as the school year drew to its close, some of these former students would gather in Miss Loftus's classroom (usually on a Saturday) for cake, ice cream, and cultivated conversation. At her behest I would descend to the downtown and, supplied with money that she gave me, would buy the cake (ordered in advance) and a quart or more of ice cream, not just any flavor, but always maple nut, a special favorite. Both cake and ice cream came from the same elegant boutique. In this way, thanks to Miss Loftus, I discovered new friends and acquaintances from among the special circle of students she had fostered in times past, a group that remained singularly faithful to her. Here I must mention by name the painter-singer Henry James.

Meanwhile, as I did in all my classes (except algebra), I performed very well in her Latin class, perusing Caesar's Gallic commentaries and Cicero's orations. Gradually Miss Loftus and I built up a special bond. She knew that I derived from the working poor, and often helped me attend cultural events by buying me tickets for them. We continued our friendship even when I studied Latin in my third and fourth high-school years under the instruction of Miss Ryan, a very different kind of teacher and person.

Among other cultural delights Miss Loftus paid for me to travel to Boston (we journeyed by train in those days) to witness a performance (my first live one) of Mozart's divine masterpiece *The Magic Flute*, as presented by the Metropolitan Opera of New York in the old Boston Opera House (alas, now no more) with its marvelous acoustics. Jerome Hines, the basso profundo, sang the role of the high priest Amonasro, and Eleanor Stieber that of the Queen of the Night. I can still recall the thrill I felt when she sang the character's first and spectacular aria. The overall high-quality performance of the rest of the cast, no less than that of the large orchestra, also deeply impressed me.

Speaking on a practical level—since I could not return to New Bedford after the opera finished rather late in the evening—I stayed overnight with a friend whom I had met at one of the extracurricular events put on by Miss Loftus for former students. No less than the redoubtable Joseph Perry Ponte III, then a graduate student at Harvard, this friend had a small apartment on campus, with bedroom and living room, kitchen and bathroom. At Miss Loftus's kind urging he had volunteered to let me stay with him overnight whenever I came up to Boston for some theatrical event that with intermissions ran for three hours or more, actually the standard length. This happened on at least three occasions, and Joseph honestly did not appear to consider it a bother, a very generous thing for him to do.

The two greatest theatrical experiences of my life up to that time took place at the same Boston Opera House later in the same year, when I was a junior in high school (1951–52). Again Miss Loftus's largesse made them possible. I had become fascinated with ballet as a dramatic spectacle in the theatre, first through a movie of illustrious facture, *The Red Shoes* (1948), with authentic ballet performers Moira Shearer and Leonide Massine. I first witnessed this film during the seventh grade, the school year of 1947–48 at Mt. Pleasant Grammar School. But I had already become aware of this unique art form through excerpts from the music that Tchaikovsky furnished for three landmark ballets: *Le Lac des cygnes* (*Swan Lake,* Moscow, 1877; St. Petersburg, 1895), *La Belle au bois dormant* (*The Sleeping Beauty,* 1890), and *Casse-noisette* (*The Nutcracker,* 1892).

Leopold Stokowski and a hand-picked symphonic ensemble recorded and released through RCA Victor Records, around 1950, about a third of the score for *The Sleeping Beauty*. This was a sumptuous, tonally incandescent affair that I bought and played numerous times. Not to be outdone, André Kostalanetz with his own regular orchestra recorded and released a major portion (again about a third) of the score for *Swan Lake,* later during the early 1950s, through Columbia Records. This was an exciting, dynamic performance. As for *The Nutcracker,* a choice selection (made by the composer himself) from that score had long made itself known and celebrated under the name of the *Nutcracker Suite*. Still later, during the mid-1950s, Mercury (London) Records released the three entire scores as performed by Antal Dorati (an experienced ballet conductor, i.e., in the theatre) leading the Minneapolis Symphony Orchestra.

I bought and also played numerous times all these landmark scores in these landmark recordings. The beauty of the entire scores, as recorded, lay in the fact that they provided the listener the opportunity to perceive their construction from act to act, their ebb and flow, their dynamic alternation from dramatic scene to suite of dances, from overture to finale, something not readily apparent from mere excerpts or even from a performance of the ballet in the theatre, when the spectator's attention focusses on the stage action, thus distracted from the music.

As a result of *The Red Shoes* and then all these recordings, I had turned into a nascent balletomane. However, during all this time, Cyril W. Beaumont and his mammoth and magisterial monograph, the *Complete Book of Ballets* (G. P. Putnam's Sons, London, 1937, and New York, 1938—revised edition 1949), had been aiding and abetting my knowledge of and appetite for ballet, particularly as a story form as told through story ballets, or *ballets d'action*.

As I had soon discovered, the principal tradition in ballet before the modern innovation of abstract choreography had in fact concentrated on story ballets; people like to be entertained, and a choreographer can hang almost anything upon a narrative, as Beaumont's monograph informs us. Thus a direct tradition of storytelling in dance and mime has existed at least since the seventeenth century, and probably even before then—that is, for a very long time, as computed in human terms, as a tradition handed down from generation to generation, a fact worthy of respect.

Thus my next experience of ballet, live in the old opera house in downtown Boston, made me a confirmed aficionado and eventually a ballet scholar. This came about via the performances of the complete

Swan Lake and *The Sleeping Beauty* (among other works maintained in their repertoire) by the Sadler's Wells Ballet (later the Royal Ballet of England) during their second tour in the U.S. in 1952 (their first had taken place in 1947). In conjunction with Beaumont's eye-witness and very full account of *The Sleeping Beauty* as performed at the Alhambra Theatre, London, by Diaghilev's Ballets Russes, in 1921—under the title *The Sleeping Princess*—I had studied the ballet in relation to Tchaikovsky's music by listening to it many times via Stokowski's first major recording of about a third of the score. I had thus prepared myself thoroughly for a live performance of *The Sleeping Beauty*, and (through other means and recordings) of *Swan Lake* in the same fashion as well. When Miss Loftus's largesse gave me the chance to see them on stage, I would not waste it!

I witnessed *The Sleeping Beauty* with Moira Shearer herself on Tuesday, and *Swan Lake* with Margot Fonteyn on the following Saturday, overall an *embarras de richesse*. To my surprise, delight, and approval, the Sadler's Wells company in their production of the first opus had retained the original division into a prologue, three acts, and four tableaux (or five, counting the prologue). They had also done the same for the second opus and its Moscow division into the original four acts. The main revelation for me came in the form of the original choreography, and as reproduced via the dance notation done under the sponsorship of N. G. Sergheyev, the stage manager at the Maryinsky Theatre during 1903-17. (The same sponsorship appears to have notated the entire repertoire as left in place by Marius Petipa before World War I, an invaluable treasure.) The other and concomitant revelation for me came in the expert performances of the prima ballerinas. How much of the success of these *grands ballets d'action* utterly depends on these women, even when supported by an exceptional company and orchestra!

Of the two evenings, the one devoted to *The Sleeping Beauty* somehow seemed more magical to me than the one given to *Swan Lake*, although both appeared equally professional. Years later I found out that the performance of *The Sleeping Beauty* that I witnessed was regarded by the company itself as one of their very best. What do I particularly remember about that first "full-length, evening-long" ballet that I experienced, surely Petipa's greatest masterpiece? Well, not just the performance and production, but the ambiance itself included.

The old Boston Opera House! The ticket that Miss Loftus had bought for me (she knew the ambiance from prior experience begun long ago) put me in the front right-hand box of the first row of the several rows of opera boxes. (Remember that this was a so-called horseshoe-shaped theatre that, with all its admitted disadvantages, also had its peculiar advantages, such as I found out firsthand.) I sat poised over the orchestra pit, and almost over the stage, once the curtain rose up. In the ordinary light of the regular house lights the musicians filed into the pit, tuned up their instruments, and arranged their particularized parts of the score for ease of access. From where I sat in my separate movable chair (nobody sat in front of me), I could see the house interior, the orchestra pit, and the main part of the stage once the curtain ascended.

Anon the house lights dimmed, and a roseate glow took over the theatre emanating from pit and curtained stage. A bit of subdued applause and murmured appreciation rippled through the audience as the conductor filed into the pit, looked around, and picked up the baton. The already legendary Constant Lambert, long the chief conductor for the Sadler's Wells, would lead the orchestra on this particular evening. Even with cuts it would make for a long evening, say, around three hours, including the intermissions after the prologue and the second and third tableaux. Lambert lifted his baton; all those highly trained musicians had fixed their eyes upon him; and all at once they plunged into the brief but commanding introduction, the loud theme of the evil fairy Carabosse, contrasting nicely with the theme of the supremely good entity, the Lilac Fairy, always embodied in one of Tchaikovsky's most expressive slow melodies. The curtain revealed the throne hall of King Florestan XXIV (a long-reigning dynasty, and a nice play upon the name and number of Louis XIV).

And so the story ballet unfurled *comme il faut* before our eyes all through that memorable evening. The christening of the Princess Aurora, the curse laid upon her by Carabosse, and the slight improvement of it by the Lilac Fairy. The princess's coming-of-age sixteen years later and the spectacular moment effected by the four princes as they court and pay homage to her. Then, as the curse goes into action, the falling-asleep or putting-to-sleep of Florestan's court and kingdom for one hundred years. The arrival of the Prince Désiré out hunting with his numerous escort of courtiers and retainers in the forest surrounding the enchanted palace, his voyage in the little barque guided by the Lilac Fairy, the arrival at the palace, and the awakening of the princess and the entire court from their enchanted sleep, a moment of great suspense and then climactic jubilation. Finally the splendiferous wedding celebration of Désiré and Aurora leading up the magnificent and more than dramatically justified apotheosis.

Borne on the successive flux and ebb, the propulsive waves and melodies, of Tchaikovsky's music, I sat there as enchanted as the enchanted princess, court, and palace. Exquisite as a rose and evidently strong as a sumo wrestler (speaking of her legs), Moira Shearer made a perfect fairy-tale princess. Robert Helpman made a superb evil fairy: I sat so close overlooking the stage that I perceived the broad stripes of his vivid Kabuki-type makeup, adding to the sense of make-believe being created before our very eyes. He reappeared in the last act, dancing the demanding role of the Bluebird in the Bluebird *pas de deux*. Michael Somes played the role of the prince with perfect aplomb and as the handsome and ardent cavalier, and played it to the hilt.

The highlight of the evening for me came during Aurora's coming-of-age in the second tableau (the first full act): that ultimate *pas d'action*, the Rose Adagio, one of Petipa's most commanding pieces of choreography. With practiced poise and expertise Moira Shearer absolutely riveted the audience's focus during this daunting first challenge to any prima ballerina, especially while she accepts one by one the roses from each of the four princes (of the north, south, east, and west); and as they manoeuver her around, she stands *sur la pointe* (of her right foot), that is, rock solid on the tip of that toe. The music expands this rare moment on toward its triumphant conclusion, a climax that expands even further into an ultimate flowering of all the courtly imagery of the rose from *The Romaunt of the Rose* onward into the late nineteenth and early twentieth centuries (until World War I). The rest of the ballet unfurled beautifully as well. The entire company and the orchestra performed beyond expectation and nobly supported Shearer. By the time performers and audience alike attained the end, the mazurka and the hymnlike apotheosis, we had surely reached a consummation devoutly to be wished and enjoyed, a pure theatrical sacrament; and thus returning the dramatic element back to its now remote source in the sacred chorus of Greek drama, strictly religious in origin.

After the triumphal procession of dances and action scenes that constitute *The Sleeping Beauty*, *Swan Lake* on the following Saturday, with Margot Fonteyn as the Swan Queen and Michael Somes as the Hamlet-like Prince Siegfried, did in fact register with me, if not as a disappointment, then as a distinct anticlimax, through no fault of production or performance. Leslie Hurry's costumes and sets in scenic worth equaled those by Oliver Messel for *The Sleeping Beauty*. I can't quite recall, but I believe that Robert Helpman once again played the grand villain (the evil enchanter Von Rothbart) to the limit, as he did with Carabosse in *The Sleeping Beauty*. In her lovingly modulated performance, I recognized Fonteyn as the exceptional prima ballerina she had proven herself over and over again to be. Michael Somes revealed himself as even a deeper and better dancer-actor than he had in *The Sleeping Beauty* as the Prince Désiré. Again Constant Lambert conducted the orchestra with his accustomed expertise, not to mention flair and panache.

However, despite all these positive elements, something about this "authentic" *Swan Lake* bothered me, and profoundly. The discrepancies between the original Moscow score (1877) and the adaptation of it by Marius Petipa and Riccardo Drigo for the St. Petersburg production (1895) appeared too glaring for me to ignore, if for a fact Tchaikovsky's music per se provided the chief incentive for the St. Petersburg revival following the ineffectual Moscow première, as chroniclers have recorded over and over. Petipa was adapting a rather different kind of dance drama onto his own tradition established long since, beginning with the danced melodramas of Jules Perrot (active in Russia, 1848–58) and then Petipa's expanded version of this beginning with *Pharaoh's Daughter* (1862).

Another factor operated in the case of *Swan Lake*, which I did not understand until I studied and assimilated *Giselle* a few years later, and—as a fact—which Tchaikovsky intended in dead seriousness as a romantic ballet that would surpass *Giselle* (Paris, 1841), which had reappeared in St. Petersburg with the original creators, Jules Perrot as the real choreographer and Carlotta Grisi as the original dancer-actress. As a student in St. Petersburg during the 1850s, Tchaikovsky witnessed *Giselle* and other story ballets (created or recreated by Perrot after their first appearance in Western Europe); *Giselle* became a special ballet for Tchaikovsky, a favorite of favorites. (It had already become that for Delibes, Bizet, and Berlioz.) Indeed, Tchaikovsky seemed to know this ballet by heart. During the protracted composition and orchestration of the music for both *Swan Lake* and *The Sleeping Beauty*, the Russian composer as part of his homework studied the score of the older ballet for technical instruction, the accompaniment that Benjamin Lumley (the director of Her Majesty's Theatre in London during the 1840s and half of the 1850s) once rightly described as "the truly captivating music" by Adolphe Adam.

As with *Giselle*, Tchaikovsky purposed the Moscow *Swan Lake* as another tragedy, but as a tragedy that in starkness outdoes the relatively sugarcoated *Giselle*. As published, the original scenario does not make explicit some important aspects of the drama (or melodrama), as revealed, for example, by the music for the *Pas de six* in Act III. The weak and ineffectual "happy ending" apotheosis that custom forced

Petipa to tack on at the ballet's very end obscures the intended starkness of the dramatic effect. Moscow's Bolshoi Theatre seems to have restored the original music in its original order—first in 1953 via Vladimir Bourmeister—otherwise retaining the original St. Petersburg choreography (1895) by Petipa and Ivanov, which functions just as well as laid out in accord with the music's original order. The inspired choreography by Lev Ivanov for Acts II and IV easily surpasses the brilliance of the movements devised by Petipa for Acts I and III.

For me Tchaikovsky's original intention for his own dance drama (as revealed in his music) far outweighs whatever else others have done with the ballet since 1877 and 1895, especially since the original published scenario does not always make the drama clear vis-à-vis the music, above all anent Act III, and also to some extent Act II. Tchaikovsky had been wanting to write the music for a ballet evidently for quite a while, since the latter 1860s or early 1870s. Building on the basis of a one-act "house ballet," *The Lake of Swans*, organized for his nieces and nephews (for which he provided both subject and music that he would have played on the piano), Tchaikovsky somehow managed to obtain the commission from the Moscow Directorate of the Imperial Theatres for a full-fledged, four-act ballet *Le Lac des cygnes* (*Lebedinoye Ozero*), which we have come to know under the title *Swan Lake* outside Russia. He had managed to do this by sometime the midsummer of 1875.

Although credited originally to the ballet-master first involved, Julius (or Wentzel) Reisinger, apparently the Russian composer himself created the libretto and then laid out the dances and action scenes without a choreographer. But he consulted closely with two experienced theatre people, both working for and at the Moscow Bolshoi Theatre: as credited by his brother Modeste, these were V. P. Beghichev, the Intendant of the Moscow Imperial Theatres, and V. F. Geltser, the famous dancer-actor. Both these people, especially the latter, could or would have advised Tchaikovsky in regard to technical or practical matters, such as length and suitability of the individual numbers making up the libretto and score, so that the ballet-master, whoever he turned out to be, could readily stage it. Inspired by the danced melodramas of Jules Perrot in St. Petersburg during the 1850s, it would have required a genius like him to have staged the dramatic concept that Tchaikovsky had in mind, and that has never quite come into existence. It was this discrepancy that I sensed at that first witnessing of *Swan Lake* that made the ballet less satisfying for me than *The Sleeping Beauty*, all of which I reported in due course to Miss Loftus, even if originally I did not know any of these basic facts or logical suppositions, that is, during my junior year of high school in 1951–52.

(I should add that Modeste Tchaikovsky's revised libretto for the 1895 St. Petersburg production represents a superior and much needed simplification of the original published scenario for the 1877 Moscow production.)

I have discussed at some length these first two major story ballets that I witnessed not just because of their impact on my life at that impressionable age but above all because of the aesthetic orientation it has given my life and career ever since, again all because of dear Miss Loftus. The relationship and exchange between her and myself as it developed over my four years of high school, I should emphasize, did not go just from her to me, but increasingly, as time went on, from me to her.

When after two years of Ancient History (one year but done twice) I mentioned to Mr. Whitmarsh that, although his course did indeed feature Ancient Egypt and Mesopotamia (Chaldeans, Babylonians, Assyrians, Medes, Persians, etc.), it did not include civilizations at least as old or as great as Egypt —to wit, India and China. He conceded my point and then told me that, if I had a serious interest, I should go look up on my own the ancient and modern history of these respective cultures, which also covered enormous geographic areas. I did. Luckily I discovered, as my very first books, accessible and easy histories for the average reader, each somewhat along the lines of "the pageant of" Indic history and Chinese history, respectively. I became enthused by what I learned and shared that enthusiasm with Miss Loftus; in turn she asked me to check the books out for her from the downtown central library. I did, and she read them, becoming duly impressed as had I. Her interest and enthusiasm fully justified my own.

One other teacher taught at our high school with whom I developed a friendship, Miss Gladys Blackmer, who taught me English language and literature during my second and third years. We even went on several special excursions, driving in her own car, most notably to an early-dawn (or sunrise) Easter celebration at Fort Phoenix over at the southern end of the main part of Fairhaven; this took place during my senior and last year in high school (1952-53) before I finally graduated in June 1953. In fact, she became the closest thing as a teacher to a teenage buddy that I might have had. (Of course, I did have several teenage buddies all through high school, the most notable stemming from the Boy Scouts.) But beside English we had another and even more immediate link that involved geographical distance. At first my brother and I went to high school (several miles away from our home at least) by the local bus near our housing project, but later, and mostly by station wagon, via our Uncle Roland, who would drop us off in front of the high school while on his way to work in Fairhaven.

Early on, during my freshman year, I started going home on foot—it saved bus fare—but it proved to be great exercise, and also something that I loved to do per se. In this way I began my lifelong preference (literally career) for walking, which continues to this very day, and which has helped me to keep in shape, on into the advanced adolescence of eighty. Much of this walk home from high school I conducted along County Street, going past Miss Blackmer's residence on the same thoroughfare, and not far from the Common. We would sometimes observe and salute each other, she coming out of her first-floor front door onto the porch, and I rapidly going past. On a rare occasion we might casually chat, and this deepened the camaraderie and bond between us. I also walked by her house, of course, at other times of the day or night, but we would not necessarily run into each other on these occasions. Miss Blackmer remained special to me, but in a way different from Miss Loftus. We stayed friends into our later lives.

My junior year turned out as the best and richest of the entire four-year span. The Honor Society elected me into its rarified ranks via a special ceremony on the stage of the auditorium. The entire school, teachers and students, had assembled for the event, a nice recognition for us all being inducted. It might have happened for me during my sophomore year except for the problem with the outline that I failed to complete and hand over to "Professor" Whitmarsh at the end of my freshman year, but that I did complete when I repeated the course the next school year.

Meanwhile, thanks to the fervent sponsorship of Miss Loftus behind the scenes, I won a summer scholarship to Phillips Academy, Andover, Massachusetts (not the related one of the same name in Exeter, New Hampshire). Even though not quite summer camp, I found the campus rather idyllic, I did well enough academically (English and Art History), and I passed as much time as possible in the school's excellent library, finding books and subjects unavailable at home. The scholarship furnished me with room and board, not to mention tuition. I shared a chamber with another but agreeable student, and each of us had his own private sleeping space (with a single bed and bureau), marginally better than the bedroom at home with twin beds. As part of the scholarship arrangement, I had to perform kitchen duty, washing dishes and/or pots and pans, rather than peeling potatoes.

At the end of the summer, before going back home, Phillips Academy offered me gratis my senior year there, including once more tuition, room, and board. A tempting offer considering the ambiance: many trees, vast lawns, and attractive brick buildings. Nevertheless, despite the honor, I graciously if reluctantly refused it. I very much wanted to graduate from New Bedford High School. Also, as a lesser but genuine factor, the difference in income between me (as a poor person on a special scholarship) and most of the other students (who came from wealthy parents) might have become a "sensitive" issue for me, an issue that I instinctively avoided and would never have discussed with anyone there. To their credit the wealthier kids never mentioned my obvious poverty, albeit I appeared neat and clean and had good manners thanks to my mother.

After the major efflorescence that I had experienced in my junior year, my senior one seemed flat, simply because nothing extraordinary happened for me during 1952-53, nothing but continued hard study and high grades, that is, with one remarkable and sad exception. Just as the death of Jean Teillière, my mother's father, and my favorite close relative, had marked my junior year (1951-52), so now yet another death signalized my final year, a death that hit me far harder even than his own, because it happened so unexpectedly. So far as I can recall, it happened in autumn. Struck by a severe abdominal complaint, Miss Loftus went into St. Luke's Hospital on an emergency basis. The father of one of her best students, the excellent surgeon Joseph Perry Ponte II, operated on her, only to find that she suffered from advanced intestinal cancer, so developed that he could do nothing for her, and simply closed the abdominal flap. Heavily sedated, Miss Loftus died sometime soon after that.

I remember quite clearly the day at school when I learned of her death. My teachers and fellow students all had long known of the special friendship between Miss Loftus and myself. Amazingly, many students came up to me to express their sympathy over my loss, probably the first great friend whom I had cultivated in my life up to that point. Even more amazingly, as I entered their classes one after another, my teachers also took me to one side, briefly before instruction began, to sympathize with my loss. Despite this emotional outpouring from others, I managed to keep control over my grief until I walked back home that afternoon. I sat me down in the living room, picked up the telephone, and called my mother at work, not to talk long, just to give her the sad news. I simply stated that Miss Loftus died, giving only the barest facts. My mother said, "Oh no!" I replied, "Oh yes!" Then I broke down sobbing and weeping. She expressed her sympathy, and we hung up at once, while I continued weeping violently.

The death of Miss Loftus did make one thing easier for me. I did not apply for college, something that she would not have understood. If I had applied, I could only have done so as a special scholarship student; and one applies as early as possible during the senior year. Miss Loftus died before she could have noticed this deliberate neglect on my part. I had my reasons not to apply for college at that time. Nonetheless, I graduated in due course in June 1953. Another major phase of my life had ended. I was eighteen.

I recall attending my junior prom, but I found this teenage ritual so inane and insipid that I did not bother to attend my senior one. Given the depressed level of social dancing in those pre-rock-and-roll days, it held no appeal for me. I always enjoyed square dancing because of its purposeful animation and energy. Nor did teenage petting hold any charms for me: "All tease and no release," leading to a painful case of "blue balls." Inane and insipid indeed, especially after all the hot sex that I had known growing up with males.

Chapter VI. Military Service and Young Adulthood

College or not, scholarship or not, I got me a summer job edging into autumn, just a job for the time being, at a store on a main street in the North End, a store that sold fresh produce and its specialty, horsemeat, then a novelty, but leaner and better than beef as a source of protein. The owner, Nate Greenstein, a great good guy, made for entertaining company and in general was a pretty good boss. He and his family lived in a newer housing project west of Presidential Heights and the big cemetery. I did all kinds of odd jobs for him, moving produce around, waiting on customers, and so forth. Of course, I realized that I could go nowhere in this or any other dead-end job, nor anywhere else professionally or scholastically without college. I had vague plans of teaching or entering the theatre.

The Korean War had not quite finished, and if a young man did not go to college and get good grades, then he ran a good chance that the U.S. military would induct him into one of its branches. Joining a branch seemed somehow much less passive than waiting for induction, and conferred a few privileges. If I joined, then I could bank on the G.I. Bill to put me through four or five years of college, carefully living on limited funds and supplementing my income with odd jobs during the summer, or even part-time during the school year. That way I would not need to depend on scholarships, provided I got ordinary good grades. As my first choice, I wanted to go to sea, given the marine background of New Bedford, but the Navy had a waiting list. Then I fancied the Air Force as the next best thing, but again a waiting list.

Apparently I could not avoid the Army as my last and least preference. At the last minute I noticed a poster for the U.S. Marines. I knew its traditional (very close) relationship with the Navy, and so the U.S.M.C. became the choice: it had no waiting list. I signed the necessary papers, and after induction in late October I went to boot camp at Parris Island off the southern coast of South Carolina. My tour of duty would extend for three years ending in October 1956, but I would get an early discharge in August of that year so that I could begin my freshman year (1956-57) in September. Because I had worked as a clerk in my uncle's dry-cleaning store, someone in Washington, D.C., assigned me, after boot camp (and boot leave), to a Navy Air Supply school, to become a clerk in Marine Air Supply, thus combining elements of Navy and Air Force all into one. In a sense I did obtain my wish for duty at sea or in the air.

Boot camp turned out to be a real challenge both physically and emotionally, but memories of home, school, and family sustained me both morally and in terms of morale. Oddly enough, memories of historical New Bedford in particular buoyed my spirits up despite the harsh ambiance of Quonset hut and bare parade ground, not to mention the severe discipline of boot camp. During that last summer or so that I spent in my native city, I talked with friends, and we walked around for what would turn into the very last phase of my residence there, from birth to late adolescence. I must have anticipated leaving.

On my time off I still hiked around the town and, as it turned out, for a last look at certain special buildings and sites that I had previously visited, and that had long fascinated me. Chief among them there stand out the mansions and other structures made out of granite, sporting multicolumned porticos, and often endowed with cupolas and widow's walks. A prime example sits at the eastern bottom of William Street, the lordly Custom House with a portico of Ionic columns. Along County Street to the south there sits the Grinnell mansion with four colossal Doric columns, and across from it on the east there sits the superb mansion with Corinthian columns that survives as the Jewish Community Center, beautifully maintained.

On County Street right next to the Common on the south there formerly stood the most stunning example of a granite mansion, with wings on the north and south, and with impressive porticos of Ionic columns on the west and east, the latter overlooking not just its own wide, multiple, descending terraces, but much of the town and harbor. Its demolishment before World War I represents a great architectural loss. Perhaps another and unique building makes up for the loss. The essence of picturesqueness, this more modern building, the Jonathan Bourne Whaling Museum, conceived in the Georgian style, made out of handsome red brick with white trim, rises atop Johnnycake Hill across from the Seamen's Bethel (not far from the harbor), mentioned by Herman Melville in his romance of the ocean, *Moby-Dick*.

In this accounting I can only allude marginally to the many handsome and just a bit less impressive whaling mansions made out of wood, most of them extremely picturesque with modest porch or portico, cupola and widow's walk, and surrounding trees and other verdure. In addition to these architectural recollections, needless to mention, memories of friends and family also lifted my spirits during the three months of boot camp, November 1953 to January 1954, but I have already mentioned these, and they need no further description or emphasis beyond the names of my mother, Miss Loftus, and my painter-singer friend Henry James. After her death I often dreamed of Miss Loftus, and in these dreams otherwise realistic we often visited back and forth, truly consoling fantasies, especially when I had them in Marine boot camp.

Halfway through boot camp, my mother's boyfriend Lee Hebert, who happened to be traveling for some reason through the South, drove onto the island; and the people in charge allowed me to go out to the parking lot and to visit with him in his car. A big beam of transcendent light, something reassuringly civilian, suddenly illuminated the rather austere life that I along with other recruits was leading. What a sense of change and relief his visit and talking with Lee, gave me! He noticed that I had lost weight, looked trim and fit, and stood and walked ramrod straight with broad shoulders, none of which I myself could observe. We recruits had only small mirrors for shaving. His spoken observations made me feel good about myself at last. I had gained in confidence.

Something quite negative had happened to me in my last two years of Latin, those with Miss Ryan, which had made me lose all or most of my confidence, whereby I had gone from having a normal faith or belief in myself to virtually none. When Miss Ryan realized what she had unintentionally done, she did her best to make me feel better about myself. (I made my translated homework as polished and correct as possible, but when I came to read it aloud in class, I developed extreme speech hesitation, and Miss Ryan interpreted this as unpreparedness, rather than the nervousness that it was.) I did somewhat recover from this nervousness and speech hesitation (I did not suffer from it in any of my other classes), but boot camp helped me recover from it completely. The discipline in boot camp, which at first can make the recruits lose all their confidence, can then later build it back in them. Thus, as the others recovered from their funk, I also did the same, but in my case I recovered as well from the other funk going back to high school. This represented for me a major step forward.

Despite the severe contrast that boot camp makes with civilian life, I personally derived an enormous amount of good out of the experience both physically and psychically, the latter quite unexpectedly. By the time I finished boot camp and went home on my first furlough, I had become transformed into a better and healthier person. Still, what an exuberance I felt when I left the strict prison of boot camp and then briefly tasted civilian life again during my leave! Even if it seemed to pass too quickly, the furlough lasted some three weeks. I had plenty of time to travel by train (how most people journeyed in those pre-airflight years), first going home to New England and then returning to Florida, but only after spending several blessèd weeks with my mother at our old apartment in Presidential Heights.

I must say something about the trains that went up and down the Atlantic or Eastern Seaboard as well as other parts of the U.S. in those flightless days. These passenger trains pulled various cars, those old Pullman coaches: the drawing-room cars, the dining and sleeping cars, the day coaches (the ordinary passenger cars), etc. We have all seen in movies of the 1930s and 1940s the drawing-room cars, out of reach for people of limited funds, who mostly traveled in the day coaches. By lucky coincidence the Marine Corps had us travel via sleeping car, which resembled a day coach, but which transformed at night into sleeping cars with nice, comfy, private bunk beds, one above the other. Unless one brought one's own food (many did), the passengers in the sleeping car ate the three meals per day in the dining car.

I usually traveled by sleeping car and ordinarily slept well despite or because of the sleep-inducing clickety-clack of the train wheels moving over the hard iron rails. When the train stopped at night for whatever reason, one might wake up and wonder at the delay, but one would normally fall right back to sleep. All in all, the passenger trains represented a generally comfortable mode of travel. They simply took more time to go from one place to another than an airplane. During the day most people read, napped, or looked out the window at the ever-changing landscape.

Apart from the essential engineers who made the trains actually move, the porters, and only the porters, made life comfortable for the passengers journeying on the Pullman cars. They transformed the seats into the curtained sleeping berths and waited on the passengers in their seats or in the dining cars. They, and only they, provided an irreplaceable service; and when I traveled going north or south, I always realized the important role they played in the comfort and enjoyment of the passengers. The trains usually hired as porters mostly Afro-American males; most of those I encountered I found to be middle-aged and seasoned employees, the personification of charm and accommodation. Upon leaving the train after a journey, many passengers usually gave a tip to the porter, or porters, who had given them generally excellent service. I must accord those old-time porters the highest praise and pay them the highest compliments.

The powers that be had assigned me to the Naval Air School at the Naval Air Station west of Jacksonville, Florida, across the St. Johns River. There I would spend the next three months, approximately March through May, learning what would become my regular job of Marine Air Supply clerk. After the schooling they would assign me to the Third Marine Air Wing at Opa-locka in northwest Miami, where I would remain from June 1954 until September 1955, some fifteen months. Meanwhile I enjoyed going to school at the Naval Air Station near Jacksonville, and often on my own time I would spend the day in the big city nearby, haunting the libraries and used bookstores as usual, unless I went to see some feature film at some first-run or second-run house.

While in high school, I began my first serious book-collecting, in this case, certain juvenile so-called series books, with some of which (like the novels of Edgar Rice Burroughs) I had grown up; and eventually I had made complete, or almost complete, collections of them. To the original first fifteen titles of the Tom Swift Series (which I inherited from Uncle Roland), I eventually added all the other titles of the forty-volume series, apart from the very last one (yes, volume forty), *Tom Swift and His Magnetic Silencer*. Edward Stratemeyer, who plotted the series as a highly successful writer of boys' books, also went on to establish the Stratemeyer Literary Syndicate. He conceived and plotted most of a huge variety of series, but had them actually written by other authors under pseudonyms. Thus, for example, Howard Garis, Jr., who wrote the Uncle Wiggly books (about a rabbit), really scrivened most of the Tom Swift Series under the pen name of Victor Appleton. Stratemeyer himself authored the Rover Boys Series (which became enormously popular) under the pen name of Arthur M. Winfield. I chose the Tom Swift Series as the one representative classic Stratemeyer Literary Syndicate series to collect par excellence.

Published mostly by Grosset & Dunlap (*the* publishers par excellence of all manner of popular-style fiction), some of these other Stratemeyer syndicate series gained an enormous vogue, selling thousands or even millions of copies despite the objurgations or objections of librarians and serious-minded literary people. Librarians in public libraries refused to put them on their shelves, objecting to their highly formulaic nature, however otherwise competently written. The Stratemeyer syndicate books need no apology, defense, or detailed account from me. The titles and series appear to be legion, and the older reader will easily recognize them: the Motor Boys, the Don Sturdy series, the Bobbsey Twins, the Hardy Boys series, the Ted Scott Flying Stories, the Nancy Drew Mystery Stories, etc., etc., ad infinitum and ad nauseam! Some of them, updated, continue to sell.

Apart from the Tom Swift Series, I largely concentrated on collecting the books of two original authors who actually wrote their own titles, even if published (ironically) under the imprint of Grosset & Dunlap! The first of these two authors, Percy Keese Fitzhugh, laid most of his books, most of them about Boy Scouts, in the northeast U.S. (the author's own native area), largely New Jersey and New York State. His chief series include the Tom Slade Books, the Roy Blakeley Books, the Pee-wee Harris Books, the Westy Martin Books, and so forth, most of them "Published with the approval of THE BOY SCOUTS OF AMERICA," as it usually read under the author's name on any given title page. Sir R. S. S. Baden-Powell, the British general, established the Boy Scouts in England in 1908, followed by the Boy Scouts of America, established in 1910. Rather than a mere cynical ploy to sell copies of Fitzhugh's titles (that is, with the approval of the Boy Scouts), the books actually played the major role in popularizing the early Boy Scout movement. P. K. F., I should add, wrote in a very entertaining manner with much word-play and banter, whether in the dialogue or in the narrative.

The other original author (of series books) whose titles I collected, Leo Edwards (Edward Edson Lee), laid his narratives in the general Midwest area, but largely northern Illinois and southern Wisconsin (the author's own native region, where he lived in Cambridge), at the time principally the land of lakes and forests, as well as the canals that linked the local rivers. His own series include two major ones, the Jerry Todd Books and the Poppy Ott Books, and the three minor ones built around Andy Blake (a young salesman), Trigger Berg, and Tuffy Bean (a likeable canine). With the very first Jerry Todd book, Leo Edwards established the principal "conceit" of his boy-centered fiction, that the featured heroes themselves actually wrote their own stories (usually told in the first person singular), and that Edwards merely edited and/or touched them up to make them suitable for publication.

Ingeniously structured and plotted, and sounding as if indeed the boys had written them, the books, like those by Fitzhugh, became very popular, a real vogue greatly assisted and enhanced by the delightful caricature-like illustrations done by Bert Salg, a popular-style artist of the 1920s and later. The author included a special feature at the end (sometimes at the start) in many or most of the books, a feature called "The Chatter-Box." Therein Edwards would include fan letters and poems by the young aficionados of his two chief series, material usually written in admiration of the boy heroes and their fairly plausible adventures, even if presented as low-key fantasy.

My introduction to P. K. Fitzhugh and Leo Edwards I owe to the old Y.M.C.A. with its gables and corner tower, built of mixed brick and stone in (Henry Hobson) Richardson style, located just west of City Hall in the civic center of New Bedford. On the third floor, a collection of boys' books, mostly series books, existed in a revolving bookcase, where I found a good number of titles by both Fitzhugh and Edwards. Although the often fanciful titles of the Jerry Todd and Poppy Ott books caught my attention, I first picked up and read *Tom Slade on the River*. The kind young man who managed the top or third floor let me borrow books (no strings attached) to take and read at home. I always returned them after a few days, or however long it took me to read them. I began with Fitzhugh, and then continued with Edwards. Since that first experience, I have read and re-read most of the titles by both authors, a low-key pleasure but solid and substantial in a way that many adult novels rarely accomplish.

Although the series by P. K. F. and Leo Edwards never sold in the immense quantities enjoyed by the Stratemeyer syndicate products, they still managed to do quite creditably on their own. The overall genre of the series books dwindled in the 1930s during the Great Depression. I began my serious collecting of these books while at or near Jacksonville, Florida, and I more or less finished while in Southern California, mostly via the old Acres of Books in Long Beach, then still under the enlightened ownership of Frank and Charles Cotten. I bought a huge amount of the series books (most of them for less than a dollar) at that used bookstore in the spring or summer of 1956.

After boot camp at Parris Island, any other military base would have seemed an improvement, but N.A.S. Jacksonville became and remained my favorite base of all those that I came to know from personal residence. The Air Supply School gave me no problems; I had a big city nearby for my escape valve, but most of all I had a big luxurious base to discover and explore, including three libraries and three swimming pools, one for the enlisted men, one for the noncommissioned officers, one for the brass, the regular or commissioned officers; and in each case for their families as well, if they had them. By luxurious I mean lush, verdant lawns and attractive landscapes, and with an exotic new detail for me from New England, tropical palm trees—not to mention well-designed and well-maintained hangars, houses, and other structures.

Again, after Parris Island, what a contrast and what a relief! Here on my time off I could wander and make discoveries at will—all the while enjoying equable warm weather not yet hot. I would find tropical hot weather (with blessèd air conditioning indoors) once I arrived at the Marine Air Station at Opa-locka. Meanwhile I enjoyed the swimming pool for enlisted men and the three libraries: those for commissioned and noncommissioned officers did not bar enlisted men from using their respective collections and other resources. Following another brief leave at home, I finally reached what would turn into my chief locale of military obligation, located at Opa-locka. It had taken me some seven months from the time of enlistment until June 1954 to get there.

My new locale of assignment soon transformed into a great good place for me, not as big and beautiful as N.A.S. Jacksonville, but, as I would soon discover, with other even more exceptional amenities. Once I got established in my new barracks on the first of two floors—with bunk (I had the top one), duffel bag, foot locker, upright locker (for once, close by)—I went to work in the huge hangar not far away (whose gigantic doors rarely closed), in one of the upstairs offices on the south side of the main, enormous, open, indoor space, where the mechanics repaired and serviced the airplanes, mostly fighter jets. I worked in an inner office as an accountant who kept the books, noting down expenses and expenditures in big ledgers. The paperwork came in, I processed it, and then it went somewhere else. My job, simplicity itself, gave me no problem, I did it well, and my superiors complimented me, including the colonel in charge of everything who presided in the outer office, and who gave me occasionally a ride in his cute little three-wheel Isetta.

I had a great new boss as my immediate superior, an old sea dog and a career man. I could have had no one better than genial, smiling, but savvy Sergeant Turnipseed, who seemed always to have a coffee cup in hand. He made everyone feel good around him. He would often make me smile and laugh when he would begin some command or advice with "Now you just listen to your old sea dad here." Often I had extra time while at work, and I took advantage of it to do surreptitious reading. I would place a smaller book on or inside an opened ledger, and if a superior came into my space unexpectedly, I would simply close the ledger, thus hiding the clandestine book. Sergeant Turnipseed subtly let me know that he had noted my secret reading, but he simply grinned and looked the other way. And as ever, I did a helluva lot of reading on my own time.

I usually took my meals in the mess hall (overall pretty good, the breakfast often with fresh fruit salad, including pineapple, a real treat for me coming from New England), but on occasion I would eat in the commissary (payment required) in case I missed my meal for some reason in the mess hall. It did not cost that much, and the hamburgers and cheeseburgers with crisp French fries made for a refreshing change. We had an hour and a half or two hours for lunch and an extended break from the workplace. Literally right around the corner from the commissary (going south and then west) stood the base library, relatively small but packed with many books, either fiction or fact. I had begun reading science fiction while at N.A.S. Jacksonville, and I sought such fascinating new material at this new base. It would seem that the base library had had a number of enlightened librarians in charge before I arrived on the scene, because the fiction shelves had quite a few volumes of fantasy and science fiction, either single titles or anthologies. I well remember the thrill I got when I first read *Childhood's End* by Arthur C. Clarke; this book made me a lifelong fan of Clarke and of science fiction in general. The directness and simplicity of style also provided me with some pleasant and unexpected revelations.

Once I had exhausted the available sci-fi novels (to use Forrie Ackerman's adroit neologism, punning on hi-fi, however much unloved by Harlan Ellison), I turned my focus on the available sci-fi and other anthologies, wherein I soon discovered some very different stories as created by some very different writers, and of a type such as I had not suspected actually existed: obviously modern, but who did not write like most modern writers, and who reminded me somewhat of Edgar Allan Poe. I noted the name of the editor, one August Derleth, who provided brief but sufficient notes on the authors before the given stories. In one anthology one story really hit me hard, "The Rats in the Walls" by one H. P. Lovecraft, which I assumed to be a pseudonym ("He loves his craft," ha-ha!)—and soon after that, in another anthology, by the same author, "The Colour out of Space," which hit me equally hard as the first. Who was this Lovecraft? In another anthology I discovered an equally powerful story, "The Black Stone," by Robert E. Howard. My, what extraordinary fictioneers! In still another anthology I read "The Return of the Sorcerer" by one Clark Ashton Smith, which, while competent, only impressed me moderately.

However, soon after this, in an anthology called *The Other Side of the Moon*, also edited by the same Derleth, I experienced quite a long story (actually two stories joined together, as I found out later), "The City of the Singing Flame" by the same Clark Ashton Smith.

Emotionally and spiritually this last narrative, written in quite a remarkable and highly poetic prose, the like of which I had never quite encountered before, bowled me over and knocked me down, not just because of the colorful, vivid, and intense imagination that had shaped the story but equally because of the uncommon vocabulary without which the story could not have come into existence. Because I had studied Latin, French, and English each for four years in high school, particularly Latin, the vocabulary per se gave me no real problem. However, I had almost never before encountered such uncommon words, obviously Latinate, employed in a piece of fiction—words like ineffable, supernal, primordial, incalculable, vertiginous, and so forth. I clearly recall when I first read "The City of the Singing Flame" (linked with "Beyond the Singing Flame"). Midmorning I had begun reading it surreptitiously at my desk, the anthology placed upon one of my ledgers opened out flat, in case I needed to hide it, should a superior look in upon me. No one intruded. Even though I had not quite finished it when lunchtime came, I stayed at my desk until I had read the narrative in its entirety. When I finally went to lunch, I really needed something edible and substantial to anchor me down! I seemed to be walking on air, so completely taken out of myself had I become, my head filled with strange phrases and outré prose rhythms, not to mention the extravagant imagery carefully implanted in my memory.

Where could I get yet further tales like these existential parables of dread and wonder? Would these intimations of the otherworldly, as expressed in fiction, somehow connect me back to my early recollections of the Other Side? I needed them. I had a spiritual thirst for them. My childhood religion had never satisfied me, but I still had this need for something supra-natural and beyond-the-mundane. Why had these modern fantastic tales hit me so hard? I had this void within me that needed, nay, demanded fulfillment. Instead of turning to any conventional religion, I sought solace and a sense of spiritual possibility in these metaphysically substantial fables or modern myths. So then, where could I find further examples of these marvelous tales? I had noticed in the books edited by Derleth, in his notes on the authors, the frequent mention of a certain Arkham House. In what locale did this publisher have his place of business? I would never have thought of the Midwest.

I checked the list of publishers and their addresses in a volume called *Books in Print*. I found that the address for Arkham House simply consisted of the same name followed by Sauk City, Wisconsin—and coincidentally in the same general region as Cambridge, the same town where Leo Edwards had once lived and authored his fanciful stories. I wrote a letter of inquiry to Arkham House, and not long afterward I received a personal note from the owner-scrivener-editor, who turned out to be the same August Derleth, who had edited the anthologies I had just read! He also thoughtfully enclosed some advertising materials listing the inventory of the titles that Arkham House had in stock. In his letter Derleth warmly encouraged my interest in the kind of fiction that his Arkham House published, and stated that he very much understood my desire to read a lot more of such imaginative tales. Later I discovered that Derleth had an excellent reputation as an all-around literary man, as fictioneer, poet, and serious regionalist writer.

The inventory materials that I had received with great enthusiasm I now studied with equally great care. Disappointingly, Arkham House had almost no titles by Lovecraft for sale that summer of 1954. *The Outsider and Others* and *Beyond the Wall of Sleep* had long since gone out of print. It did have some remaindered copies of *The Best Supernatural Stories of H. P. Lovecraft* put out by the World Publishing Company during World War II. It did have one book by Ashton Smith, *Genius Loci*, and one big book by Robert E. Howard, the fine omnibus of his best fantastic tales, *Skull-Face and Others*. Many earlier titles had already gone out of print, but a sizeable inventory remained. From this I selected quite a few titles, if not indeed most of the available stock, including the two years of Derleth's periodical, the *Arkham Sampler*. Some of the authors I already knew from Derleth's anthologies; and a few turned out to be outstanding, especially Henry S. Whitehead with the second posthumous collection of his short stories, *West India Lights*. An earlier one, *Jumbee and Other Uncanny Tales*, had already gone out of print.

The order I sent to Derleth after due study turned into quite a large one, and as he told me in a separate letter, it required a full two boxes. Several weeks later I received both of them in my workplace at the base in Opa-locka, moreover with great eagerness. Although I began reading some of the books at once, I found it inconvenient as a serviceman to keep them with me personally, and I eventually shipped them in the same boxes re-addressed to my mother's care at our old home in Presidential Heights. Much later, once I reached California and attained civilian status again, I would have them shipped to me, but by then I would have a more or less permanent address care of a close friend in Santa Monica.

Arkham House had begun in 1939 as a kind of experimental sideline by Derleth, never intended as a major moneymaker, but once established it did okay for what Derleth purposed. Other people then imitated his example, and a whole bunch of small specialist publishing houses came into being in the 1940s. But not enough of a market for such books existed then, and most of these other publishers went out of business. Arkham House endured, not just because of better editorial policies but because during the 1950s (when I discovered their books) Derleth himself supported the house (located in his own large dwelling, Place of Hawks, outside Sauk City) out of the earnings from his voluminous writings (books and magazine articles), which circumstances compelled him to produce: he had to earn a living and had to support his family. However, in the 1960s, the process reversed: Arkham House became successful enough so that Derleth could depend on it as a source of income.

It merits particular mention that Derleth gave first book publication to many authors who might not have attained it from anyone but him, and who then went on to have special careers, becoming well-known, e. g., Ray Bradbury, Fritz Leiber, Robert Bloch, and others. By the time he died in July 1971, Arkham House had continued its commercial success, but again for a small specialist publishing house. His two children, William Walden and April Rose, inherited the business, but the daughter it was who took it over and managed it, at first with the paid help of Derleth's former assistant Roderick Meng. Unfortunately no one in the family of children, grandchildren, and great-grandchildren has ever actually learned the editorial or creative side of the business, a thing absolutely strategic or essential, and April has had to hire well-informed people to perform the editorial function. Derleth did it out of love for the genre of fantasy and science fiction, not to mention hypernatural horror. Since April's death, Arkham House appears to have lapsed into some kind of standstill or impasse.

What with marvelous reading adventures, exotic discoveries, aesthetic thrills, and so forth—not to mention the demands made on me by my military service (not that bad)—my life proceeded apace. I would sometimes take the long bus ride from Opa-locka (passing through Hialeah with its racetrack and its bevies of spectacular scarlet flamingos) to downtown Miami, unless I got a ride in the car of some buddy on the base. Downtown Miami appeared very different in those days from what it has become since then, one of the great Latin American cities. Back then it seemed small, almost provincial (I say this in a complimentary sense), but pleasant and charming in an unpretentious manner. It did not have very many highrises, but it did have much attractive Art Deco architecture, even if it could not compare to all the Art Deco hotels in Miami Beach. The downtown public library, a beautiful white or off-white structure broader than tall, did not have very many books compared to the urban libraries up north, and so I began using the much better-stocked library at the University of Miami in Coral Gables. There I could usually find adequate books on whatever subject happened to interest me. The trip there and back made for a very long day, but eminently worth it in every way.

Thanks to a buddy who also wanted to do the same thing, I began working out with weights in the base gym at Opa-locka. We both built our bodies up to an impressive level over a period of six months or so. In addition on my own, I did a lot of situps, eventually building up to 500 at one session. Once I achieved this—my abdominal muscles did in fact look like the traditional washboard—I dropped down to an easier 50 or 100; it took much less time. Otherwise it took me half an hour to do 500! I also continued my extended walks, hiking several times around the base outside the chain-link fence, and making a rather startling discovery on the north side (the ground plan of the base formed a square or squarish rectangle). A small but significant section of the fence completely lacked the diamond-shaped mesh, making it possible to slip out and back in with utter ease. But since the personnel could just as easily go through the main gate, why would one go out of one's way to pass through this open, even if unguarded, section of fence?

To break the enjoyable monotony of our military existence, once a year we had to qualify with the rifle. To do so, we went north to the navy base at Green Cove Springs on the western shore of the St. Johns River, about twenty-five miles due south of Jacksonville. Once again, the base had a small but adequate library, but the base itself on this occasion provided the chief interest. The navy used only a small part of it, but here on the river (several miles wide, it seems more like a bay than a river) the naval establishment kept a large fleet of ships of various types not in active use, maintaining them, in the quaint phrase, in mothballs (that is, in protective storage). The chefs in the mess hall, all old salts (that is, well-seasoned sailors), made the standard navy food, but made it very well. Great chow!

Nevertheless, despite this agreeable existence, when we learned that our Third Marine Air Wing would be moving, one part to Japan, one part to El Toro, south of Los Angeles, most of us (at least those unattached to boyfriend or girlfriend) prepared eagerly for the big move. The powers that be gave us a choice, Japan or California, a rather hard choice as it shaped up. Exotic, far-off Japan had its ancient culture and charm (not to mention its women, many of them of legendary beauty) to entice us. However, exotic, not so distant California had its own old Californio culture and enchantment to lure us. I chose California almost without a moment's consideration. The Golden State (a creative name, since much of it is desert, dry and dun) had fascinated me since my youth, as soon as I could assimilate both text and photos in any article on California featured in the *National Geographic*. Furthermore, one of my favorite authors during my youth lived there, Edgar Rice Burroughs, who resided in Tarzana. The big move would take place in early September.

The big day finally came to pass: 5 September 1955. We got up extra early, all our personal gear in duffel bags, etc., ready to be moved and shipped by air, of course, along with ourselves. It would turn out to be a long, not quite all-day-long flight from Opa-locka to El Toro. We would travel in military transport planes, not the essence of comfort, but at least we would have enclosed toilets. Our transports took off, and soon we found ourselves aloft. The flight went as directly as possible, weather permitting: northwest over the Gulf of Mexico, across southern Louisiana, central Texas, southern New Mexico, and southern Arizona, and then due west to El Toro south of L.A. I remember flying over New Orleans and looking down, but I could identify very little from that height, except the mile-wide Mississippi. We landed at our new Marine Air Base in early or middle afternoon.

What a contrast to luxuriantly verdant Florida with its abundant water, palm trees, and lush tropicality! In their place desert and aridity seemed to reign, even allowing for the orange groves and other orchards between the base and the small city of Santa Ana. I never learned to like the new base, but perforce I tolerated it. It did have a few amenities. After the sweet, the delicious drinking water in Florida, we had this alkaline or acidic water that tasted like chalk and never seemed to quench my thirst. The base did have a gym with a weightlifting area that I used until it became too crowded, a real problem, and annoying. However, there I met and made a great new buddy of Louisiana French nativity who also disliked the base's crowded gym. We decided to patronize a commercial gym in Santa Ana just to the north. He had a car, and besides English we could speak a little French together. We went to the off-base gym two or three times per week. What a pleasure to drive through the sweet-smelling orange groves (some of the few that still survived), going to Santa Ana and then back to the base.

As already stated, the base did have some but not many amenities. Chief among them I discovered the base library, surprisingly large and quite well stocked. In this especial refuge away from the military world, I found some great new writers and great new books, paramount among them the omnibus *The Collected Writings of Ambrose Bierce* (put out by Citadel) with a trenchant and extended essay by Clifton Fadiman. However, after tasting the strong and flavorful brew concocted by master brewer Bierce, Fadiman's essay left me so dissatisfied with his rather conventional mainstream perceptions and opinions (he simply did not really comprehend Bierce in depth) that I began reading articles and books about Bierce much closer to the truth about this remarkable writer, whose magisterial lexicon *The Devil's Dictionary* delighted me beyond measure, including quite a few belly laughs. His brief humorous macabre stories delighted me no less, while his grim and savage *Tales of Soldiers and Civilians*, especially "Chickamauga," horrified me with their uncompromising vision of the hell that is war.

If he had come to some unflattering conclusions about humanity, about life, about people, Bierce had certainly merited the right to make such conclusions. Taking part in the Civil War from its beginning to its end, he had risen in the ranks from a mere enlisted man, and on the field of battle had become a commissioned officer, ascending to the rank of a brevetted major. If he had accomplished that, then Bierce must have proven himself a disciplined and competent soldier over and over again. Reportedly, he participated in many of the major battles of that internecine conflict between the North and the South, the Union and the Confederacy. Unequivocally he had to act bravely under fire, under the threat of death and serious injury from bullet, bayonet, and cannonball. Among other battles he fought at Chickamauga, the ferociousness of which he captures indelibly in his powerful and unforgettable short story of the same name. Thus he had witnessed, had known intimately, both the best and the worst of what men at war could achieve under nearly unbearable stress. The unflattering conclusions about humanity that he reached with some justice and propriety deserve our careful consideration and respect. Few of us could have withstood what Bierce endured without such experience forever leaving its mark on our psyche and subsequent emotional existence. I cannot help but wonder just how the desk-bound Mr. Fadiman would have reacted in the same nightmare situations through which Bierce passed, and which he survived.

Perhaps his overall experience in the Civil War can help us understand why Bierce preferred for his own special reading pleasure a certain type of fantasy to other forms of literature, in order to satisfy his own sardonic sense of humor and his own rather severe doctrine of aesthetics. We use the term fantasy here in its pre-Tolkien exemplification as imaginative projection as embodied, for example, in the plays of Kit Marlowe and Will Shakespeare, or as in Spenser's hodgepodge epic *The Faerie Queene*. Bierce clearly preferred as his escape literature a poem like *A Wine of Wizardry* (1907) or *The Testimony of the Suns* (1903), both by his poetic "pupil" George Sterling, or (in the genre of prose fiction) a compilation like that huge Saracenic mixture of poetry, wonder, humor, and horror, the *Arabian Nights*, or by extension, William Beckford's hilarious *History of the Caliph Vathek*. We can gauge and further plumb many of Bierce's tastes and preferences by reading the essays that accompanied the first major publication of

A Wine of Wizardry (in *Cosmopolitan*, a national magazine): "A Poet and His Poem" and "An Insurrection of the Peasantry." Somewhat later both Bierce and Ashton Smith gradually led me to investigate and appreciate George Sterling and his own poetic output.

With delights and revelations like these, I beguiled my third and last year in the Marine Corps. Apart from the workweek, Monday through Friday, I began spending every weekend up in L.A., even when the schedule dictated once-a-month weekend duty. I hired some buddy to stand by for me. Although not bored by military routine, it interested me much less. Since I was planning on the G.I. Bill to fund my room and board while attending college (I had been saving money for my tuition and books), I took great care not to fool around sexually with other Marines despite temptation and opportunity coming from several quite attractive guys obviously willing. I would not run the risk of detection, a dishonorable discharge, and the loss of my G.I. Bill. However, I could have sex off the base with man or woman so long as I behaved with discretion. Dear old Sergeant Turnipseed sometimes teased me about what I did to dip my wick, asking with a twinkle in his eye. For answer I would grin, put my two fists one above the other, as if grabbing onto a flashlight, and hold them just above my crotch. He got the message, ahem: self-actualization.

It goes without emphasis, I still noticed guys in general, and like them would merely glance in the showers at other genitals, but without staring, and making it obvious. Sometimes it took real will power not to stare, since a few of the guys carried impressive equipment. One kid in our barracks aroused universal interest. Like others, I had noticed him even before moving from Florida to El Toro. Hailing from some rural town in the South, this cute little white guy—he had an amiable, somewhat sleepy look about him—kind of reminded me of Dopey or Sleepy, one of the seven dwarfs in Disney's pioneer film *Snow White* (1937). He always amazed the other guys. This kid sported, flaccid, an unusually long and thick member like a regular-sized flashlight, or like a long and very thick piece of hose hanging down—easily bigger, flaccid, than the erections of most white males, or than even most well-hung Afro-Americans, that is, when flaccid. One could not help but notice such a phenomenal organ. How did he get it?

Once or twice a month in the barracks we would perform a complete general cleaning known as a field day in the Navy and Marine Corps. This happened in the workweek but not in the workday, rather in the evening after supper and before sunset. On one occasion, on our second floor, we had finished the cleaning except for those few guys buffing the lightly waxed floor with those giant round buffing machines. Most of us were sitting on the bunks with our feet well off the floor. We would give no problems or interference for the buffers. We were talking and making jokes. Good-naturedly I addressed the little kid with the giant penis, who sat not far from me, and asked him how he had gotten such an enormous member. Other guys all at once asked the same thing, almost in a chorus, one voice after another, "Yeah, how come such a little guy like you has such a great big dick?"

The kid grinned, and answered. "When I was a little boy, I ran around naked like other kids. One day I was sitting on a rock. A great big spider crawled up my leg and bit me on my dick. It swelled up real big, and it hurt a lot. My daddy and mommy took me to the doctor. He looked at me and my dick, and told them not to worry, that the swelling would go down. Finally it did after a couple of days. But it stayed big like this ever since." We all looked at each other and asked again, almost in a chorus, "What kind of spider was *that*?" The kid laughed and said that he did not know, but that it was not a black widow. I am positive that there was not a single one of us who would not have experimented with such a spider if we could have known what kind it was. Whenever I tell this anecdote to gay people, they too always ask the same question.

That first month (September 1955) or so of weekends in L.A. I mostly spent in and around the then downtown (minus all the highrises that would pop up later), getting acquainted with some of the landmarks. The idiosyncratic Pershing Square: I had had no concept of how many eccentrics and genuine individuals this big city possessed—big surprise! The Biltmore Hotel on the plaza's north side. A street nearby that had all the old magnificent movie palaces in a row, theatres that had witnessed many splendiferous premières. The Art Deco masterpiece that the main L.A. Public Library remains to this day both inside and out. The superb Richfield Building, another early highrise in black and gold, another Art Deco masterpiece, but stiflingly hot inside in the summer, now demolished, alas! To the east of the Biltmore, in the same city block (the northeast corner of Pershing Square), there was a cozy old coffee shop that made very good sandwiches, salads, breakfast, and lunch, and that I patronized in that first month of weekends. If I stayed overnight, I would have done so in some cheap but decent hotel, certainly not at the Biltmore, more suited to very wealthy people than to myself as ever on limited funds.

By mail from Florida I had already contacted Bob Mizer, the male physique photographer, the owner of the Athletic Model Guild, and the owner-editor of the magazine *Physique Pictorial*, but also a pioneer champion of gay rights in the 1950s and later, a period when it was rather dangerous to be a spokesman even in a modest way. Gay people, to keep their jobs and survive, did not dare avow their identity. By mail from El Toro I contacted Bob again, and he invited me to visit him during one of my weekends. He included the phone number for his photo studio, and soon in due course I showed up at his doorstep. He made me feel at home immediately, and I began spending all my weekends in his photo studio, where he usually entertained, sitting at his desk, typing, when not photographing. I had just turned twenty at the time, and he must have been in his thirties or so. I realized at once that Bob Mizer was an exceptional individual, perhaps a genius in his own genre.

Bob lived with his mother on the good-sized family property northwest of the immediate downtown. It consisted of a big two-story family house (a swimming pool he added later), his photography studio, and a structure combining a garage below and a photo lab above, where his brother-in-law developed the physique photos that earned the money to keep the whole enterprise going. Bob turned out to be a lot of fun, a great companion, unusually intelligent, and very well informed. He would often include me on the jaunts and errands that he ran in his car, eating out at restaurants, and so forth. He introduced me to two places that turned into a special treat, Clifton's Cafeterias in downtown L.A. They both boasted the most outrageous décor: one was the Redwood Forest, and the other the Tropical Island or some such. They both had several floors. The tropical one became my favorite: it had make-believe palm trees and other plants outlined with neon lighting. Both restaurants had pretty good food, especially for cafeterias; and they both had warm and welcoming atmospheres. What a great ambiance! I loved it, and I loved going there whether with Bob Mizer or other friends.

Here I want to pay a real and well-deserved compliment to Bob, particularly now that he hath transcended back to the Other Side. He was a brave and magnificent human being. If he became tired of me, he never let me know. I usually overnighted on Saturday and returned to El Toro on Sunday late afternoon or evening. I was young, handsome, well muscled, well educated, unpretentious, and people told me then and later that I had a lot of charm. At last through Bob Mizer I began to find partners for sex and socializing, not the least debt that I owed and still owe him. He knew that I was looking for a special partner, and again through him I eventually found that partner, another Bob, or his name in full, Robert G. Crook. He taught high school mathematics and originally came from an upper middle-class family in Lincoln, Nebraska. Like me he was a bodybuilder, well educated and cultivated. He lived and worked in Santa Monica. Bob Mizer phoned him, told him about me, and Bob Crook drove over to meet me on a Saturday afternoon.

The new Bob turned out to be neat, clean, well groomed, unassuming, and very pleasant with a ready smile. While no slouch myself at twenty, I can only describe Bob Crook at twenty-six as what most people would call a pretty man, that is, as physically beautiful. We felt an instant attraction to each other, and after socializing with Bob Mizer for an hour or so, by mutual agreement between the new Bob and myself, we drove to Santa Monica. I must admit that I felt a certain reluctance at leaving Bob Mizer, as if I were deserting him and the photo studio, which had served as my weekend home for several months. I mentioned this to Mizer, but he dismissed my qualms and wished Bob Crook and me the best, adding that I would still be seeing him on occasion, of course, at his photo studio. He had his eye on both Bob Crook and myself as future (and superior) athletic models. Whether or not we actually posed for Mizer, I can't recall.

Soon, after an hour or so, Bob Crook and I found ourselves at his apartment in Santa Monica above the garage where he parked his four-door passenger car. His apartment, one of several built around a lovely garden-court with trees and flowers, contained a living room with the ubiquitous television set, a kitchen with eating area, a bathroom with bathtub and shower, and a good-sized bedroom with a big double bed. I believe that we went out to eat at some quality cafeteria not far away. Returning to what would become my new home on the weekends, and then full-time while I went to U.C.L.A., Bob and I relaxed in front of the television.

Without further ado, we kissed a very long kiss, embraced, went to bed, and made love. The sex per se resulted in something deeply satisfying for both of us, and we fell asleep close to each other. I had rarely, if ever, soul-kissed anybody, man or woman; and such intimate build-up to the sex act itself turned into a major and exciting revelation for me. With the right person French kissing can become sensational and spectacular! Between my weekends first at Bob Mizer's and then those at Bob Crook's, the twelve months from September 1955 to August 1956 went by rapidly and agreeably. In fact, because of my relationship with Bob Crook, it really became an enchanted period for me, and it continued on into my first and second years at U.C.L.A. I could hardly wait to get out of the military, and to start college. U.C.L.A. had already accepted me with no problem, given my excellent grades in high school. Even though I still had two months to go beyond August to fulfill my three-year enlistment contract (that is, September and October), the Marine Corps was giving me an early and honorable discharge so that I could start attending school at the regular time in September.

I had taken an examination for the University of Chicago (an expensive private school, I should add) and had won an honorary entrance scholarship of $800, but the same problem arose for me that had arisen when I had contemplated going to Harvard on a scholarship. Could I perform academically well enough so that I could continue to apply and receive scholarships? I chose instead to go to U.C.L.A., and on the G.I. Bill, the benefits of which I had earned by my enlistment and my good conduct. It would be cheaper over four years to go there, even if I had to pay full out-of-state tuition for my first year. My year of California residence at El Toro did not count because I had lived there under military auspices.

Like most people soon to leave the military, I too counted, and crossed off, on a calendar the last hundred days of my enlistment time left, a little over three months. I too had the irrational fears and worries that, if a war might break out in those last hundred days, I might need to remain in the military longer than planned. The international scene remained steady. Nevertheless, the great and long-awaited release finally came. I believe that it happened on a Saturday or Sunday, because Bob came down from L.A. to get me and bring me to the new home that I would now be sharing with him full-time. Even though my new status in the Marine Corps Reserve obliged me to hold on to my military gear (my uniforms and so forth) for several years, I sold them to someone in my barracks; and he stood there and took the very last pieces as I took them off and changed into civilian clothes.

I distinctly recall that last day. It was later morning. When I passed through the front gate with such gear as I still retained, stowed in some overnight bag, Bob was waiting for me in his car, bless him, just as planned and promised. I put my bag in the back seat, sat myself down in the seat next to the driver's, and then it hit me. I was free at last. I was free to live my life as I wished. The sudden release from the emotional tension that had been building up for months made me burst into tears. I sobbed, so overwrought had I become despite myself. Bob held and comforted me, and when the tempest passed, we drove off en route to Santa Monica. I never saw El Toro again. One major period in my life had ended and another had begun.

Chapter VII. U.C.L.A. and Odd Jobs

The theatre with its associated and secondary arts had long fascinated me, so that for the initial two years at U.C.L.A. I became a theatre arts major and language minor (in this case, French). A few years later, for my final two years, I became a French major and Spanish minor. Heigh-ho and ho-hum, from aspiring toward a career in the theatre (always a creative ferment) I switched to serious plans to teach languages. I had a much greater interest in the theatre than I did in the movies, but New York remains the big city for theatre arts of all kinds than L.A.—at least it was back in the 1950s. I did not pursue the theatre arts curriculum with greater avidity for a variety of reasons, but I suspect that it had something to do with Bob.

I started taking ballet lessons in the evening with Tatiana Riabushchinskaya, otherwise Riabouchinska, one of the three former baby ballerinas (so called) of the Ballets Russes, and the wife of dancer-choreographer David Lichine. They had a dancing studio in Beverly Hills. Even if I could not have become a ballet dancer at twenty or twenty-one, I knew the value of rigorous dance training in shaping a capable all-around performer. I took ballet lessons for some six months, and also took some adagio classes (in the evening as well), learning how to support women as they execute the disciplined ballet movements (supporting them this way is a real art), for which Tatiana and David even enlisted Bob (they needed men specifically for this demanding style of physical maneuver), who good-naturedly performed this yeoman service along with me.

The biggest chance from which I walked away came in my first or second year. The theatre arts department was putting on some kind of Aztec-themed spectacle, and I tried out for the part of some important character in the drama. I had all the right ingredients: looks, movements, and general abilities. But then I let Bob persuade me not to pursue this great opportunity, his arguments tending as follows:

rehearsals would use up most of my spare time whether diurnal or nocturnal, especially my evenings; I would be returning home from U.C.L.A. rather late; how could Bob and I have a life together if I dedicated my life to the theatre, etc., etc. Since the relationship with Bob had become the much-needed anchor in my life, I heeded what he said, but most reluctantly. I refused the singular chance represented by the part in this curious drama.

I also anticipated, erroneously, that other similar opportunities would arise, but they never did. Moreover, like the young fool into which I had metamorphosed, I changed, at the end of my sophomore year, my major to French, my minor to Spanish. I had chosen to become a teacher of languages, which I have never taught except privately as a tutor. I realized later that, compared to high school, I had lost my focus in college. Also, high school had spoiled me, a time when I had so many great friends among my teachers, who took a real interest in my academic progress, who gave me good advice, and who participated actively in my life. For all of which I never found a genuine substitute in college, which I missed and evidently needed. However, obviously I survived this poor decision, and I continued my academic life at U.C.L.A.

After living about a year at his apartment in Santa Monica, Bob suggested that we find a new residence in West L.A. to make it easier for me to go back and forth to U.C.L.A. We found a neat little house in the desired area, rather smaller than his apartment, but viable enough, south of Santa Monica Boulevard, and southwest of U.C.L.A., within easy reach of the campus by foot or bus along Westwood Boulevard; and also southwest of the marvelously grandiose Mormon Temple nearby on Santa Monica Boulevard. The little house had its own fenced-in walkway to and from the street (the place backed up against an alley), and thus had privacy from the main house on the property to the immediate north or northeast of us, the residence of the owners from whom we were renting. The new place had in its northern half a good-sized living room, and in its southern half a kitchen with eating area, a bathroom, and then a bedroom, into which Bob's big double bed could just fit. We could also build bookcases made out of bricks supporting wide flat boards for my growing collection of series books, and now that of my Arkham House titles.

Meanwhile I had prepared my books (in storage at my mother's apartment in New Bedford) for shipment to me at Bob's place in Santa Monica, where I received and put them out on the shelves available in that residence, while still in the Marine Corps. I had already augmented my collection of series books with my large purchases from Acres of Books in Long Beach. Also, separate but significant, I had also bought by mail (while at El Toro) a very good copy with dust jacket of Smith's second Arkham House collection of short stories (long out of print), *Lost Worlds* (1944), for an inexpensive price. I did not at once devour the book as I had anticipated, but read the tales at my leisure, from time to time, savoring the originality of the imagination and the beauty of Smith's prose style. The delight and pleasure that I received from his remarkable tales proved only a little bit less than those that I had gotten from "The City of the Singing Flame" in Derleth's anthology *The Other Side of the Moon*.

At U.C.L.A., while I did not do as well as I had in high school, I kept up a good enough average, B's and C's, and A's on occasion, in order to continue getting my G.I. Bill benefits. The theatre arts classes did not turn out as dynamic as I had hoped. My French classes after those in high school gave me no problem, but still held my interest. I would not find my French classes of any great concern until my second year, when we began studying systematically the history of French literature from Medieval through Renaissance into Modern, and I enjoyed the great pleasure of having Professor Hubert as the instructor. He proved to be a wonderful guide and a delightful humane being, as well as incredibly erudite. He knew his material so well that he never used notes in his classes. He taught several of my classes, always a treat, and an extraordinary learning experience.

Another remarkable teacher, Madame Lenard (in my second or third year), taught us advanced grammar and composition. A fascinating and beautiful woman, she somehow reminded me of a personage at the court of Louis XV or Louis XVI, someone who might have served as an intimate companion of Marie Antoinette. Madame Lenard once had us each choose one of several classical poems to memorize, and I chose "La Beauté" by Baudelaire, and intimately tasted for the first time the special quality and purity of that poet whose work plays for many Frenchmen in our modern period the same role as the dramas of Shakespeare do for Anglophones since about the time of poet laureate John Dryden.

But let me state it again: after the extraordinary experience I had in high school, and then the major change afforded by the Marine Corps, college seemed rather flat, lacking the intellectual excitement and sense of discovery that I felt in high school, or on my own in military service, or simply when I found and explored a new library, or a series of new libraries, as I did while attending U.C.L.A., which possesses fabulous collections with untold and unsuspected riches of all kinds. In case I forgot to mention it in chronological sequence, I add it here now as an important afterthought: not only did I receive an honorable discharge, but I performed otherwise quite all right while in the Marine Corps: I went from private to private first class to corporal to sergeant, the last rank not long before I mustered out of the military.

Meanwhile and always I maintained my interest in libraries wherever I found myself, whether in Santa Monica or in Westwood, above all in the fabulous libraries created and sustained at U.C.L.A. These latter, where I discovered them in situ (rather like archaeological sites), I soon put to good use: the college or undergraduate library, the research library, and the music library (aptly situated in the Music Building). Growing out of my long-held fascination with Tchaikovsky and his music for ballet (for three specific and extraordinary ballets), I had long nurtured a special interest in the tradition or traditions of the Romantic Ballet (from 1832 through the early 1900s), attaining its original apogée in the magisterial dance dramas of Jules Perrot first in London, Milan, and Paris (1842-49), and their final flowering in St. Petersburg (1848-58); and last but not least, in the same city, the safeguarding of this tradition under the long but creative "intendantship" of Marius Petipa from 1862 to 1903. The late or last creativity of Petipa overlaps the earliest work of Michel Fokine, whose choreography led to the renaissance of ballet (in Western Europe) under the aegis of Diaghilev's Ballets Russes (the new Romantic Ballet) beginning in 1909.

However, a special problem has long existed in regard to this tradition, that of the Romantic Ballet from 1832 until its rebirth in the Ballets Russes from 1909 onward. The problem centers around the music from the 1840s on into the later nineteenth and early twentieth centuries, music largely written by specialist composers for the productions in this ongoing tradition, music supplied to order, that is, according to the precise order or command of the given ballet-master or choreographer. In general the specialist composers worked as part of a team in collaboration with specific choreographers. The names of certain composers claim prominence in this regard because they worked with outstanding ballet-masters at prominent theatres in prominent cities across Europe. Even so, because ballet remains a collaborative art, the chief emphasis fell on the dancing as embodied in the dancers, who could not move without the tunes and rhythms furnished by the music, obviously enough.

Two specialist composers in particular claim the attention of the student of ballet history by their prominence due to their long association with the Imperial Theatres in St. Petersburg and Moscow, the Italian Cesare Pugni and the Austro-Polish Ludwig Minkus. Even if originally well regarded in their own period, their music over time increasingly became anathema to an important and vocal group of aesthetes and other critics. Cesare Pugni perhaps typifies this artistic problem at its most pronounced because of his very long career. Starting in Milan around 1818 or 1820, he worked with a long line of distinguished *coreografi*, moving from Milan to Paris, London, and St. Petersburg, where he ended his life and career in 1870. He collaborated with the most prominent ballet-masters of his period. He also composed symphonies (i.e., orchestral pieces like operatic overtures, and not like the four-movement symphonies of the Austro-German tradition), ten operas, and forty masses. Reportedly he supplied the music for 312 ballets (even if only a little more than one hundred have made themselves known).

I became intrigued. How could a composer have earned such a dismal reputation as a musician and orchestrator, and still have continued working with so many distinguished *coreografi*, many of them composers and musicians themselves? From the middle to the latter 1950s I did some initial research on Pugni in a variety of published sources (here the libraries at U.C.L.A. came in handy) and compiled a checklist (with essential data) of the known dance productions for which he wrote the scores. Using mostly hired researchers in London and Milan during the 1960s and then the 1970s, I unearthed much more information on Pugni and his career. Much later (during the 1980s and 1990s), working with the Library of Congress, I expanded the checklist into a major monograph on him, actually a full-fledged history of ballet during the 1800s as perceived through the prism of his life and career. The actual writing and assembling of the manuscript (in regular typescript form) took place from 1980 through 2000, and totalled over 5,000 pages, a major opus on the scale of Edward Gibbon's history *The Decline and Fall of the Roman Empire*. It has yet to see publication, but it has found a possible publisher.

However, during the latter 1950s, the checklist and initial research for this project remained all that I could achieve, preoccupied as I was with college, with odd jobs, with regular full-time employment, and so forth. At the end of the 1950s I privately printed the checklist in a limited edition and airmailed six copies of it to one of the two preeminent writer-scholars of ballet history (that is, in English), Ivor Guest, following in the tradition of the other one (chronologically the first), Cyril W. Beaumont, and the latter's magnum opus, the *Complete Book of Ballets* (not to mention his many other books on the subject). Retaining one copy for his own use, Guest then kindly distributed the other five to various ballet scholars and historians throughout Europe, as follows: Beaumont himself, Marie-Françoise Christout in France, Vittoria Ottolenghi in Italy, and Vera Krasovskaya and Yuri Slonimsky in Russia. (Beaumont and Guest lived in England.) I had based my own list on several titles by Guest and Serge Lifar as my primary sources, duly credited at the end of the checklist.

During 1954-62 the well-known publishers in Rome, the Casa Editrice Le Maschere, brought out the nine volumes of their massive encyclopedia of the theatrical arts, a first of its kind, the *Enciclopedia dello spettacolo*. One of the editors and writers preparing entries for this pioneer reference work, Vittoria Ottolenghi, put together the generally favorable entry on Pugni, which appears in Volume VIII. This editor directly based her list of "Principali balletti con mus. di P. e loro principali riprese" on my own checklist. (See pages 587-89 of Volume VIII for both entry and list of dance productions.) Not only does the encyclopaedia credit my work and name, but the publishers even sent me $100 for the use of my checklist. Of course, this pleased me, especially the scrupulous evenhandedness of it all, but I also cherished the fact that it should have appeared in such a superb opus. In a sense it represented my first professional publication! Thank you, dear Vittoria Ottolenghi, as well as dear Casa Editrice Le Maschere, in Roma! I should mention for completeness that the publishers brought out an Appendix volume in 1963, and then a Supplement, covering the years 1955-65, in 1965.

Let us continue the chronicle of my life now near midway through my four years at U.C.L.A. If college to me seemed rather flat after high school and then the military, I was performing well enough to go forward under the G.I. Bill, I was learning in whatever courses that I had undertaken, I was deriving much benefit and pleasure while roaming freely in the library stacks with a stack pass, and I was enjoying new friendships among the student body, the teaching staff, and the given library staff. In one sense all was going well, but now life outside school suddenly became richer and more rewarding. I had no complaints.

In late August and early September 1957, Bob and I began a sort of tradition for us during several years, while we still had the freedom to travel before the school year began. We took our first trip to Northern California. Usually we would stop first in the Monterey area for several nights and then continue to the Bay Area, spending a week or so in San Francisco. During our first sojourn there I picked up three copies of Ashton Smith's rather special *Odes and Sonnets* for $3 each, published by the private and prestigious Book Club of California in 1918 with a special preface by George Sterling.

While Bob stayed behind in the City, I took the Greyhound bus to Sacramento and then to Auburn, expecting to find and meet Ashton Smith himself in the latter town. I went at once to the Auburn Public Library, one of many funded by Andrew Carnegie; but as I did not know very much about Smith, the staff referred me to someone else who also did not know, but did refer me in turn to someone who did, Ethel Heiple, an old friend of his and of his family. The cutest little old lady whom I had met up to that time, Ethel turned out to be a delight, and we became fast friends almost at once. She resided in a neat little house at the intersection of High Street (running north and south) and Sacramento Street (running east and west) coming up from Auburn's picturesque Old Town, where the very old post office that Smith had invariably used until he left Auburn (as I discovered from Ethel) was still functioning.

More than that, he had married, the reason for his departure, and was living in Pacific Grove in the Monterey area with his new spouse, Carol Jones Dorman, in her own house (along with three teenage children). Ethel gave me his new address and said that she would write him about me, and that I would probably come up to visit him from L.A. in the later summer of 1958, again late August and early September. I had a momentous meeting to anticipate during the school year of 1957–58.

Meanwhile I had waxed very tired of surviving on the G.I. Bill and did not attend U.C.L.A. the spring semester of 1958. I wanted and needed to earn some real money. I found a job at the field office of Southern Counties Gas Company in Venice. I did little sketches of where the gas pipes lay (street to building) for the ground crews. I held the job until I returned to Northern California with Bob in August. I had earned and saved enough money to make some needed big purchases, including copies of Ashton Smith's early poetry volumes (1912, 1922, and 1925).

Probably sometime between my sophomore and junior years at U.C.L.A., Bob and I moved for a third time, that is, from the little rented house in West L.A. to Pacific Palisades, into a detached house at the high terminus of Monument Street, a modest but modern-style home, which Bob's kind parents in Lincoln, Nebraska, helped him purchase. The house and property sat on a cut-out shelf or terrace that overlooked, as from a cliff, the deep and winding Temescal Canyon (owned and operated as a summer camp by some Christian fraternal group).

Our new house would serve as my home until I moved to Northern California on my own sometime during the mid-1960s. Bob and I would still continue our friendship even after I moved north. Once we had settled in at the new house, Bob brought home one day a pair of the cutest little dogs I had ever encountered, two Boston Terriers and sisters, whom Bob named Suzie and Tippie. They became our close and cherished companions for many years, whether I lived by myself or in a larger place with several housemates.

During the latter spring of 1958 I circulated a wanted-book list among a circle of established antiquarian book dealers, and as a result I acquired one or more copies (all in fairly good shape) of Ashton Smith's early and (as I discovered soon) epochal poetry collections:

The Star-Treader (1912), *Ebony and Crystal* (1922), and *Sandalwood* (1925). The prices for all of them turned out very inexpensive, a big surprise. I had hardly begun reading and assimilating them before I realized (thanks to my background in language and literature) that Smith ranked as a great and unique poet both in terms of technique and (more importantly) in terms of depth and breadth of subject matter and vision. Even more than in Lovecraft's most original tales, the cosmic-astronomic element or component in Smith's poetry (as in his prose fictions) grabbed my attention and made me ponder the implications of what he projects, as indicated by his painstaking but not laborious craft as a poet.

When Bob and I overnighted near Monterey for several days in August 1958, I seized the opportunity to make the long-planned meeting and visit with Ashton Smith and his wife Carol at her small but spacious enough house in Pacific Grove, not far from so-called Lovers Point with its "municipal plunge" or swimming pool—the home sitting on a street high and well removed above the beach and the ocean just to the north. The city of Monterey lies to the northeast. I rang the doorbell in the early evening, once we had secured a motel room, and Bob drove me to the Dorman-Smith residence.

Carol answered the door and graciously admitted me into the front chamber (the living and dining rooms combined into one). With another couple Smith and she were sitting next to a fire in the rubblestone fireplace. The Monterey and Carmel area has cool or cold weather most of the year due to the ocean's nearness. I introduced myself as a serious admirer of Smith's poetry and prose, and received recognition, once I mentioned Ethel Heiple. We arranged a visit for the later morning of the next day. The graciousness and urbanity shown by both Carol and Clark charmed and impressed me. I left my bag of books by C.A.S. with him so that he could sign them for me overnight, and then I would pick them up the next day.

The next morning I presented myself in due course and had an extended and rewarding conversation with Ashton Smith. We discussed literature in general and his contributions to it. His deep voice and understated behavior took me by surprise. As a person he struck me by his genteel quietude. I recognized him at once as a true and exceptional individual. I had already become a fervent admirer of his poetry, and in this new enthusiasm I tended to slight his marvelous prose fictions. Gently but firmly he corrected me by stating that his best work in prose equaled his poetry in value.

We must have talked several hours—we may have eaten lunch in the house—and Bob came back to pick me up in the early afternoon. Bob and I wanted to get to San Francisco before nightfall. Smith nodded and said that he understood. I mentioned that I hoped to visit him again in August 1959, and he readily gave his assent. I picked up my bag of his books that he had signed to me, and we said goodbye. In this way went my first extended meeting with an exceptional fictioneer and poet. I would soon meet another one. I had found somewhere a copy of an unusual and humorous account of one man's involvement in the world of fantasy and science fiction fandom: *Ah Sweet Idiocy! The Fan Memoirs of Francis T. Laney*. This account alerted me to the fact that Fritz and Jonquil Leiber lived somewhere in L.A.'s Westside, perhaps Santa Monica. Accordingly, sometime during my junior year I looked up his name in the Santa Monica telephone directory. Lo and behold, I found his name, address, and phone number. This happened in February 1961.

Fritz and his wife were living right across from Palisades Park (running north and south) that sits quite high above the ocean. They did not reside in the big family house in the front that some owner had divided into very small apartments, but in one of the upper apartments in the two carriage houses at the back. The day that I went to meet the Leibers, Jonquil answered my knock, and at my inquiry told me that Fritz was out on some errand; and so we arranged that I should come by again some other morning.

From that first visit onward, the Leibers and I became fast friends and exchanged many visits, especially when finances forced them to move back in with Fritz's mother in Huntington Palisades, the fancy southwest sector of Pacific Palisades. The medium-sized house where they resided thus off and on had been built by Fritz's father, and the floor plan resembled a capital H, two wings joined in the middle by a large living room with fireplace. The wing on the north had more or less equal-sized rooms, both spacious, one a bedroom, the other a kind of library-den that could serve as a bedroom. The wing on the south had a similar arrangement with bedroom and kitchen, and both wings had each a bathroom between the two larger rooms. A garden with roses spread out in the back yard. The house had gone up back in the 1930s.

Fritz's actor-father, after he disbanded his Shakespearean acting company following the Great Depression of 1929, had gone to L.A., to work in the burgeoning movie industry. He soon established himself as a leading character actor and acted in many quality studio films of the 1930s. Fritz Junior, the fantasy and science fiction author, had acted in his father's company during one season, and his mother Virginia Bronson Leiber had also acted in the company on a regular basis before the Great Depression. Among other things, Fritz Senior had painted the broad kitchen walls with some charming murals illustrating fairy tales or Mother Goose rhymes. A charming, functional house and a great family! Raised on Shakespeare as it were, Fritz Junior became not only an outstanding writer of imaginative fiction but also one of the best critics in the fantasy and science fiction field, one of the most insightful, articulate, and evenhanded. His critical essays remain some of the very best.

Fritz, Jonquil, and I had many fruitful discussions of literature and the arts in general, not to mention sharing many fine home-cooked meals, and going out to see here and there in L.A. some extraordinary foreign film. We rarely attended live theatre, however. We would remain close friends until death intervened, first with Jonquil in L.A., and then Fritz in San Francisco. In addition to Fritz and Jonquil, I would meet yet another remarkable artistic, literary, and musical figure when I encountered him in May 1961: Robert Arthur Hoffman, or as he preferred, Rah.

Meanwhile, during my junior year of 1958-59, under the instruction of Professor Clint Humiston, I had what was probably my single best, or most favorite, year-long French course: that is, Renaissance French, the elegant poetry of which, for freshness and innovation, vies in interest and enjoyment with the other greatest period in French poetry, the nineteenth century, first with the great Romantic figures like Victor Hugo and Théophile Gautier, who like Chateaubriand diffused his particular brand of poetic sensibility into his prose but wrote for newspapers for more than forty years. Nor should we overlook such superb and evenhanded critics like Sainte-Beuve, who focussed the attention of the literati and the reading public in general, among much else, on the brilliance, charm, and, yes, the enchantment of the Pléiade and other outstanding poets of the sixteenth and seventeenth centuries, from Clément Marot to Agrippa d'Aubigné, that French Milton who reflected the tumultuous events of the Renaissance in France (meaning the religious wars) in his idiosyncratic epic *Les Tragiques*. At the end of the school year in June Professor Humiston invited our entire class (a small group) to come to his house off Sunset Boulevard, where he had prepared a fabulous Chinese dinner to celebrate our completion of his class, and served with the fabulous white wine Château d'Yquem. We liked the wine so much that he opened a few more bottles from his private reserve—astonishing inasmuch as it does not come cheap!

As I had already discovered from experience (often the best instructor), college and full-time employment do not readily mix or coexist. But part-time employment and odd jobs can more easily do so. Thus during my junior and senior years I did both to supplement my G.I. Bill monthly stipend, first by working at the student bookstore at U.C.L.A. in the charmingly Gothic Student Union building down the slope from Royce Hall and the main plaza of the campus. Following that, I got jobs as a grocery packer (or box boy or bag boy) at the two supermarkets, both on Sunset Boulevard, in Pacific Palisades, first at Hughes Market and then Mayfair Market. Among other notable occasions at the former I had the pleasure of packing the groceries of no one less than Francis X. Bushman, the big star (as Messala), among others, of MGM's first *Ben-Hur* (1926)—a man of large presence, flamboyant charm, and big, deep, rich, ripe voice. After packing his groceries, I brought them out to his car in a shopping basket and put them into the trunk, all under his beaming and beneficent gaze. A big thrill for me, yes! At the other emporium I packed more than once the groceries of another MGM star more to my own taste, above all in *Tom Thumb* (1958), the nimble and buoyant actor-dancer-tumbler, the inimitably trim and cute Russ Tamblyn—usually accompanied by his beautiful and full-bosomed young wife, quite a looker, indeed. Yes, I also took their groceries out to their car and put them into the trunk.

Howdee! The bus that I usually took to U.C.L.A. from Pacific Palisades ran along Sunset Boulevard, but at other times I used the busses into and out of Santa Monica. On one occasion I could not help but notice a very friendly, well-built, and stunningly handsome teenager, all smiles and projecting a special radiance. In turn he noticed me; we began to talk and exchanged names. Like myself, Harald Hoeffding (he preferred his self-adopted name of Howdee) lived in the Palisades. Whereas I attended U.C.L.A., he went to University High in West L.A. Although understandable enough, he had some special qualities to his speech, and indeed attended some special speech therapy classes at U.C.L.A.

Born—during the Blitz of World War II in London—of an Anglo-British mother and a Russian-born father (who spoke perfect, British-inflected English), he had his hearing damaged by all the noise; and when he learned to speak, he reproduced the sounds as he heard them with his damaged hearing, and not as others did. Thus he spoke in his own proper way, which imparted to many of his words and phrases a peculiar pronunciation, almost like baby talk. For Bob and me this peculiarity only added to his charm, which he had in buckets.

It seems that everyone loved Howdee, no one could resist that charm!

As much as his busy schedule allowed, he visited us, and over time he became a fabulous friend to Bob and me. Later he went to Iowa State University in Iowa City (the old capital of that state), where he met an Iowan native, an English major, one Marvin R. Hiemstra, who later became, as he remains to this day, a distinguished poet and critic. Later still, Howdee went to the Big Apple, where he worked as a fashion designer. At some point, after Marvin moved to San Francisco, Howdee introduced us by mail, and Marvin in turn became the best of friends to me, as he still remains. Yet later still, when I needed to go to New York City to do research in the Berg Collection at the New York Public Library (for my Ashton Smith bibliography), Howdee always insisted that I stay overnight with him. We spent many marvelous weekends together, going out to places, for example, like the Bronx Botanical Gardens, a veritable paradise, or holed up sometimes in his warm and welcoming apartment, where we often made our own meals.

Another school year ended, and once again Bob and I headed north, stopping once again in the Monterey area. We had failed to make any motel or hotel reservations—it was the Labor Day weekend!—and we could not find any commercial shelter. This meant that I could only have a brief visit with Clark and Carol. I presented my problem to them. They invited me to stay overnight with them for several days. While I was doing this, Bob would go ahead to San Francisco and await me there, when I would arrive by Greyhound bus. This arrangement permitted me much more time with Clark for our discussions. During our first visit in August 1958, when I asked him what poet meant to him what he meant to me, he turned around to a bookcase behind him and picked out a volume that had a dark blue Art Nouveau cover with a pictorial design and printing etched in silver: *The House of Orchids* (1911), by George Sterling. He opened the book and read aloud therefrom a dozen magnificently sonorous lines, which deeply impressed me. I commented on them quite favorably, and Clark handed me his copy. I looked it over, reading here and there to myself, and then I opined, "This is great stuff!" Clark nodded his head in assent and approval.

I vowed to myself and to Clark to obtain this volume, and to investigate Sterling's oeuvre further. During the interlude between my two visits I had accomplished just that. I had obtained a copy of *The House of Orchids*, and had also studied his first two volumes of poetry, *The Testimony of the Suns* (1903) and *A Wine of Wizardry* (1909). Smith's high opinion of Sterling's poetry remains vindicated up to our present time.

This second visit, August 1959, turned out even better than the first, since Clark and I could have longer talks about poetry as well as other genres of literature, in addition to art in general. Carol had complained about the dirty kitchen ceiling and the need to clean it. I delayed my departure for San Francisco by a little, so that I could clean (I offered to do this) the *blackened* kitchen ceiling for her, removing the accumulated grease and smoke while standing on a ladder and using a pail of hot water and ammonia with assorted rags and sponges. Quite a task!—and it required much more time than anticipated. Once again we arranged for my third visit in August 1960, following the school year of 1959-60. We said goodbye, and then I went up by bus to San Francisco, where I continued my vacation with Bob.

My senior year at U.C.L.A., 1959-60, proceeded as it should, from beginning to end—with my studies, with odd and part-time jobs, and with private passions of all types—when in June 1960 I received quite a big surprise. I did not graduate and get my B.A. in the humanities, as I had anticipated. I had not received adequate counseling, or I had failed to figure it out myself. That meant that I would need to return to U.C.L.A., say, during some summer or double summer session, which I now planned to do during the early 1960s, to make up the courses and credits I had missed. The summer of 1960 I worked as an aircraft-parts assembler for Aerojet in West L.A. and got a taste of the factory work that my immediate forebears had needed to do to pay bills and survive, whether married or unmarried.

Another disappointment awaited me. Upon my advance inquiry by mail I learned from Clark and Carol that my third visit with them could not take place for whatever reason they had, I have forgotten. Instead, I would have a longer and very welcome period to spend with Ethel Heiple in the Sierras northeast of Auburn by some fifty miles. She had arranged matters so that she and I would have the use of a vacant operator's house at the P.G. and E. power installation or "camp" at Lake Spaulding, about seventy-five miles northeast of Sacramento. She had a friend, a young man at the camp, drive down to meet me getting off the bus. After being penned up in a West L.A. factory for most of the summer, I could only consider the ambiance at Lake Spaulding, and the several weeks that Ethel and I spent there together, to be a fresh-air and ecological paradise. I did not really want to leave when the time came for me to depart!

One special and quite unanticipated event happened while I stayed at that power camp, and in that operator's house. These rectangular structures with pitched or A-framed roofs stood two stories high, the windowless ground floor serving as the storage space for the huge supplies, the many cords, of wood indispensable for the wood-burning stoves in winter. The floor above, the second story, served as the regular living quarters, fairly spacious, but without high ceilings, making them more efficient for heating during the long cold season.

Not far away, but on a non-official basis, stood a small community of summer homes belonging to former officials of P.G. and E. and/or their wives. A group of elderly women and their friends was vacationing there while Ethel and I were staying nearby. Ethel had a friend in the group, and she arranged with her for us to visit them. We spent several hours in their company during a warm and golden afternoon (as of yet it had not turned cold). Once I met them (they seemed to be in their seventies, maybe a little older), these women assumed a special status for me. I brought up the subject of the great San Francisco earthquake and fire of 1906. The catastrophe took place at a time when all or most of them were attending some college or university in the Bay Area, several at Stanford University in Palo Alto. One woman described her awakening through the violence of the earthquake tremors, even if the strongest made themselves felt much further north in the City. She recalled seeing the door to her room opening and closing, swinging back and forth.

Quite apart from MGM's excellent feature film *San Francisco* (1936), this recollection, and those from the other women present, made that catastrophe all the more vivid for me. Then I realized almost with shock, all in a big flash, that these women were all attending college while Sterling was making his first reputation as a poet and man about town. I mentioned his name, which all of them recognized at once, some still impressed by him as a remarkable poet, and some not so much. Still, they knew who he was and what he had accomplished. This became my first immediate link to Sterling, Bierce, and their coterie of writers and poets, that is, apart from the primary and living link with Ashton Smith.

Thus it was that I found myself in an indeterminate position starting that summer of 1960, sometimes working, sometimes not, usually eligible for unemployment benefits. The academic year of 1960-61, which I did not spend in school—it might otherwise have served as my first graduate year—nonetheless found its redemption when I finally met dear old Rah in May 1961. He was not old at the time, but much younger, even if older than myself, say, by fourteen or fifteen years. 1960-61 also found its redemption, between my odd jobs and unemployment, when I began the research (among the materials most easily available) needed for the bibliography of Ashton Smith's writings. Yes, by the late 1950s, I had rather portentously determined to compile a C.A.S. bibliography, as nothing less deserved or valuable on behalf of such a neglected but utterly great artist-poet-fictioneer.

The summer of 1961 proved strategic, if not pivotal, to the research that I was attempting. My job as night watchman at the Mendelson-Zeller Fruit-Packing Shed allowed me to check out and utilize the resources of the Auburn Public Library, the old Carnegie-funded institution, which had become very well known to, and utilized by, Ashton Smith himself. Ethel had obtained the job for me from the manager of the Auburn fruit-packing shed, Angelo Lemos. She also let me use her deceased Grandma Atkins's house (next to Ethel's) as my residence the summer of 1961, an "interesting" place to live even without a regular bathroom and with only an outhouse. Summer camp not so long ago in my past had certainly gotten me accustomed to outhouses! Besides the old-fashioned furniture and lace curtains, the old house had several very large Maxfield Parrish prints in full color here and there around the place, and all beautifully mounted and under glass with big wide frames.

Although he had the typescript ready for publication in the mid-1960s, Donald M. Grant (then of West Kingston, Rhode Island) did not actually bring my bibliography out until the summer of 1978 as *Emperor of Dreams: A Clark Ashton Smith Bibliography*, as compiled by Donald Sidney-Fryer ("and Divers Hands"). I purposed it as more than just a bibliography: it would also be a compendium of all kinds of information about C.A.S., still primarily known at that time either to connoisseurs of Californian poetry on the one hand or on the other to connoisseurs of modern fantasy and science fiction. The research necessitated many trips to Northern California (mostly Auburn and Sacramento), but this first research laid the foundation for my later research during 1960-61, especially the coming winter of 1961-62 at the State Library in Sacramento. Because of my indeterminate status between odd jobs and unemployment, I could arrange my time so as to concentrate major periods of it exclusively to do the research, something that I could not have done if I had had a regular job, 9 A.M. to 5 P.M., Monday through Friday.

Chapter VIII. Later Life and Sexual Experience

The Clark Ashton Smith bibliography! I should attempt here to give some kind of coherent account of how the research evolved. At some point before the winter of 1960-61, I had accomplished a significant portion of the research, using the large, bound, ledger-like volumes of the *Auburn Journal,* kept on some very sturdy shelves in the western or further part of the complete basement (on ground level) under the Auburn Public Library. But this collection at the old Carnegie-founded structure represented only a relatively small portion of the newspaper that needed perusing. Therefore I planned to do the remainder, the bulk, of the research at the State Library (located inside the gorgeous Library-Courts Building, officially Building No. Two) in Sacramento; and furthermore, in the California Section, where one obtained access to *their* large, bound, ledger-like volumes, that is, in those pre-microfilm days.

I would achieve this main part of the research in the *Auburn Journal* during the first two months of 1961, looking for materials both by and about Ashton Smith, *turning over every page* (very carefully, as the sheets could rip easily) from about 1911 or 1912 on through 1942. After 1942 I would check only selectively for reviews of Smith's Arkham House books. I also checked, but only selectively as well, in the *Placer Herald* and the *Placer County Republican*. Meanwhile I had met Robert (Baker) Elder through Ethel Heiple. Bob lived in his inherited family dwelling in the middle of a large city block amid the relatively newer part of Auburn (that is, as compared to Old Town), not far from the Auburn Public Library.

I needed a place to stay overnight while doing this research at the State Library. (I could not afford to stay in a hotel or motel.) When I explained my project and my need to stay with a friend (to stay within my means), Bob realized the value of my endeavor and readily agreed to let me sleep in his house, in the bedroom downstairs just off the bathroom. I would get my own meals or eat out somewhere (breakfast or supper, no lunch), but Bob sometimes would share one of his meals with me. He grasped the fact of my limited funds. I took the Greyhound bus back and forth between Auburn and Sacramento. The State Library opened at 8 A.M. and closed at 5 P.M., Monday through Friday.

Much later (but not that winter of 1960–61) I would check selectively through the then leading San Francisco newspapers for the articles in 1912 about Smith's being "discovered" by Boutwell Dunlop, as well as for any reviews of Smith's poetry and prose volumes. I would also check in magazines like the *Argonaut*, the *Overland Monthly*, as well as *Town Talk*, the *Pacific Weekly*, the last-cited from 1910 until the periodical's demise in the early 1920s upon the death of the owner-editor, Theodore F. Bonnet. I searched the first two only selectively, but *Town Talk* page by page. Like the *Auburn Journal*, it contained quite a bit of material about George Sterling and (by extension) Ashton Smith.

As I discovered and had suspected, the *Auburn Journal* contained considerable material by C.A.S., above all what he contributed during 1923–25, in the form of "Clark Ashton Smith's Column," mostly poetry but also epigrams and pensées (the very last column appeared in January 1926). Most of the poems reappeared in *Sandalwood*, Smith's third major collection, published in October 1925. Much later I collected all of Smith's known epigrams and pensées (apart from those in *The Black Book*), and Don Herron had them published as the collection *The Devil's Notebook* (a title à la *The Devil's Dictionary* by Ambrose Bierce). It would seem that titles with the word devil have a better chance of selling, and selling well.

When I had almost reached the end of my page-by-page search in the *Auburn Journal* for 1942, I discovered or re-discovered a long and important article in the issue for Monday, November 3, 1941, "Local Boy Makes Good." (Whoever wrote it, and it was not Bob Elder, did not know of Smith's earlier and rather spectacular fame as a poet, beginning in the early 1910s.) This article contains the full text of "About Clark Ashton Smith," which originally appeared on the dust jacket of *Out of Space and Time* (published August 1942); it reappeared in *Weird Tales* for March 1942 as "Clark Ashton Smith—His Life and Letters." A New Zealand correspondent, Thomas G. L. Cockcroft, had already sent me a copy from its reprinted appearance in *Weird Tales*. However, rediscovering it made me refocus on it to my advantage.

It contains what seems like a complete list of the periodicals to which Smith had contributed some prose but mostly poetry (magazines either American or British). Somewhat later (Spring 1961) I would use this list, an invaluable tool, in conjunction with the *Union List of Serials*, to locate Smith's appearances in these and other magazines. This reference work lists which libraries possess which holdings of the periodicals in question, as well as the addresses of the public or college libraries with their holdings, particularly the so-called little magazines from the 1920s onward. This involved writing many letters of inquiry to many libraries and to the owner-editors of the little magazines. In many cases I needed to write three or four letters per item: thus, I had to mount a major epistolary campaign!

Alas and alack, Ashton Smith had also contributed an unguessable amount of stuff to many fantasy and science fiction fan magazines, beginning in the 1930s, and including the *Fantasy Fan*, the *Science Fiction Fan*, etc. This presented a special problem inasmuch as very few regular libraries had ever collected the fanzines. Fortunately I knew of Forrest J Ackerman, "the world's foremost science fiction fan," who was then living in or near the southern reaches of Beverly Hills, on South Sherbourne Drive. In fact, Fritz Leiber himself pointed me to Ackerman and his then modest first Ackermansion, when I told Fritz of my need to find and search through a representative collection of these curious fanzines.

In his residence Forrie not only possessed a fabulous collection of modern imaginative fiction, but also in the office wing extending back out of the main house an almost complete collection of the desiderated fanzines. I visited Forrie in person, and after I explained my project, he kindly and happily gave me unlimited access to his collection whether fiction or fanzines, in case I needed to do any cross-referencing. Like Ray Bradbury, Forrie seemed the soul of affability and amiability. Well groomed, tall, and thin, Forrie always appeared to dress up in formal office attire: shirt and tie, jacket and slacks. As others have remarked, with his trim pencil moustache, he bore a strong resemblance to the actor Vincent Price. Like old Will (Shakespeare) himself, we both shared a love of puns, and Forrie remained a master punner all the time that I knew him. The punning became just one more component in our friendship.

The next step of my diligent research ensued. During the entire month of March 1961 I looked through the entire collection of fanzines, page by page, for materials by and about C.A.S. Once again a significant amount of stuff rewarded my search. I duly copied it by hand and then transcribed it into typescript. The overall accumulation of fanzines, if piled vertically, one issue upon another, would have amounted to circa twenty-five feet of hectographed paper! Even though I had completed my search, I still needed to go back to Forrie's house to re-check on a few random items here and there in April and May. The last time that I went back to re-check on something took place in May.

On this occasion Forrie mentioned (for the first time) his close friend Rah Hoffman as a dedicated Smith admirer, in the same way as myself. Forrie said, "It seems to me that you two Klarkash-Tonophiles [Forrie's coinage] should get to know each other." And so we did. Forrie gave us each the other's phone number, and soon Rah and I arranged an assignation. He came up to my residence in Pacific Palisades, and after a brief visit among Rah, Bob, and me, I went with Rah back to his then home in West L.A., south of Santa Monica Boulevard and the Mormon Temple, and just off Westwood Boulevard. There he lived in one of three apartments that he owned, in one side of a duplex (the other he rented out); the third apartment sat atop a three-car garage.

At the time we met, Rah appeared young at about forty years old, seemed rather handsome, and wore his hair in a becoming brush cut. While he was warm and friendly, he cultivated a disarming sense of humor, if not drollery. Overall a delightful companion, he made you feel as if he were letting you in on some irreverent joke. We spent a wonderful evening together, talking our heads off—and by the time we finished, we decided that I should sleep on the sofa in the living room, and Rah would return me home in the morning. I phoned Bob to let him know the reason for my not returning home that evening. Rah worked as a film editor in movie or television studios (MGM, CBS, and so forth), but every year he became seasonally unemployed for four to six months, when he could legitimately draw unemployment and could otherwise do what he wanted on his own time off. Thus Rah and I began a friendship that would only end when he died in early 2013 at the age of ninety-two.

I had informed Rah at once about my Smith bibliography and mentioned that just as he had visited Smith in the early 1940s, so had I visited him (and his wife Carol) in the latter 1950s. 1961 turned out as a bad time to visit Smith, since he was experiencing poor health including heart trouble. Then that summer the word came from Forrie: Ashton Smith died on 14 August 1961. Of course, this occurrence made a great impact on both Rah and myself. Meanwhile we had continued visiting back and forth between West L.A. and the Palisades. We had already spent many fine evenings together during May on into August.

While Smith was passing through the very last weeks of his life, a stage of terminal illness, a young British couple, Ian and Eileen Law, had just married and had planned an extended honeymoon in the U.S., traveling from and then back to England via ship. Once they arrived in the States, they bought tickets to travel via Greyhound bus at a rather special price, "90 days for 90 dollars," as the advertising slogan ran. Obviously the dollar then had a higher value than it does today, even allowing for the slow but steady inflation it has undergone since then until now. A veteran reader and admirer of such

Arkham House authors as H. P. Lovecraft, C. A. Smith, R. E. Howard, and so forth, Ian had long nurtured a plan to visit Ashton Smith at his home whether Auburn or Pacific Grove. The young British couple was journeying initially during August aboard their ship from England. While they did so, Smith died, alas for Ian's plan to visit the Californian poet and fictioneer. Meanwhile Ian was communicating with Forrie Ackerman. Once the couple reached L.A., Ian contacted Forrie, who gave him the news about Smith's death, thus dictating a change of plans.

Although disappointed, of course, and saddened by the news, Ian then decided, as the next best step, to visit several people, friends and admirers, who had known Smith. Forrie thought at once of Rah and myself. After several phone calls between Forrie and Rah, the latter called me, and we both agreed to meet Ian, quite happily so. Ian and Eileen were staying in an inexpensive hotel in downtown L.A. Via Forrie, Ian arranged with Rah to visit us at Rah's place in West L.A. Instructed how to get there, Ian arrived at the nearest bus stop on Santa Monica Boulevard near the imposing and otherworldly Mormon Temple. We met him there and brought him down to Rah's apartment just off Westwood Boulevard. By the time we had settled in Rah's living room, the clock registered about 7 P.M., or maybe a little bit later. Handsome with a trim moustache, Ian manifested enthusiasm, intelligence, and knowledgeability about some of our mutually favorite authors ancient and modern, as well as about the arts in general.

In short, the three of us were discovering kindred spirits, always an exciting and agreeable experience. We passed a long and marvelous evening from about 7 P.M. to midnight, or beyond. Of course we ate, drank alcoholic beverages, and talked our heads off. Rah volunteered to return Ian to his downtown hotel. We drove him there, and then we returned to Rah's place. Ian probably spent several other evenings at Rah's apartment, which turned out equally well. We could not have had a better comrade than Ian! Ian and I became the best of friends and great correspondents, writing back and forth to each other from 1961 until his death a decade into the twenty-first century. We corresponded for half a century, sharing literary and other aesthetic enthusiasms.

Ian and Eileen went on to create three children, two daughters and one son: Sarah, Rachel, and Matthew, all remarkable each in their own way. Sarah has become a real friend to me. Her job takes her back and forth between the U.S. and the U.K., giving seminars and pep talks to business groups, as I understand it. At some point Ian ended his relationship with Eileen, and began a new one with an especially warm and friendly woman, Maureen. When I sojourned in England in 1972, I stayed with Ian and Eileen. I also stayed with Ian's friends Jack and Audrey Hesketh, who lived nearby in the same development of New Ash Green in southeast England. During that first English sojourn I also met Ian's handsome and fascinating brother, who shared many of Ian's literary and other enthusiasms. Ian's second partner Maureen died in mid-December 2009, and Ian did not long outlive her, dying in early July 2010. He had become one of my best and most cherished friends ever.

I have met some of my best friends through my fascination with Ashton Smith's artistic output, not to mention Clark and Carol themselves. Grief-stricken, traveling to recover from the loss of her husband, Carol passed through L.A. and sojourned for about a month with some friends in Beverly Hills. She carried with her a paramount literary treasure, safeguarding it at all times close to her person: her husband's commonplace book, already known as *The Black Book of Clark Ashton Smith*, thanks to some excerpts published in the *Acolyte* in the issues for Spring and Fall 1944, respectively. While in the L.A. region, she spent much time not only with her hosts in Beverly Hills but also with Forrie and Wendy ("Wendayne") Ackerman, and above everyone else, with Rah. I had myself already perceived the exceptional worth of *The Black Book*, when Smith had read to me from it several plot-sketches (of stories that he never managed to write), such as "The Oracle of Sadoqua," one of his tales of Averoigne when known as Averonia during the Roman period, otherwise based on the Auvergne.

Sometime before she left L.A. Carol entrusted the notebook to Rah, who had expressed a strong interest in it. Clandestinely Rah consulted me, and even before she departed, together we began deciphering and transcribing this valuable literary artifact. We started in mid-October and finished the considerable task in mid-November, checking the transcription always against the original. The transcription and its multiple proofreading alone also represented a considerable task. Together Rah and I proofread it during the latter half of November. We then proofread it individually during December, Rah in the first half of the month and I in the second half. Together again, during the new year of 1962, we proofread it during the last week of January, the entire month of February, and the first week of March, again always checking it against the original, I repeat with the strongest emphasis. I then prepared my own version of the text during the latter half of March and intentionally annotated it as lightly or minimally as possible, so as not to interfere with the reading experience of the dedicated Smith aficionado, student, or scholar.

Meanwhile Mrs. Clark Ashton Smith had suffered an extraordinary loss during that August of 1961. I must speak out here in the warmest possible appreciation of Carol as Smith's wife. The relationship between Clark and herself had lasted from the early 1950s on into the early 1960s. They had met, initially and exclusively, through two other friends, another couple: the dancer and dance teacher Madelynne Greene and her husband, the poet Eric Barker. Madelynne first had her dance studio in San Raphael and later moved herself and her studio to North Beach in San Francisco, the then Italian section north of the downtown area. Due to financial reasons the couple often lived apart, and Eric maintained himself by living as a caretaker on the estate of some friends at Little Sur south of the Monterey area. Madelynne needed the city, Eric the countryside.

Clark and Madelynne on one occasion had driven down in her vehicle from the City to Little Sur to visit with Eric in the early 1950s. The couple introduced Clark to Carol, one of their close friends. Carol, now alone, had a house in Pacific Grove, where she lived with her three children, two sons and one daughter. Instantly smitten with each other, Clark and Carol fell in love, and with a rare and fulfilled erotic passion. Each had met their match in the other! They married in November 1954, and Clark moved down to Pacific Grove from his lonely family cabin on Indian or Boulder Ridge outside Auburn. Carol thus provided a warm and comfortable home for Clark in the final decade of his life, a not unimportant consideration.

The couple shared certain domestic arts, and both could cook and garden. They both could fend for themselves in her house. Carol did all she could to maintain a fine ambiance where Smith could live and write, or otherwise create, even if during his sixties he wrote little prose and only a little more poetry. From 1910 or 1911 into the 1930s he had already achieved an impressive corpus of writing, his exceptional poetry and his equally exceptional prose fictions. We should not begrudge C.A.S. a well-deserved rest in the final decade of his life. Carol did all she could not only to encourage Clark in his creativity, but also to facilitate the visits of his admirers, his aficionados, either well-known like L. Sprague de Camp or little-known like Donald Sidney Fryer. Thank you very much, dear Carol!

After Rah and myself finished with *The Black Book*, Rah with a close friend drove to Northern California, taking with him Smith's commonplace book. Among other places and persons, Rah stayed overnight in Berkeley with George F. Haas, an eminent Smith aficionado and, apart from Carol herself, probably the closest of Smith's friends. When he departed from George's domicile, Rah left *The Black Book* with him. Sometime later George handed it back to Carol at one of her visits with him in Berkeley. At that time George lived with his mother on Dwight Way. In time, after I moved to San Francisco, I myself became acquainted with George, who became in turn one of my own best friends.

One never knows where one will find a fellow balletomane, and to my surprise I found one in George! Will surprises never cease? During the latter 1950s and the early 1960s, before I moved to San Francisco, I had pursued my passionate interest in ballet as time and funds allowed, the latter always minimal, what with my bare survival as I went to school, on the G.I. Bill, or managed with odd or temporary jobs. Despite various handicaps I did get to experience several magnificent productions of a few superb story ballets as embodied by several magnificent ballet companies, and with excellent or even legendary lead performers.

First, the Royal Ballet of England presented Frederick Ashton's exemplary version of *Sylvia*, with Svetlana Beriosova in the title role, in the immense theatre that is the Shrine Auditorium not far from downtown L.A. Constant Lambert conducted the unique and glorious music by Léo Delibes. First performed at the then new Paris Opéra with choreography by Louis Mérante, *Sylvia* in fact opened what was then the brand-new *Palais Garnier*, and in a sumptuous production that evoked the splendors of both antiquity and Graeco-Roman mythology. As Tchaikovsky remarked, on witnessing a performance at the Hofoper in Vienna, *Sylvia* represented the only ballet at that period in which the music for the first time furnished the paramount interest. Quite a feat!

Next, at the same Shrine Auditorium, as performed by the same Royal Ballet of England, I witnessed Ashton's delicious new version of *La Fille mal gardée* (the oldest story ballet, created by Jean Dauberval in 1786 at Bordeaux—that is, the oldest in continuous performance since then). Ashton had completely revivified and rethought the work in all its particulars, with a delightful new score by conductor-composer John Lanchbury. When Dauberval's pupil Jean Aumer became chief ballet-master at the old Paris Opéra, then housed in the theatre on the Rue Lepelletier (utilized 1822–73), he produced a new version of this comedy ballet during the latter 1820s, and with a mostly new score by Louis-Ferdinand Hérold, that is, as composed and arranged incorporating a hatful of suitable tunes from the original potpourri or medley score probably put together by the conductor at the original theatre in Bordeaux (and probably in collaboration with Dauberval himself).

Lanchbury based his renewed score (magnificently orchestrated) on Hérold's music, which otherwise has become the ballet's chief accompaniment in most theatres during the nineteenth and twentieth centuries. Sometime during the mid-nineteenth century, or somewhat earlier, Paul Taglioni created a new, or renewed, version of *La Fille mal gardée* with new or rehandled music by Peter Ludwig Hertel, the regular composer-collaborator of this ballet-master at the Berlin Opera House, that is, the Königliches Opernhaus, during Taglioni's long engagement there, c. 1830–60. Ashton's version remains one of his best pieces of narrative choreography and ranks as his masterpiece deserving of every praise. I cannot remember the names of the chief dancers in the performance I saw, but the entire company danced and acted as if possessed, including the genial conductor, Lanchbury himself. After the performance I waited by the stage door to speak with the conductor-composer. Lanchbury revealed himself as a kind, witty, and gracious individual. I have never forgotten this performance nor my brief interview-visit with Lanchbury.

Later, at the same Shrine Auditorium, the Bolshoi Ballet from Moscow performed their exemplary version of *Giselle*, the dramatic masterpiece of Jules Perrot with the then innovative music by Adolphe Adam (although not credited to Perrot when first performed at the Paris Opéra in 1841). I had long wanted to see this dance drama despite many excellent modern productions of it, but I had waited to witness an unexampled one. At long last I found it in the legendary version from the Bolshoi Theatre with the legendary Galina Ulanova as Giselle, and with her usual conductor-collaborator, the equally legendary Yuri Fayer. However, both the entire company and the orchestra performed in unparalleled style and in a sumptuous production that was pure theatrical magic. I suffered no disappointment but rather enjoyed a veritable epiphany!

The very last narrative ballet that I witnessed at this time was one that I had first seen in 1952, *Swan Lake*, with Margot Fonteyn in the dual role of Odette-Odile and with Michael Somes as Prince Siegfried in the then production by the Sadler's Wells Ballet, a production that I could not fault in any way. However, this version, once again with the same company but renamed the Royal Ballet of England, seemed transformed. It had the same wonderful prima ballerina, but who now danced and acted with the legendary Rudolf Nureyev, who transformed and galvanized Fonteyn's long-since excellent interpretation to stratospheric heights. Alas, the performance at the Hollywood Bowl in and of itself left something to be desired in terms of theatrical illusion—through no fault of the production, but simply because the unusual venue created a strange compromise. The company had to perform on a stage built out over where the orchestra usually played, but instead now played behind the dancers, and thus between them and the celebrated acoustic shell, the large sounding board or structure shaped like a huge concave seashell. Despite this bizarre disadvantage the company gave it their best, and Fonteyn and Nureyev danced and acted sublimely.

Here I must correct or otherwise amend the recollections that I presented about the last year I spent in the Marine Corps, that is, from September 1955 through August 1956, on the Marine Air Base at El Toro in Southern California outside Santa Ana. This amendment serves as a good example of how a memory, reliable and vivid in detail, can sometimes fail in terms of its precise location in an extended timeframe. During the months (September into December) of that first autumn of mine in California, I did not at first seek out Bob Mizer and his Athletic Model Guild. Rather, I sought out the few relatives I had in the Golden State, and luckily for me they lived in Southern California not very far from El Toro, perhaps no more than fifty miles as the bird flies from southeast to northwest.

My mother had a cousin, Margery Krumholz, born Dufresne, who remained a very close friend to her from childhood as long as they both lived. Although she was technically a second cousin to Ronald and myself but of the same age as my mother, we always regarded and called her Aunt Marge. I personally always felt very close to her—she had witnessed my birth as I emerged from my mother, and this closeness continued on into my adulthood. Physically trim and handsome, Aunt Marge had a particularly warm and attractive tone of voice. We socialized with her off and on, especially throughout our childhood. Eventually Aunt Marge and Uncle George (Krumholz) retired to Southern California from New Jersey.

Although as a child I rarely, if ever, saw them, through Aunt Marge I had three aunts, or great-aunts, Marge's mother Aunt Suzie and her two sisters, originally Canadian or Anglo- British, who just happened to reside each in one of the beach towns along the coast north of Long Beach, that is, Redondo Beach, Hermosa Beach, Manhattan Beach. To these towns they and their husbands, incidentally all grand people, had retired. Thus it came about that during my first autumn (1955) in California, after establishing my first contact with them (probably by mail and then by phone), I went off the base to visit my three great-aunts on several intermittent weekends, invariably staying overnight with Aunt Suzie and her second husband Donald. These visits provided some very pleasant and emotionally warm interludes for me.

Aunt Marge had actually informed them in advance of my presence at El Toro, so that my communicating with them, and then showing up, certainly proved no shock, but rather a welcome novelty. Aunt Marge also had a brother Edson Dufresne, with whom I also socialized, who thus qualified in some way as an uncle, who lived not far from his mother Aunt Suzie, and who had long since become a favorite with my mother, my brother, and me. A cultivated man, Edson and I had far more in common with each other than I had with most of my other relatives. Eventually, although I kept in touch, I ceased visiting the Dufresne family as I discovered some friends much closer to my own age and interests. This I primarily did through Bob

Mizer, whom I sought out somewhat later that first autumn of mine in 1955, but thus only after I had visited my relatives, this extended family, along the coast in Southern California.

In a certain sense the Cub Scouts and then the Boy Scouts (originally quasi-military social organizations for boys) prepared me for my actual military service in the Marine Corps, not that the military aspect of the Boy Scouts proved a burden. In the transitional period between the Boy Scouts and the latter years of high school, I had locally one best buddy, Walter Sidlowski, Polish-American as his name indicates. He lived with his family in a big quality flat in a two-flat building on County Street just south of a fine old wooden mansion of the whaling period with a mansard roof. The mansion with a big yard and carriage house (which became a garage) occupied the whole eastern end of a city block. Its architecture suggested something vaguely Chinese due to certain curvilinear aspects of the roof. Perhaps the several old but healthy Chinese elms with their fan-shaped leaves that turned yellow in the autumn contributed to this Chinese quality.

The old Holy Name church (largely made out of wood but very sturdily constructed) stood further north but adown County Street as it descended—no longer used as a church but as a parish hall for Catholic community events, and also by the Cub Scouts and Boy Scouts. The new Holy Name church (attractively designed, and constructed out of stone and beige-colored bricks) stood much further west on a wide residential street that boasted big, handsome, upper middle-class dwellings with ample space and lawns around them. I recall attending mass at both the old and the new churches. Next to the new one a two-story rectory rose immediately to the north.

I remember several unusual adventures that I passed with Walter, or Sid, as I sometimes called him, as did others. One evening as connected with some special holy day, Walter and I (both Catholics) visited a dozen churches or more, either in autumn or spring, one church after another, a long and finally rather tiring hike; even young people become tired. A special blessing (but not emanating directly from any priest) would presumably descend upon us for accomplishing this ecclesiastical pilgrimage. We started in the north end of New Bedford, encompassing St. Anthony's cathedral-like structure, and our own Holy Name temple, the new church; the old one, changed into a parish hall, did not qualify. Gradually we wended our way, mostly along County Street, through the central residential and commercial area, and at last completed our pilgrimage at some Portuguese parish church. At that period the ecclesiastical authorities did not need to worry about vandalism and kept the churches open all night long, thus allowing the faithful easy access for private prayer and individual devotion. At each church we duly crossed ourselves, and each said a prayer, generally addressed to the Virgin Mary (often easier to address a female figure rather than a patriarch).

By the time that we reached the last church somewhere along near the southern end of County Street, Walter and I had become purty tuckered out, but still we each duly uttered our respective prayers. We must have made more noise than what seemed strictly needed, because some deacon or other emerged from near the altar and admonished us to maintain the quiet. We explained our mission, our pilgrimage, and he acted aptly mollified, leaving us to our own devices. But as soon as he departed, each of us in his own pew across the aisle from each other not far from the altar, we stretched out full-length on the wide cushioned seats and fell asleep, not intending to do so. Undetected and undisturbed, we woke after a brief nap and wended our way back north along County Street, all the way to Walter's family flat, where I stayed the rest of the night, sleeping in an extra bedroom. I returned home the next day, duly blessed and edified.

Another notable adventure befell Walter and myself on a later occasion. Although we never went to summer camp as Boy Scouts together, we did camp out just the two of us on several occasions, usually during the warmer weather in the summer or on a school vacation. Finding a suitable spot in which to camp, not far from our city, proved the first challenge. We had both happened to notice, each on his own, a certain spot south of the big highway going west out of New Bedford toward Lincoln Park and Fall River. The site lay back some little distance from the road, a spot that promised both privacy and novelty.

There we could camp out quite unobserved, hard by the man-made crater of an abandoned quarry, part of which had long since flooded, making a little lake or pond. There in this pool of water we could wash our dishes, etc. The water proved basically safe to use, to brush our teeth, and what have you. We would bring with us not only our supplies but also some drinking water. We would use a certain predetermined spot as our latrine away from our tent and behind some bushes. Once we had prepared, Walter's father dropped us off with all our gear at the designated site and then drove away in his car. We planned to camp out for no longer than a week, or until we grew tired of camping and campsite.

We carried our stuff over to what looked like a good place to camp, pitched our pup tent, dug a little ditch around it in case of rain, arranged our sleeping bags inside the tent, and at a lower elevation established the spot for our campfire for cooking (certainly not for heat) and encircled it with small rocks, to keep the fire well within it. We also removed any miscellaneous debris from our immediate area. We then scavenged for about an hour all around the quarry, finding many small pieces of old arid wood that could burn easily enough, and brought them back to our hearth, covering them up with a small tarpaulin. We had also prudently brought with us other food that we could prepare, such as canned food or sandwiches, in case of rain when we could not easily make a fire for cooking. When we did not remain in camp during the day, we could explore the surrounding area, including limited parts of the abandoned quarry. With a little effort the first few days went okay, no problems, no complaints.

But one day soon enough we made a singular mistake. We had prepared our campfire to cook us another meal, and then we realized that we had not cleaned our dishes and pans after our last meal, probably breakfast. Without thinking, together we went down to our little lake to do the cleaning. We had hardly done so when with a flash I remembered the campfire that we had left unattended. We, the Boy Scouts? I exclaimed, "The fire!" We looked at each other in consternation. We left the dishes and utensils right there by the pond. Lickety-split we both ran back to our little encampment. We found our worst fears confirmed.

Sparks from our fire had jumped outside the circle of stones and had ignited the dry grass around it. The flames were racing up toward our little pup tent. Horrors! Then, like maniacs, we grabbed whatever we could to smother the flames and put them out, including with the tarpaulin. We danced about like men possessed, and after several minutes of panic-inspired labor we managed to put out both the campfire and the unwanted fire outside it. With a small bucket that we had with us, and with several pots and pans, we doused the burned areas here and there. Had we returned any later, our tent, our sleeping bags, and our supplies would have all gone up in flames and suffered ruin or destruction. What a close call! As Boy Scouts we would not have wanted any firemen to have rescued us. Besides, it would have happened too late. How embarrassing! We had become so shook up that we contented ourselves quite happily by making cold sandwiches for our supper.

The next few days it rained heavily. We could not cook, and we could not explore the surrounding environment to any real degree. The rains more or less confined us to our little tent except when absolute need forced us to use our latrine, luckily not far away. After several such sodden days of discomfort and confinement, we hiked to the nearest phone booth and phoned Walter's parents. His dad came to pick up us and our bedraggled gear as we waited by the side of the highway. So much for the would-be resolute pioneer Boy Scout campers—ha! Since that fiasco, I have often camped with one or more friends in special places of great natural beauty. While in Marine Corps boot camp I bivouacked as required with no problem, and otherwise my camping out has gone well and smoothly. Now as an older man, if I have the urge to go camping, then I camp out in my bedroom near the convenient bathroom!

On occasion I still saw Walter Sidlowski—we remained firm friends—but as I necessarily became preoccupied with my serious high school studies, I fell away from the Boy Scouts. At the same time I formed another important friendship until I joined the Marine Corps and finally left New Bedford behind. I have only mentioned his name, but Henry James (coincidentally with the same name as the celebrated novelist) stood out, and still stands out, even if (as I fear) he is now deceased, albeit he was not much older than myself. I first met him at the first of the extracurricular events put on by Miss Loftus for her former students—in June at the end of my freshman year at New Bedford High School (1949-50). By a strange coincidence (he never married) he lived with his family, with his brother and his three sisters, in a big beautiful family house, painted a very deep chocolate brown, not far from where Walter Sidlowski lived with his parents, and hence just off County Street.

His father apparently had already died, perhaps worn out working as a wage slave to support his large family, to which he had evidently devoted his life, noble man! Once Henry and I met, we became fast friends, often visiting back and forth between his family house and the apartment that I shared with mother and brother at Presidential Heights. He remained my closest and single best friend during the rest of my high school years, whatever the season of the year. We kept in touch even after I joined the Marine Corps, and after I never came back to live permanently in New Bedford; but when I went back home to visit, I still went over from Presidential Heights to visit him and his very dear family.

Extraordinarily talented, nay, gifted (although he did not think so), Henry seemed to have no regular job until much later in his life, as teacher under the auspices of the federal government. Extraordinarily cultured and cultivated, as an individual artist he could paint, and quite individually (the emphasis demands reiteration); several paintings of his art (oil paintings) hung in the living room. He possessed a deep bass voice and could sing magnificently. A devout Christian (but not a Catholic), he sang with tremendous fervor on more than one occasion some famous religious song, which begins with the words, "Were you there when they crucified my Lord?" As I told Henry on more than one occasion, had he pursued a singing career, he would have ended up amid the roster of the most celebrated singing stars working for the Metropolitan Opera of New York.

Like myself and Miss Loftus, as a veteran listener, he heard and assimilated the Saturday afternoon broadcasts with Milton Cross. Henry knew and loved all the arts in the curriculum of the classical repertoire, opera, ballet, symphony concerts, etc. Extraordinarily well read, he knew the received classical masterpieces in English or in translation. Although I had long since almost abandoned my Catholic religious beliefs, I could still respect his firm and fervid Christian faith. The many long and enjoyable discussions that we had on life, metaphysics, literature, and the arts helped form my own religious convictions or non-convictions, my perspective on life and the cosmos, and (not least) my own character.

Thin, small, but strong and wiry, Henry was around five foot eight inches tall. He wore a small moustache, a small close beard around his chin, and sideburns. His hair tight and kinky, and his physiognomy, revealed his ethnic derivation, an evolved family mixture of West Indian Negro and some Amerindian tribe. Handsome, he had a ready and good-natured smile, and the rest of his cultivated family appeared similarly exotic. Perceived in retrospect, Henry's ready wit, his rather ironic sense of humor, and his always pleasant companionship stand out brighter than ever.

The saga of Homespun House! I have had many jobs, including many dead-end ones, but the (ahem!) professional jobs (utilizing my college degree) that gave me the most money gave me the least satisfaction—odd but veracious! The job that I had as linen draper (in this case, cloth cutter) at Homespun House, which gave me only minimal wages, gave me nonetheless the maximal pleasure and satisfaction. Why can I say this? Because Homespun House turned out as a truly fun place to work thanks to the highly individual owner-manager Henry Knowlton, who became friends with selected employees, including myself. I had gone down from Pacific Palisades to Bob Mizer's place on the edge of downtown L.A., looking for work through Mizer's auspices. I had already worked for him one summer, and he knew me, for sure, as a dependable worker who got the job done to the employer's own satisfaction. Therefore he could recommend me without reservation to some other employer, straight or gay.

Homespun House—hmm, an interesting and evocative name! Armed with the address and phone number, I took a bus that moseyed along Wilshire Boulevard not far from Mizer's place and got off at South Robertson Boulevard (another major artery). I walked south for several blocks before I discovered on my right (that is, on the western side of the street) a modern one-story structure lifted up from the paved ground level on solid cement supports. The glass-walled showroom just off the sidewalk, and the parking lot (for both customers and employees), lay under the flat-roofed main floor. A staircase in the front went up from the showroom to the main floor that had no windows, but did have several skylights and brilliant fluorescent lights as the regular illumination for the interior. I noticed that a staircase at the back went up for the use of the employees.

I went in through the showroom (no one in sight) and then up the front free-standing staircase. A middle-aged woman, Valerie Forbes (a great gal, by the way), the secretary, sat at a desk in the main office space at the front, from which there opened other rooms, including the boss's corner office (on the northeast). Mizer had already phoned ahead about me as a potential employee, and so I introduced myself at once. Valerie called out to the boss. He came out of his office, one

Henry Knowlton. We introduced ourselves. It seems that I came along as merely the latest in a long line of would-be youthful employees, many of whom did not pan out. Henry seemed pleasant enough, a thin, middle-aged man with a deep voice and a rather mocking smile. He took me out into the main working space and explained the job to me, that of a linen draper (he used this term—Henry had a very developed sense of language). The job didn't seem hard, but it would keep me busy most of the day—fine! It was during the work week, and I would begin the very next day—excellent! Henry and I got along famously from the very start. As we soon discovered, we had a complementary sense of humor. He loved nonsense and verbal play.

I felt comfortable at once in the big bright working space, a positive ambiance in which to spend much or most of the day. On the south side (on the left as one emerged from the front office space), as arranged on giant shelves, a series of giant rolls (or bolts) of cloth appeared in longitudinal array, the ends toward the onlooker. In front of the shelves holding the big rolls, there stood several sturdy, and very wide (six or eight feet), cloth-covered tables (very tightly covered, out of necessity), one after another, thus all lined up on the left. On these tables the linen draper would hoist himself in his stocking feet (or in special slippers never worn anywhere else) due to the need to keep tables and fabrics as clean as possible during the actual handling of the big bolts.

While reclining on his left forearm or elbow, the linen draper would use a pair of special cloth-cutting scissors to separate the needed yardage from off the given roll of the desiderated cloth, which roll he would take down from its usual resting place on the given shelf according to the individual order. Valerie would write up the orders for the linen draper: these came in the mail or came up from the showroom off the street. To the right of the aisle separating the cutting tables from the rest of the big working space, there stood a complete packaging or wrapping area, another big bench or table, with everything needed to send out the individual orders, usually via the United

Parcel Service or the U.S. Post Office. One very large chamber contained this overall workplace.

To the right of the main workplace, accessible through several doors, at east and west, there lay another very large chamber, in which some two dozen seamstresses were busily working at their individual sewing machines, making draperies from the unusual cloth in which Homespun House specialized, and which some textile mill (in the Old South) manufactured to Henry Knowlton's exact specifications. The unusual width of each bolt facilitated making the cloth into drapes and other curtains. For tax reasons Henry ran this major side of the business separately, or someone else may simply have handled it as a separate business in itself. I forget, or I never knew.

Unusual cloth, indeed! In addition to the agreeably coarse basket-weave of cotton, light gray or off-white in color, known as monk's cloth, the chief stock of fabrics, almost all of cotton, included many of simple but colorful design often using primary hues, often suggesting plaids but without imitating official Scottish tartans. Nevertheless, whatever the design, any given cloth overtly looked as if echt-homespun, that is, woven on some loom in Appalachia, with a deliberate but attractive coarseness, as if to adumbrate something actually made on a primitive wooden frame for interweaving spun yarn or thread.

Beyond this fundamental quality of the fabrics themselves, this echt-homespun aspect, a special built-in feature played a strategic role in the amount and measurement of the cloth as merchandised by Homespun House, as made into draperies with perfect ease, or as put to any other use that a customer might wish—such as luxurious lining for a doghouse! Doris Day, a customer more than once, purchased on one occasion several yards of one of the more vivid fabrics for this purpose. Of what did this special built-in feature consist? For each regular square yard that the customer bought or wanted made into drapes (as for the living room or wherever), the said client actually got three square yards. The width of all the fabrics thus measured at around nine feet, but for ease of handling these extra-large or extra-long bolts, as conceived or designed by Henry Knowlton, the textile manufacturer folded all the fabrics (that is, all the length of the bolts as they unrolled) exactly once down the middle and then rolled the fabrics into what became extra-thick bolts. Despite this inherent condition, the bolts did not seem extra-heavy to handle for the linen draper. All that he had to do was to exercise all due caution in moving the bolts from shelf to cutting table and back. One soon developed speed and facility at it; the cutting itself demanded minimal care.

I personally found it a great physical, if not a great sensual, pleasure to move the bolts around, to cut from them, and otherwise to handle them: a pleasure to feel, a pleasure to smell (a nice, clean, cotton smell), a pleasure to see close up. I loved the job, and my co-workers headed by the boss created a positive ambiance in which to function. I looked forward to going to work and enjoyed the bus or car ride to and from Homespun House. I often got a ride to and from Pacific Palisades as provided by a co-worker (by name of Dean) who lived not far away. If I used the bus, I generally took with me some big Arkham House book and read it en route: the chief manner in which I first experienced *Skull-Face and Others*, the R. E. Howard supernatural omnibus selected and edited by August Derleth. Henry Knowlton as the boss, the big man, made all this possible. As we got to know each other better, I came to discover in Henry an exceptionally kind, congenial, gregarious, and well-informed companion. In addition, he had an infectious and slightly raucous laugh!

We often visited back and forth, between Pacific Palisades and wherever Henry had his home (not far from the shop), making meals for each other or eating out somewhere. If you spent the evening at Henry's house after a meal, he would sit you down opposite him across a chessboard or checkerboard: in my case, the latter, since I always found chess too regulated and complicated to play, albeit I love the chess pieces themselves as historical, heraldic, or aesthetic artifacts. While you figured out your chess or checker manipulations, Henry would play on his hi-fi set some of his favorite musical entertainment, one of the masterpieces of sheer theatrical silliness purveyed under the names of Gilbert and Sullivan. I have always enjoyed their shows, but Henry made me into a genuine aficionado.

I recall one winter when business had come to what seemed like a standstill. Henry closed up shop early, posted an out-for-vacation sign on the showroom door, and then we all went out to experience the then delightful new movie *Tom Jones* (1963). The boss treated us all to the feature film, about six or eight people—the movie remains a high-spirited masterpiece—and then he treated us to a very good meal at some quality cafeteria nearby. Wow, what a boss! Homespun House boasted several other exceptional individuals. There was Dean (I can't recall his full name), who worked as a kind of salesman at large. He worked hard and had great social skills, selling the clients on Henry's unusual fabrics. Dean resided in Santa Monica Canyon and drove up from his home (which he shared with a special male partner) to pick me up at my home in Pacific Palisades, and then often brought me back. According to Don Williams, Dean boasted some mind-boggling and other-boggling equipment.

Then there was Don Williams himself, the ultimate cute guy, blond hair, blue eyes, sometimes with an endearingly squeaky but basically masculine voice, and surely not under-endowed as I learned from a few chance but intense encounters. When I first met him as quite a competent and clever co-worker, he served as paramour to the boss, who made him the vice-president of his business. From the position of paramour Don graduated to a relationship that lasted several years with a beautiful French youth. I spent several weekends with them in their apartment in Hollywood, and we all three had a lot of fun. Then from that relationship Don graduated to an unending line of beautiful and willing young women, whom he picked up with impressive ease at the Whiskey-a-Go-Go on the Sunset Strip. He brought them to his apartment, made love to them, and then returned them to the dance club where he had met them. A real go-getter, or go-get-her! He worked at Homespun House all during my several years there, as well as before and after. He played and he worked hard.

As just announced, I held my job at Homespun House for several years during the first half of the 1960s, and enjoyed every moment of it. Henry had a branch store in the fashionable area of San Francisco east of Van Ness Avenue and north of the Civic Center. He seriously contemplated making me the manager of it (a job that I could have handled very well); but the then manager, after mentioning to Henry that he wanted to move on, changed his mind, and this wonderful opportunity failed to materialize for me. I had long since fallen in love with San Francisco and had wanted to live and work there. Then Henry's volume of business underwent a temporary decline, he had to lay some of his employees off, and I, good old Sid, became one of those elected for this honor. At least I could legitimately draw unemployment benefits, always a great help. Like most people I lived from paycheck to paycheck.

Meanwhile, early in the 1960s, Henry had allowed me a brief leave of absence during one summer, when I went back to U.C.L.A. for a double summer session, took the classes that I needed to complete my B.A., and in fact did receive my degree at the end of that summer. Whether I used it or not, I had actually come into possession of it, which sometimes helped when I applied for a job. Also, at about the same time, I continued the research for the C.A.S. bibliography, going back and forth between L.A. and Northern California, on sojourns at public and private libraries in Auburn, Sacramento, San Francisco, and other locations. I had it more or less ready for publication by the mid-1960s. Indeed, I had gone back and forth so many times, falling in love with Northern California, that it became just a matter of time before I would have moved there anyway. I would first move to Auburn for the last six months of 1965, and then would move to San Francisco sometime during early 1966.

The assassination of President John Kennedy took place in Dallas in late 1963, an event that depressed and amazed me as it did most people in the U.S. at that period. It also may have acted as a catalyst in my decision to move north out of L.A. I had been chafing for some few years under the restrictions imposed by a one-on-one relationship. Although I still loved Bob Crook, I had already begun catting around with other guys in Santa Monica, Venice, West L.A., and Westwood, and sometimes further afield in and around the overall downtown of L.A. proper or improper. Despite this mild promiscuity I never contacted a venereal disease at that period, luckily for me—and for Bob!

At some point in the latter 1960s Henry Knowlton sold his business and retired to the unusual if unassuming residence that he had had some contractor build for him in Topanga Canyon. I had seen the plans before I left Homespun House, plans that featured a long, low series of interconnected rooms all opening from a colonnade of simple wooden pillars (four inches by four inches), all arranged to make square or rectangular openings in the porch. Henry's gregarious nature led him to rent some of the rooms out to the then burgeoning hippies, mostly young adults. Whether this left him burned out and bitter as it did some elderly propertied friends of mine, I don't know, but I doubt it. (These especial friends of mine, in Auburn, swore that they would never rent to any hippies again because in every instance when they had, the young people had left the rental properties in a shambles, even requiring sometimes actual reconstruction!) Henry had a pretty realistic grasp of the world and knew how to survive with grace and joy. As for whatever happened to the inimitable Don Williams, his erstwhile paramour, Henry did not know, and I knew no one else who had known Master Williams who could have told me.

To give the reader another idea of the whimsical atmosphere that reigned at Homespun House in its heyday, I recount a special little episode that I have never forgotten. One day Henry came out of his office at lunchtime eating a sandwich and talking to Valerie at the same time. "Valerie, when Don comes in, tell him to come into my office." (Of course, we all knew about the special relationship between Don and Henry, no big secret.) I was passing through the front office space to another room and witnessed the whole episode. Since Henry was talking and chewing at the same time, the last part of his request came out as "Tell him to come into my orifice." When Henry realized what he had said, he broke out laughing, and Valerie and I howled, Valerie wiping tears out of her eyes.

I should close this chapter with an important aside. Even if I have had some outstanding friendships with men whether straight or gay, that does not mean that I pursued sex with all or even most of them. My friendships with Walter Sidlowski, Henry James, and Henry Knowlton, to cite some immediate examples, absolutely did not include any sexual exchange. If the individual is reasonably attractive, he will always find willing partners whether he deals with men or with women. A person of great sexual passion but of good intuition never needs to force himself or herself on anyone. It all boils down to an alert sensitivity. You don't need a billboard with giant letters to let you know when something is afoot or amiss!

Because of the very positive experience that I had at Homespun House due to Henry Knowlton and my co-workers, when I left L.A. and Southern California I left with an overall positive feeling about the southern half of the Golden State, much less crowded then than now during the winter of 2014-15.

Chapter IX. Northern California: Auburn and San Francisco

After my big move to Northern California, to live in Auburn, I worked as a salesman at the old Montgomery Ward department store downtown, in the newer part of the small city, as contrasted with picturesque Old Town. I had settled in a little house on Linden Court at the top of the little hill to the east of High Street, not far from the State Theatre, Auburn's nifty movie house, with the old *Auburn Journal* building next to it. Eventually Bob (Crook) would visit me there in my new dwelling, accompanied by dear little Tippie and Suzie, those wee special canine friends. When I moved to the City, I knew that Bob would eventually move there himself.

My move to Northern California had become inevitable, not just because I far preferred the overall ambiance—I could negotiate these towns the same way I had those older cities and villages in New England—but also I knew that the move would give me greater opportunity to cat around with other guys. (Hey, there are a lot of fish in the ocean, and you only live once—well, at least in a given incarnation!) After the usual Christmas shopping mania late in 1965, business predictably fell off at Monkey Ward's, the manager laid me off, and this gave me my direct opportunity to move to the City by the Golden Gate, as soon as possible, as if I needed any prodding.

In truth I had been spending most of my weekends in San Francisco, staying at the Y.M.C.A. on the Embarcadero, a neat refuge from Straightsville (the heterosexual world), and it had a purty good, inexpensive cafeteria. Y.M.C.A., of course, means Young Men's Christian Association, but the gay men who spent the night there, mostly on the weekends, had irreverently nicknamed it Young Men's Cocksucking Association. Believe you me, some of these guys turned out to be real experts at the art! The restrooms on every floor became places to meet other guys and sample the wares on display, some of which appeared *rather* impressive. The individual rooms also became hot beds of desire and sexual exchange, where people could conduct their activities in utter privacy so long as they kept their conversations, groans, and moans down to a discreet level. Also about this time, the early-to-middle 1960s, the institution of the gay baths, above all in San Francisco, really took off as very convenient places for sexual meeting and hook-up among men.

Sometime after the New Year—I forget exactly when during that winter of 1965-66—I moved yet again, but it happened fairly early on. I had arranged to move in with certain male friends in an old unpretentious Victorian house located in Diamond Heights, conveniently close (apart from a slight climb up to the house) to the Church Street streetcar line. However, to walk to the gorgeous Art Deco Mint Building on Market Street seemed like a trifle to me, who walked and who continues to walk as much as possible. In San Francisco one can easily walk in and around from Market Street near the Civic Center, or from the Ferry Building for that matter, to the Castro-Market area or down along Dolores and Church Streets. I did not find it easy at first, but I persevered and found a job in some downtown office building. I loved exploring the City, which the diagonal of Market Street cutting across the town's street grid greatly facilitates.

A dear friend in Auburn, a young man only a little younger than I, had kindly driven me and my stuff (oh, the boxes of all those heavy books!) all the way from Linden Court in Auburn down to the City, and then up to the flat on Diamond Heights. I would miss my few close friends in Auburn (not to mention the beautiful countryside around it), but the greater chance of adventure sexual and otherwise in my novel environment far outweighed any nostalgia that I would feel for the little city and its denizens. While residing in Auburn, I had intensified my close friendships there: with Ethel Heiple, Helen Farmer (her son, William, a special compadre, had moved away), Bob Elder, Genevieve Sully, and her two daughters Marion and Helen, both of whom played violin (and if needed, viola) in the Sacramento Symphony, and in fact over a long period of time.

Concerned about my living in the evil Big City, Genevieve (many blessings on her!) had not wanted me to leave, and put on a big dinner in my honor, which she made herself in her charming and unique house, the garden of which her close friend Clark Ashton Smith had often watered in the hot arid summer whenever she had gone away. The evening meal, the dinner that she made, turned out as tasty and filling: meatloaf, baked potatoes, and salad, with dessert later. The evening itself overall resulted in something quite emotionally fulfilling. She had invited her closest family: her daughters and their husbands, and her grandson, Geoffrey, Helen's only child, who had studied music as had Helen and Marion, and who played Spanish guitar extremely well. We had all gathered in the living room by the fireplace, where a crackling fire gave off a warm glow to the proceedings. After he tuned his guitar, Geoffrey went ahead and performed a short concert (his instrument had a gorgeous tone), twenty or thirty minutes perhaps, of mostly rhapsodic flamenco pieces, a concert that enraptured and enchanted us all.

Then Helen volunteered to play the piano. She sat herself down and performed with extraordinary feeling a favorite and very slow piece by Handel, the ineffable and haunting "Largo" from the Anglo-German's opera *Xerxes*. The piece itself and Helen's exceptional performance of it had seemingly wafted us all into another dimension while we still remained in our bodies. Thereupon, after a due interval of quietude and reflection, we all begged for an encore, the same piece again. Helen obliged, and the effect of the repeat on us proved even greater than that of her first performance, so pleasantly keyed up had we all become. The silence following the second performance proved even deeper and longer. As did the others present, I found myself on the verge of demanding a third performance of the same piece. Genevieve intuitively sensed this, and before anyone could utter it, she put a stop to the potential request. She told Helen not to perform it again. As she said, Genevieve feared, half joking, that another performance would cause us all to leave our bodies and not return. Who knows what might have happened?

Genevieve certainly gave me a wonderful send-off, the memory of which I have cherished ever since. Thank you very much, dear Lady Genevieve! My love and gratitude follow you wherever you may have gone. Anyone who knows the unusual and high quality of imagination and facture characteristic of Ashton Smith's fiction and poetry can readily grasp how Clark must have found in Genevieve a rare and very cultured friend and companion. She inspired *The Jasmine Girdle*, one of his few cycles of love poems, and Ashton Smith dedicated to her *Out of Space and Time* (1942), his first major prose collection. During the several decades I knew her (starting around 1960), Genevieve physically reminded me of none other than the attenuated but elegant Karen Blixen, otherwise Isak Dinesen. Like her, Genevieve had a keen sense of humor and irony. I consider it a great honor that in my own turn I became a close friend of Genevieve.

Like Clark, she had a special regard for the poetry of Nora May French, that tragic and unfulfilled figure who died so young. During 1965-73, through the auspices of another friend, I became a close friend with Nora's only sister, Helen French Hunt. On one occasion, in the early 1970s, I tried my very best to arrange a meeting between Helen and Genevieve (they were almost the same age), a meeting that might have turned into an historic occasion. Helen came up from Pasadena several times a year to sojourn in the Bay Area. This meeting would have taken place during one of her last visits to San Francisco, if not indeed on her very last one. Alas, at the last minute all the carefully laid plans fell through. Only a few years later death had claimed both women, two of the most extraordinary individuals I could ever have met.

The single most spectacular period in my adult life now followed, the ten years that I spent in San Francisco, that is, 1966-75, during my own chronological thirties. Not that my own life proved that spectacular in that entire period. Much of it, at least the first half, I lived rather quietly. It more or less coincided rather neatly with the Hippie

Period there, or the New Age Movement. Nor was it a pure coincidence that it should have happened in San Francisco or the Bay Area at large. "The City" has always existed as a metropolis different from any other since her very beginning as a modern town with the Gold Rush of 1849. She still remains a very different place to this day, even if the circumstances have surely changed since 1849.

Even before the Hippie Movement got under way, you never knew from day to day just what you might not witness casually on the public thoroughfares, especially Market Street, the main artery. I soon got used to taking the ever convenient Muni (the Municipal Railway) from Castro or Church Streets on into the downtown, and then back. Or I would arrange my time so that I could walk the distance west to east (actually southwest to northeast), including several miles or more north or south along Van Ness Avenue. The combination of Market and Van Ness certainly facilitates the movement of vehicles and pedestrians.

For one example of an unusual public exhibit, I recall a foggy, overcast morning when I was walking back along the north side of Market Street from the Ferry Building. I had reached the plaza where once the old and gorgeous Fox Theatre stood. I was walking near the curb the way I often walk on big-city streets, and I glanced ahead to my right. While keeping my cool about it, I was startled to notice a nice-looking, well-built young man just about stark naked. Hardly anyone gave him a glance, and he and the other pedestrians acted with perfect nonchalance. Beyond a little titillation, I may have felt a little concerned because of San Francisco's eternally cool or cold weather, but the young man seemed impervious to the morning cold.

The Hippie Movement or Period that flourished from the mid-1960s to the mid-1970s! What a crazy, what a glorious, what a kaleidoscopic decade that turned out to be! In recalling the people and events in my life during that period, I shall do my best to keep everything roughly in chronological order. I shall present the Hippie or New Age Movement in San Francisco only as it chiefly impinged on my own life. The movement became a major social and cultural phenomenon that attracted active participants, mostly young people, from all across the U.S. The movement itself—its rise, its efflorescence, and its decline—more or less coincided with the time when Joe Alioto presided as mayor over what was on occasion a pretty unpredictable electorate. Whether in San Francisco or outside of it, the mantra that former Harvard professor Timothy Leary was actively declaring dominated the scene: "Turn on, tune in, drop out."

From my own point of view I regarded him as "St. Timothy," a genuine holy man or public guru of the New Age Movement. You didn't need, and you still don't need, to practice as a professional sociologist to understand that something unprecedented was taking place in the mid-to-later 1960s. As New Age troubadours, the British group of musicians, the Beatles, had initiated something novel and revolutionary with their words and music. They reminded people to feel the joy and beauty of life, to show compassion, to participate in communing and community, to live in the moment, not to obsess about the past or the future, at least not so compulsively. When they came to the U.S., these then four young men, first on the Ed Sullivan television show and then by their record-breaking tours, exerted an enormous and positive influence on our society and on society everywhere.

For people in San Francisco and the Bay Area, Candlestick Park became the great cultural arena or venue. Soon there ensued in the City the anti-Vietnam War protests, the protests against military conscription, the mass be-ins in Golden Gate Park, and other demonstrations, not to mention the rock-and-roll bands with their anti-government messages, all of which signaled a vital and active young generation protesting against an older generation, those people running things, and the culture of death and potential mass annihilation they had promulgated, perhaps not consciously, during the Cold War of the 1950s and subsequently. Despite superficial appearances to the contrary, the whole Hippie and New Age Movement represented the desperate calling out of concerned young people for a different order, a different system, a different rationality, so as to effect a reconciliation of differences between non-Russian capitalism and Soviet socialism, for something other than competition with atom and hydrogen bombs between the two major mindsets, between capitalists and socialists-communists.

We must not overlook the fact that the Beat Poets of the 1950s in San Francisco did in fact set up the foundation for the later so-called counterculture movement of the mid-1960s to the mid-1970s, the Hippies and the New Age people. Publishing many of the same poets in sturdy but elegant paperbacks, Lawrence Ferlinghetti established his bookstore in 1953, and his publishing house in 1955. (However, as an independent press away from the big houses in Manhattan, he was following, even if not consciously, in the same tradition of independent specialist presses like Arkham House, established by August Derleth in 1939.) Among much else of genuine benefit in literary terms Ferling (his real name) gave permanence and publicity to the Beat Poets, especially Allan Ginsberg. The latter's *Howl* (very well titled) captured and attracted much-needed celebrity to the cause of the Beat Poets.

Their cause? That of the disaffected politically and otherwise, the rebels against unthinking patriotic Americans in the U.S., the rebels inhering as the "flotsam and jetsam from urban America." As during the Gold Rush, San Francisco became the ultimate seacoast of Bohemia, giving shelter and refuge to the alienated and the nonconformists from Straightsville, U.S.A. (as opposed to the counterculture). Without the conventional middle class that created and nurtured them, and against which they rebelled, the people of the counterculture could not have come into being, could not have existed. Rather an odd paradox, but perfectly true.

The counterculture mostly thrived via the young people flocking to San Francisco. Needless to say, despite all this brouhaha, regular life in the City and elsewhere went on as usual. The people who did not and could not participate in the counterculture, because they had jobs and had families to support, simply went on with their lives, but did not necessarily oppose what was happening. In fact many non-participants displayed pride that all this ferment was happening in *their* San Francisco no less. I can personally testify, once I became an obvious hippie, to the good will and hospitality shown to the hippies by the population at large, as well as to myself as a case in point, and I surely remain a mixture in more ways than one.

Many different segments or components of population went into the counterculture (whose agenda could accommodate anyone and everyone, truly democratic in practice and principle). Perhaps as the largest of the minorities who had taken refuge in the City, the gay community represented the single most vocal, most organized, and most powerful of them all. In a sense the gays who had flocked to San Francisco had fled there as pariahs from elsewhere and were making a kind of "last stand" on the "last frontier" located on the western seaboard of the U.S. No one was going to dislodge this determined group of sexually disaffected people who did not lack for a certain sophistication and a certain grim sense of humor about themselves. Interestingly enough, a certain number of the Beat Poets happened to be gay, even misogynistic. So much for spiritual democracy!

During the latter half of the 1960s, the first of my decade in San Francisco, I lived at a variety of addresses, rather quietly, trying merely to survive. I had several undemanding office jobs downtown on or near Market Street, when I got to know that area pretty well—that is, from the Castro-Market intersection down to the Ferry Building, and then from Market Street to North Beach (the original Italian area) and Fisherman's Wharf, from there along the Embarcadero, across Market, onto and along Mission Street (parallel to Market) from the Transbay Terminal on into the Mission District, including Dolores Park, leaving the downtown behind. Fascinated by both the old and the new architecture, I loved and studied the old wooden Victorian houses with their characteristic and ubiquitous window bays (also called bay windows), wherever I found them during my random walks. At some point that winter or spring of 1966 I moved from the flat in Diamond Heights, settling in with a temporary lover who had a basement flat near some public school high up in the Twin Peaks area just off Market Street. This residence had no great advantage for me, lacking an immediate access to the flat area of Market Street, east of Castro. I moved again, and soon.

Meanwhile Bob Crook had himself moved from Southern California and had located a suitable residence on 18th Street, several blocks up from Castro, and close to the Castro-Market intersection. A very pleasant single man, Richard Gaines, owned a two-story house with four bedrooms and needed housemates to share the expenses. Bob took one of the three available bedrooms, one of the two at the back, and I took another, one of the two at the front. Richard on occasion would rent out the fourth bedroom at the front next to mine, but the individual renting rarely stayed for long therein. The downstairs had a living room, a dining room, a kitchen, a bathroom, and a front hall leading to the upstairs hall. The upstairs had four bedrooms and the main bathroom, not to mention adequate closets, one per bedroom. This new residence now became my home for much of the first half of the decade that I spent living in the City.

One of the nicer features of our new neighborhood came in the shape of a very large Victorian mansion with turrets and towers, an actual front yard (rare in the City) with poplar or cedar trees, the property located in a very large city block southwest, and uphill (or upslope) of my new home. This block, and a few others around it, had genuine, semi-paved alleys going upslope east and west. When I returned home after the day's work, I would take the little dogs on leash for a walk that would last about half an hour, a most agreeable interlude with which to end the day in the last lingering light. I met several oldtimers who had lived in the neighborhood since childhood, and one gentleman remembered when (apart from the large mansion) few other houses existed, and the immediate neighborhood served as a dairy farm. I had never before given any thought to the rural aspects of the once undeveloped parts of San Francisco.

As already stated, Bob had brought with him his two special canine companions, Tippie and Suzie, and thus I had the comfort and consolation not just of Bob's great and ongoing friendship but also of the two little Boston Terriers. After several nondescript jobs I finally landed a good one, a professional occupation, by which I earned a good salary, and for which my B.A. in the humanities benefited me: an agreeable change! The training period alone lasted six months, and I had to commute to Oakland every working day. Luckily I had co-workers living in San Francisco with whom I could commute, and (of course) I contributed money toward the cost of the gasoline. My new residence also served as an excellent center for catting around and otherwise for socializing, with easy access to several convenient pick-up bars. Some of the ships that passed in the night sometimes turned into real friends and/or (on occasion) repeat partners.

The Castro-Market area had not yet changed into the almost exclusively gay neighborhood it has become today. Back in the late 1960s and early '70s it still had an interesting mix of ethnicities and sexualities, not to mention a variety of shops, drugstores, bakeries, and so forth, including the Castro Theatre or movie house. There I first experienced the epic feature film *Doctor Zhivago*, sitting next to housemate Richard Gaines, one of more than half a dozen showings that I have witnessed over the years. David Lean as usual had accomplished, had created, an exemplary film, based on Boris Pasternak's extraordinary novel. I still maintain that nothing equals the witnessing of a big feature film in a first-class movie house, where the spectator can concentrate on the cinematic offering without the distractions attendant on watching a film at home, no matter how large the television screen.

The professional job that I held for several years in Oakland served me well, despite the commute (not that bad, only about half an hour either way), and also despite the usual business or office uniform that

Americans have exported, alas! around the world, inflicting it on often totally alien cultures. I worked as a claims examiner for the State of California in Disability Insurance: when workers become seriously ill or physically disabled for reasons not connected with their work, they can collect some form of compensation to pay toward their basic expenses, and up to six months. However, if their work has caused their illness, then that becomes a matter for Workman's Compensation. Besides deciding on other aspects of the given claim, the examiner needs to determine first if the claim falls into either of the two categories, "workman's comp" or disability. This interesting job gave me some space for exercising a discreet compassion that I found gratifying.

In the late 1960s the *San Francisco Chronicle*'s Sunday magazine section sported a flamboyantly colorful and vividly delineated cover depicting two macaques, a piece of art such as I had never perceived before, by one Jesse Allen. An article on him and his art graced the magazine's interior. Both the cover and the other art, together with the article, hit my aesthetic sense in a way that no other art had up to that point. Yes, an art full of fantasy and interlocking detail, as passed through the prism of imagination belonging to an original and indeed unique artist. Although certainly modern, this art also conveyed or purveyed a definite romanticism as rare as it was unique, not to mention contemporary. A thing of absolute marvel!

I simply had to sample more of this marvelous art, and I could sample it in greater abundance in a regular exhibit at the Vorpal Gallery that lay just off the Embarcadero. Therefore, one day after work I went to the gallery and saw the exhibit. I met, and talked with, the gallery owner, Muldoon Elder (himself a gifted painter), who naturally shared my enthusiasm for Jesse Allen's paintings. Alas, Muldoon was not exactly giving any of Jesse's pictures away, and had priced them all in the thousands of dollars, quite out of my reach. However, Muldoon had made, or would make, posters or other reproductions of selected paintings available to those like myself who could not afford the paintings themselves.

Muldoon also mentioned that the artist, who lived near Stanford University way south of the City, would be coming up to the gallery on a certain day soon, in case I wished to meet him. I did so wish!—and I met him on the day appointed, again probably after work. Jesse remembers me looking like a Brooks Brothers clothing advertisement, and I never wore my business or office uniform except in connection with my fancy job: dressy jacket, slacks, white shirt, and (last but not least) the tie—the last-named I particularly disliked except when I changed it to a bow tie, a clip-on, which at least had a certain flair, as well as ease of donning. The Brooks Brothers impression could not have turned out more incorrect and uncharacteristic.

Jesse, bless him, turned out as fascinating as his art. Born in Kenya but educated in England (he had studied at Oxford University), he proved to be handsome, urbane, witty, very well-informed, if not indeed erudite in some of the same areas as myself, romance languages and their respective literatures, especially the divine language of poetry in the various human vernaculars. Like myself, he had learned long passages of poetry, and by heart, he in Italian and I in French. I had studied some Italian but nothing like Jesse—I had also studied Spanish, but Jesse himself did not learn the spoken form of that language until he lived in the Mission District. I had also studied in school or on my own enough German, Russian, and Greek to pronounce them correctly.

Of course, we did not learn all this about each other all at our first meeting, but we had made a very good beginning. I have known Jesse now for forty-five years, not quite half a century. I have no better, no greater, no more cherished friend than he, quite apart from the painstakingly achieved magic of his incomparable art. As I had with Muldoon, I brought up the subject of an art book reproducing his paintings, along with a suitable text by some art critic and historian. In case I have not mentioned it before, I have pursued my considerable interest in art, architecture, and music, in the lore and history of all of them, during most of my life to date, since childhood. And even if I cannot rank myself as an expert (perish the thought!), I count myself well informed, whether Western or Eastern, ancient or modern. However, I could not write such a text, I have neither the skill nor the lingo, nor now the aptitude as an elder person. Such an art book once almost appeared from the Vorpal Gallery while still managed by Muldoon, but—alas and alack!—it did not materialize at the time, nor has it since, but it might yet do so. Let us pray, let us hope!

Meanwhile Richard Gaines had sold his house on 18th Street and moved to a house (another Victorian) on the western side of Belcher Street, not far from the convenient big Safeway Supermarket (on Market near Church), just west of the gorgeous one-story Art Deco masterpiece, the U.S. Mint Building. The new house had one story, but the main floor existed above a ground floor, an apartment of the same size and rentable. After due consultation Bob and I followed him soon after he moved; it seemed much easier to go along to the new residence than to find another suitable one elsewhere, not always easy to do. Besides, we three got along very well and had established a great rapport among us, worth its weight in gold when living with other folkses. The house had a totally private, agreeable back yard with trees, bushes, and flowers.

Somewhere during this period—I can't quite figure out or pinpoint the chronology—I became (an aberration!) disillusioned with one-on-one as well as group sex with guys, and bethought me to investigate the other gender despite my well founded misgivings, an investigation long delayed since early childhood. In reality it turned out as the best and most apposite period in which to do so, given the then facile accessibility to women, coupled with the goddess-blessèd birth-control pill. Thus I strictly disciplined myself in terms of the inevitable fateful encounter with women, with the Woman, in whatever guise she would present herself. I vowed to have no sex with any guy (solo sex with myself allowed!) until I had consummated union with a woman. Thus I passed one whole year in this benighted celibate condition.

At the end of that one year, as I had vowed and avowed, an attractive young woman, who lived in a flat just south of our new home courtesy of Richard, came up to me one day to chat (we had already met) and asked me casually, would I like to spend the night with her. What? Mirabile dictu, would I ever! After a year of enforced celibacy I would have no problem in maintaining my part of the (ahem!) exchange. The night went well, very smoothly. I might have functioned as a much more impassioned lover, but I was acting with notable caution while traversing unknown terrain. This act or action liberated me to discover and explore other unknown geographies of a human as well as humane description.

By this time I had already moved for some forgotten but significant reason to a new flat on Castro Street but at some real distance from Castro-Market-Land, even if only a half mile or so further north. Divisadero and Castro overlap each other, that is, run parallel to each other for several blocks. I had located a two-story, three-flat building, where I would share a flat with a new acquaintance. The owner (an elderly woman) resided on the top or second story, we would reside on the bottom or first story, and underneath us lay a basement flat somewhat smaller than the two above it. Here I would live for several years, during which a number of momentous events would transpire in my life. It would turn out to be almost the last residence where I would live in San Francisco. Overall, by the time that I left San Francisco to live in Sacramento, I would have moved some thirty-five times in the City. Oi vey Maria!

Sometime after I met Jesse, I began working at various gay baths, usually in the morning, a quiet period when most of the customers or clients have left the premises, when a few are sleeping in, or sleeping over, after a strenuous hormonal exchange with divers and diverse individuals. Then, at that time, I would clean up individual cubicles, as well as the steam and sauna rooms (moving from wet to dry). I worked first at the 21st Street Baths, and this resulted in a fascinating and revealing lesson in human nature. I had an excellent co-worker who let the customers in and out and otherwise dealt with them. He derived from a Jewish mother and probably Roman Catholic father, an evocative mixture on a spiritual level. This co-worker gave me one of my favorite expressions, "Oi vey Maria," instead of the more familiar "Ave Maria." He and I became allies when dealing with the customers.

I also recall the three remarkable owners of the 21st Street Baths, who acted very warm and charming toward me. I got to know them on a fairly familiar basis, and they invited me once to tour their big fancy house in Pacific Heights, west of Van Ness Avenue. It was a rectangular, three-story structure of brick, and they had furnished it in a manner not unworthy of Versailles (done well and in good taste), or as they express it in the gay world, piss-elegant. Even if their elegant mansion impressed me, I had no desire to have a house like theirs. Even after I stopped working at their baths, they let me use the premises, a very generous concession.

Despite the reputation of some gay men of being impeccably clean, I soon discovered some truly gross exceptions at the baths. I remember one particular episode. When I or some other worker would clean out a given cubicle, they would subsume any wrapping up of sheets that the customer had thoughtfully prepared, no problem, thank you very much. Either I or someone else on the staff had picked up a neatly rolled sheet that a customer had left for us and simply put it in with the other dirty sheets. Conveyed to the laundry, it fell to the female staff to handle them in turn. As they handled the towels and sheets, these big jolly black women would perforce shake them out. As a co-worker reported the story to me, when they unfurled and shook out this especial rolled-up sheet, out flew several big, healthy, well-formed stools that the customer had left behind, presumably too lazy to use the restrooms available to him. Pandemonium then, when the shit hit the fan?—No, just when the turds came to light and went flying through the air, quite without expectation. After the initial shock, accompanied by screams, every one of the laundresses burst out laughing uncontrollably.

During the several years that I worked at the 21st Street Baths (probably my favorite job after the one at Homespun House), an exceptional publishing phenomenon took place, that is, as it affected me locally, albeit emanating from New York City. Lin Carter had convinced Ian and Betty Ballantine, following the huge success of the J. R. R. Tolkien books (chiefly *The Hobbit* and *The Lord of the Rings*), that a big potential audience existed for fantasy and science fiction in regular paperback or pocketbook format. Thus began the celebrated line of pocketbooks marketed under the name of the "Adult Fantasy Series," as edited and masterminded by Lin Carter—under the logo of the unicorn's head in the upper right-hand corner of each front cover—and as discovered by me, whenever I would check out the local cigar store for any interesting novelty among their paperbacks.

Just a block or so away from the baths to the east, on the northeast corner of the intersection at 21st and Mission Streets, there stood the local cigar or tobacco store, which also carried liquor or sundries or both (you name it, and they would have it). As you would pass through the entrance at the corner of the building, in which stood the cigar store, mounting a few steps, you would encounter on the right a tall circular rack stocked with the latest pocketbooks. Lo and behold, what should I see but the first paperbacks with the soon-to-be-familiar unicorn's head logo, as they made their appearance on the rack, beginning with Arthur Machen's unique and interconnected fiction collection *The Three Imposters*—of all things!

Then there followed, one after another, the other titles in this new series, each title capably introduced and edited (oriented in time and space) by Lin Carter as the series' enthusiastic and erudite manager-editor, who published not only and mostly the worthy and worthwhile masters in the genre of modern fantasy and science fiction, but also notable new titles in the genre such as *Red Moon and Black Mountain* (1971) by Joy Chant (i.e., Eileen Joyce Rutter). Some of both the old and the new titles I bought and read, some I did not. Of particular interest for me the titles by Clark Ashton Smith, as gathered and edited by Monsieur Carter, possessed the strongest relevance, *Zothique*, *Xiccarph*, and *Poseidonis*. A fourth title, with the greatest potential for some kind of mass-audience appreciation, did not appear, alas!—*Averoigne*. I believe that the Adult Fantasy Series had ceased publication before it could release *Averoigne*. Although the series had sold well enough, it never attained the lofty status reached by Tolkien's great prose epic The Lord of the Rings.

Nevertheless, despite the lack of any gigantic commercial impact, the series under the editorship of Lin Carter had accomplished much else of genuine value. It had indeed introduced many readers to the recent achievements (in modern prose fiction) of those modern masters who had specialized in the genre(s) of fantasy and science fiction, authors as variegated as Arthur Machen, H. P. Lovecraft, C. Ashton Smith, and others. The widespread distribution and sale of these mass-market paperbacks across the U.S. but also, to some degree, across the English-speaking world around the planet—such had great value. For this fact alone we must give real credit to Lin Carter, the Adult Fantasy Series, and Ballantine Books. The series in particular turned on, and tuned in, many sensitive young minds to the potential of "sport and play" in modern imaginative fiction.

In addition, because of the association of my own name with the scholarship on behalf of C. Ashton Smith, I discovered some kindred spirits (or rather, they discovered me) who later transformed into my best and closest friends, namely two in special status, Ronald and Michelle Hilger, when we first met in the latter 1980s. In fact, I have met most of my current best friends because of our common or mutual interest in C. Ashton Smith. This friendship via literature has proven a very gratifying experience in personal terms for me. Apart from the mystery and maelstrom known or adumbrated under the name of love, great friendship remains an anchor, a consolation, and a reality that never deserves any scorn or disdain.

The significant reason why I moved from the Victorian house on Belcher Street to the one at 50 Divisadero? (The original owners had built it at a later period.) After several years of ownership Richard Gaines decided to sell this second house of his, which (once done) freed him to return to his parents' house in Riverside, to live there for a spell. I had left my job as claims examiner with the State of California and was doing just odd jobs, less remunerative but better endowed with free time (so called, but it never comes free). Richard hired me to help him move, to help prepare his possessions for moving, and to drive down to Riverside with him, and to help him unload boxes and furniture at his parents' home at the southern end of our itinerary. He sold his car and hired a medium-sized truck, into which we packed all his possessions. The drive down southward went smoothly, and without any problem we arrived at his parents' home late in the day. After a good night's rest we unpacked the truck, and after a second night Richard paid me, we said goodbye, parting as very good friends, and then he dropped me off at the nearest Greyhound bus station, from which I went back to San Francisco. We stayed in touch for a few years, and then the relationship lapsed, except when I sent him a copy (autographed to him) of my first book, the Arkham House title *Songs and Sonnets Atlantean*. He graciously acknowledged the receipt of his copy.

With several other roommates I would now reside for just a year or so at 50 Divisadero Street, maybe longer. But I had not yet quite finished with Belcher Street, since later events would return me there. I should add that, whereas Divisadero and Castro between them ran much of the distance north and south that constituted the length of the City, little Belcher covered only one city block from a street right next to Market on the south to Judah Street on the north. The chief roommate, Joe M. (I can't recall his full surname), turned out to be quite agreeable but unusually intense. When not at his job, he devoted most of his energy to writing and developing his journals, which by his creativity he had changed into a major form of literary art. On occasion he let me read them, or he read parts of them to me; and I can vouchsafe for their high quality and inherent fascination. At some point some New York publisher wanted to publish them, or at least some salient sections, but as far as I know nothing came of this possibility, alas!

During the time that I lived at 50 Divisadero, Joe and I saw a succession of other roommates, most of them young men who hailed from across the U.S., who had come to the City to sample the life and atmosphere there, to try their luck in a more sympathetic climate or environment than what obtained at home. By this time Bob Crook and I had ceased living together. Once Richard Gaines had sold his last house, Bob had moved over to Oakland with the little dogs and, finding a new simpático lover, was living with him in some rented house high in the Oakland hills. Despite the physical distance between Oakland and San Francisco, Bob and I remained in close communication via telephone. Whenever I lived for several brief periods in Oakland, we would often visit, and sometimes I would take care of Tippie and Suzie for Bob when he went back home to Lincoln, Nebraska, that is, on those occasions when Bob's new lover could not take care of them himself for some reason or other. Of course, I loved having the dogs with me again—they remained special to me then, as they still remain in memory.

Soon after I moved to 50 Divisadero, William Farmer's younger brother Noel and his pal Charles ("Charlie") Jorgenson (both simpático types, albeit ten years or so younger than myself, and both ardent rock-and-rollers: they had their own band) started coming down on the odd weekend to sample the hippie or New Bohemian lifestyle. They stayed overnight with me. Apart from bathroom and kitchen, the flat had four or five other rooms that had beds or sofas in them that could always accommodate guests. We rarely, if ever, had a full house of roommates, and Joe M. enjoyed my guests; but otherwise he usually kept to himself, holed up in his room, working on his journals. He approved of my extending hospitality to the young people from Auburn. He did need some socializing apart from that required to sustain his regular job.

Eventually Noel and Charlie had their girlfriends join us on these weekends, and eventually both young men immigrated to the City from the hinterland of Auburn and Long Valley. The hospitality turned out mutual, and I would return to Auburn to stay overnight with Noel and his girlfriend in their apartment, or with his mother Helen in her own house (where I had first met William), to which I was no stranger as she had let me use it as one of my bases when I had come up from L.A. to conduct my researches related to Ashton Smith at the State Library in Sacramento. Her property lay a very short distance away from Ethel's house at High and Sacramento Streets. High Street jogged over a bit east and then continued a little more to the south. Helen's charming medium-sized house stood on the east side, as did Ethel's house; High Street itself had otherwise continued south all the way from the then new downtown.

On one of my weekend excursions back to Auburn, during the warmer weather, I met Gloria—in full, Gloria Kathleen Braly (pronounced BRAW-lee). At this first meeting we seemed to like each other quite a bit. She was nineteen, I was thirty-five but looked much younger, as I generally have, as if in my early to middle twenties. My memory does not serve me well here, but I believe that it happened on the second excursion back to Auburn that same summer, when Gloria and I met on the second occasion, that we fell in love. We stayed with Noel Farmer and his girlfriend (the latter also a close friend to Gloria) on this second excursion. Charlie also joined us along with his ladylove. We all had a lot of fun socializing, not to mention drinking alcoholic beverages (mostly beer and in moderation) and smoking marijuana (again in moderation)—a few hits on the special cigarettes or on the bong or hubble-bubble sufficed.

Gloria and I found each other mutually attractive. Shapely, with dark blond hair and blue eyes, she certainly looked beautiful not only to me but to others as well. She had already had a number of lovers, including Pat, a strikingly beautiful young man; and the idea of this previous experience of hers only turned me on all the more. Professionally a dental technician, she helped the dentist with tools and other assistance while he worked on the patient. Evidently very good at her job, she never lacked for employment. When she left for work, she would gather her lovely, long, dark blond hair (parted in the middle) into a big knot or bun below the back of her head at the neck, which rather made her look like a ravishing schoolmarm. When on her own time, she let her hair down to float free, which did indeed make her look like a ravishing hippie chick on the one hand or on the other like some gorgeous apparition, some madonna, from the Pre-Raphaelite period of the latter nineteenth century, lacking only medieval dress. Whatever, definitely irresistible—yum!

And as for me, what did Gloria perceive? A handsome, muscular, well-formed hippie dude with passably long hair, long sideburns, moustache, and a small beard growing around the chin. I do not describe myself favorably out of any exaggerated admiration for the individual involved, but many lovers had expressed themselves about me in similar terms; and so let us assume that they were opining objectively. Let me emphasize that at eighty I describe myself at the age of thirty-five. I have a number of photos (and in color!) of myself at twenty-five or twenty-six; and apart from the general hirsuteness that accompanied the hippie period, I looked the same at thirty-five that I had looked at twenty-five or so. At any rate, Gloria found me not unworthy of her attention and love-making. Enough said!

The great moment of amorous revelation for both of us came when we had gone swimming in some lake nearby (probably Lake Folsom). It had turned rather dark at mid-evening, and we were skinny-dipping, the six of us. Sometime the next day Noel and his girlfriend let us use their bedroom (it was afternoon) so that Gloria and I could make love. We did in fact make love, and for rather an extended period, spectacularly so, during some three hours, interrupted only by the necessity to urinate on occasion, when individually or collectively we had to come up for air. Making love with Gloria generally turned into something wonderful, but that first encounter in bed with her resulted in something that proved the most profoundly satisfying for me, and that contented me on so many levels, and in so many subtle nuances and aspects. That expresses a lot, and that expresses it all.

I had enjoyed a similar experience a few years or so before the one with Gloria, which had proven as prolonged and spectacular (yes, also three hours), but with a beautiful male partner. Let us call him Jerry Holsum, who specialized in performing as a bottom, as a receptor, which requires great skill, abandon, and stamina. Since I had also performed in this latter capacity myself with various and quite well-endowed studs, I knew what the role of the receptor involved. Dear Jerry ranked as a genius at his specialty. As for me at the time of our coupling, I was finally releasing all the passion that had been building up in me for many years from late adolescence on into my early thirties. In addition, having noted my general sexiness and more than adequate equipment, Jerry had tastefully but determinedly solicited me (we had met already some little time before) while we were walking up along Castro Street north of the Castro-Market intersection.

In liberating our libidos, it also helped that Jerry had gotten both of us outrageously stoned on both eaten and inhaled marijuana. In fact, we had become so stoned that a piece of music that I knew lasted only about five minutes or so, and that played in the background on a radio while we were making love, seemed to last for about thirty minutes. Later I discovered the name of the majestic, slow-paced, full-bodied symphonic morceau: the "Intermezzo" from *Notre Dame* (yes, inspired by the famous cathedral in Paris), the first of the two unusual operas by Franz Schmidt (the other being *Fredigundis*, also inspired by French history, but much earlier).

Whether with Gloria or with Jerry, such transcendent and intense interludes rarely recur, no matter how hard we may try to duplicate them later. A much later coupling with Jerry turned out okay, but that is all. When such rare interludes happen, we simply rejoice in them and accept them for what they remain: unique breakthroughs that can sometimes occur to individuals aptly sensitive or attuned to each other. (Sigh—and alas!) As an aside to the reminiscence about Jerry Holsum, I should add that I had become so turned on by the intense breakthrough that we experienced together (it proved also that for him) that in my new-found sexual exuberance and enthusiasm I wanted to repeat our coupling the very next night, but Jerry with apologies and regrets had to say me nay: the poor kid found himself exhausted after that night of nights with me. He needed to get a full night's rest that next night. Of course, I understood (I had begged him with tears in my eyes), but I remained so horny that I found another partner that same evening after my brief interview with Jerry. So be it!

As more than one writer or poet has observed, the annals of heaven and/or happiness appear to run on without need of a recorded history, presumably because nothing happens, or at least nothing of note. Given our human or inhuman nature, nothing captures our attention so much as tension or conflict, as witness so much recorded history or many works of fiction, the latter usually based upon some premise of trouble or violence. Mystery, particularly while remaining a mystery, and thus unresolved, might make an exception. Having discovered and announced this truth (at least for myself), I shall summarize my life and experience with Gloria succinctly, or as much so as I can. One affair is like another—that is, with all proportions duly guarded. Love remains the same bizarre mixture of enthusiasm, exuberance, depression, despondency, melancholy, ups and downs, that it has always been since beyond antiquity; and sometimes the course of love may run level, compassionate, and consolatory. For a sensitive but passionate person like myself an eternal tension inheres in the equation between man and woman, the suspense inherent in depending upon someone else for regular sexual fulfillment, and release from that sometime tense expectation.

I regard the marriage or linkage between Gloria and myself as lasting four years, two years before legal marriage and two years legally married. It resulted in a great learning experience for me during the late 1960s and early 1970s. During the first two years of our relationship I followed Gloria up and down the state, as my rather flexible circumstances permitted. From her job in Auburn she got another in San Diego or somewhere in Southern California. Then eventually, and rather soon, one in San Francisco, where we lived at 50 Divisadero for a while. This early part of our marriage went smoothly and turned into something wonderful. At some point, one day while we happened to find ourselves on Belcher Street for some reason, due to the nearness of the beautiful Gloria in my presence, an inhabitant of a middle flat of three—in the middle of the eastern side of the block of ordinary Victorian houses—emerged onto the sidewalk and in pantomime invited us upstairs to partake of marijuana. We introduced ourselves all around and accepted the invitation. We tarried in the flat for a little while, as we got to know the host: one Captain Bill (otherwise William Vorwerk), head of a small hippie family (not related by blood) that the good captain called the Yellow Submarine after the Beatles-inspired animated cartoon of the same name. A great friendship had begun and would continue even after I broke up with Gloria.

Meanwhile Gloria and I had become legally married. After we got our marriage license from City Hall in the Civic Center, a friend (a duly ordained minister of some non-official New-Age religion) by the name of Vern—then residing in Mill Valley on Laverne Avenue by an odd coincidence, and as part of another hippie family—married us at 50 Divisadero. While Gloria pursued her very practical occupation as dental assistant, I continued in the part-time job working at the baths, as well as in the part-time business that I had created for myself as a fancy house-cleaner. I worked for middle-class and upper middle-class families dispersed throughout San Francisco, many of whom became close friends to me, like relatives belonging to an enormous extended family. On occasion, at their invitation, we would eat supper or dinner with some of these customer friends, all unusual but fine people.

It seemed that our little hippie family living at 50 Divisadero made too much noise for our landlady residing above us. She asked us to move in a very gracious way, with no threats of eviction, and we reassured her that we would move as soon as we could find a place. We would try to keep it quiet before we moved out. She acquiesced, and we parted on friendly terms. Thanks to a tip from Captain Bill, we found a bottom flat of a two-flat house on the southern side of Judah Street, just around the corner from Captain Bill's Yellow Submarine. We liked it and rented it. Luckily for us, we would have no trouble with the renters above us, another hippie family. Behind the main house stood a little house in the back yard, which Gloria and I claimed for ourselves as the newlyweds. We called our little hippie family the Family Sunshine.

Given the nearness, we often socialized and smoked with the generous Captain Bill. He maintained as his main business that of marijuana merchant, no less than that of supplying organic or high-quality chemical substances like LSD (or acid), peyote, magic mushrooms (psilocybin), hashish, and so forth. He turned into a very convenient friend to know! I enjoyed marijuana and hashish, but the other substances did very little for me, and for this I give thanks. Besides the real expense, they can become addictive, even if I enjoyed experimenting with them with Gloria. Of course, Captain Bill conducted his business with discretion, quite clandestinely for the most part. In addition, Bill proved a fun-loving and ever jolly companion. I maintained my friendship with the good captain long after my divorce from Gloria. In fact, after I separated from her, he became a mainstay for me, and his flat provided an ever available refuge. Thank you, dear Captain Bill, wherever you may have navigated your ship!

Gloria and I inhabited our little house quite joyfully, at the back of the bottom flat on Judah Street. The course of our marriage continued smoothly. While I would leave to do whatever job I had lined up for the day, Gloria would take the Muni trolley car to her dental occupation in the downtown. When not at work, we did have a lot of glorious times together. Once a couple travels beyond what is often the barrier of sexuality, they can find themselves, metaphorically speaking, in an occasional garden of delights, where one can share simple but real pleasures with the other, such as reading poetry to each other, and not just love poetry. Besides, to perfervid lovers madly in love with each other, love poetry might appear redundant anyway. Gloria and I often visited, and loitered in, our occasional garden of delights.

Like many hippie couples we prided ourselves on maintaining a broad tolerance of others free from the hangups and prejudices of our parents, or so we thought without much experience. Hmm! We tolerated with ease the concept of so-called open marriage, whereby one partner grants the other partner complete liberty to have an occasional fling with someone else. Unless conducted with wisdom and moderation, an open marriage can soon cease to be a marriage at all. After suitable experimentation we realized that we needed to live by ourselves for a while; and accordingly we found and moved into a small flat in the Mission District (not far from the 21st Street Baths as well as Jesse Allen's residence a little south of the baths), where all went well at first.

All went well until Gloria found that she was developing a child within her, something for which we had not prepared financially. Hmm, what to do? Compounding the problem, given our recent open marriage, with multiple partners for both of us, Gloria could not determine which partner had impregnated her. Was it I or some other man? I had very mixed feelings, alternating amid anger, betrayal, and indecision. We quarreled once, and briefly. Gloria moved out of our flat and into the apartment of some girlfriend. In one sense I felt relieved to find myself alone again. Finally, after due discussion between us, and after an extended self-examination on her part in terms of her own conflicting emotions, Gloria decided to have an abortion, probably the best decision. I could not decide for her; this was taking place in her own body. She set the operation up at U.C. Medical Center on Mount Parnassus more or less in the very middle of San Francisco. She had the abortion and recovered from it. The operation marked the end of our marriage, although we did on occasion still visit with each other again. But even that ended after a while. At some point, relatively soon, we got a divorce.

Although I have had other relationships, including some once again with both men and women, I have never repeated the act or condition of marriage with anyone else, nor have I had any desire to do so, certainly not with a woman. I learned quite a bit from my marriage with Gloria, including what makes most people tick, that is, as married adults, but they do not function exactly like clocks. Marriage is at best a very mixed bag, especially when compounded with money problems, or the lack of it. Enough said! As for me, I merely returned to my first and chief love, men in all their infinite variety. Thanks to the example bad or good that I had set, several of my gay friends (a few of them former lovers of mine) became involved with women, fell in love, got married, and found out just what heterosexuality involved. In each and every case they eventually ended the marriage (and without bitterness, no mean feat), and all of them at some point expressed explicitly to me the same sentiment. "Women are wonderful, but they are an entirely different species from men." Well, if nothing else, metaphorically true.

Meanwhile, both before and after the marriage to Gloria (many blessings upon her!), life went on elsewhere with other people, thank heaven. I found consolation or distraction with Captain Bill of H.M.S. *The Yellow Submarine*. But first I had to find a new domicile, and out of the Mission District, simply because I did not, and do not, like living by myself. Besides, it is cheaper to live with simpático friends, in addition to having the benefit of their companionship. Bachelor-style, Noel and Charlie were living in a flat somewhere not far away from Castro-Market on the northwest of that intersection, and they had an extra room. Could I please move in with them? Yes! And so I did, once again hauling all my books and bookcases with me (ugh). A very good thing that I remained as strong as an ox. Apart from my ongoing part-time business of fancy house-cleaning for elegant folks (I had met some neat people thataway), I concentrated on completing the MS. (i.e., the typescript) of my very own first book, *Songs and Sonnets Atlantean* (what turned into what I later called "The

First Series"), for publication by August Derleth via his Arkham House. Gloria had taken a lively interest in my writing. Even as and after we broke up, she did all she could to encourage me to finish that first book. By the time I completed the MS. and then had it published, it had taken me from March 1961 to June 1971, thus easily a little more than ten years.

In anticipation of the second and third series of the same ongoing trilogy, I should add an important aside here lest I forget to mention it later on. Among his immense output of highly unusual poetry in varying and almost unprecedented meters, not to mention a very large output in prose, Swinburne achieved three series of his inimitable *Poems and Ballads* (he could write as well in French, both in verse and in prose). I recall myself wondering if I could ever achieve a second and third series à la Swinburne—never mind much else in verse, given the more concentrated Muse that I worship and pursue (thanks to *The Faerie Queene* of Edmund Spenser), never mind my own limitations as a poet. (We can go into that somewhat later.) The fact that I did indeed create and publish a second and third series, and all of an equally high quality (or so people have informed me), amazes me as much as it has my friends, critics, and well-wishers.

I had already compiled several books for Arkham House on my own, that is, done at my own instigation. First, I suggested a complete collection (or as complete as was then possible) of Ashton Smith's remarkable and quite original prose-poems. Derleth approved the idea, and I rounded up all the known and unknown prose-poems wherever they existed, some of them otherwise unobtainable except via the Berg Collection at the New York Public Library. Upon explaining my project via a letter to Carol Smith, she as Ashton's widow scrivened at once for me a carte blanche statement such as I could use with any library (if it had the requisite materials) to obtain what I needed. The Berg Collection had the complete George Sterling and Ashton Smith correspondence, along with related poems and other materials, a fabulous cache.

Since I could not then go to New York for the purpose, necessity dictated that I hire a researcher (in this case, quite an intelligent and perceptive fellow) to find what I needed, but it did not cost as much as I had feared. With as much dispatch as I could muster, I typed up the MS. with great care and then sent it off to Derleth. Meanwhile I had also written an extended and incisive introduction aptly entitled "Clark Ashton Smith, Poet in Prose," which I appended with Derleth's approval to the slender volume, simply and logically called *Poems in Prose*. In the introduction I recount the history of the poem in prose as a special form (largely innovated and evolved in France) and place Ashton's achievement, quite a high one, where it belongs in such an historical cavalcade. In 1964 Derleth accepted the volume as I had put it together, and the book duly made its appearance in 1965 (despite the date on the title page, 1964, even if the copyright on the copyright page reads 1965).

As engineered by myself, the book garnered very good reviews from both Fritz Leiber and August Derleth. The latter did reviews on a regular basis for the *Madison Times*, that is, Madison as the state capital of Wisconsin, situated not far from Sauk City and Arkham House. Encouraged by this first attempt at masterminding a book, I next suggested to Derleth a collection of all of Smith's hitherto uncollected stories as an omnibus. Once more Derleth approved the idea, and as I had already gathered copies of all the stories required, I began typing the MS. at once. However, I had achieved perhaps only one third of it, when non-literary difficulties arose in my personal life (during the latter 1960s), making it, if not impossible, extremely awkward for me to continue and finish it.

Therefore I applied to Margo Skinner, who regularly typed the MSS. of Fritz Leiber for him, to finish the job for me—which she did; and although I offered to pay her, she refused any recompense, knowing as she did my impecunious condition. Wow, what a benevolent gesture! I proofed the stories against their magazine appearances and mailed the MS. of what became *Other Dimensions* off to Derleth, first making one or more photocopies, just as I had already done for *Poems in Prose*. This has become my standard procedure, in case of loss or accidental destruction of the original. I call such photocopies my insurance copies. Once more, Derleth accepted the volume as I had put it together, and the book duly made its appearance in 1970.

Apart from the part-time work that I needed to do to pay my basic expenses, I now concentrated on completing my very own first book, the first collection entitled *Songs and Sonnets Atlantean*. This completion turned into more of a task than anticipated. I did most of the work in the morning when alone in the flat that I shared with Noel and Charlie. I had already finished the main text, and the introduction under the pseudonym of Dr. Ibid M. Andor (the M. standing for Massachusetts), the latter (i.e., the introduction) very different in tone from the poetry itself. The completion of the MS. involved the creation of the notes, again under the pseudonym of Dr. Ibid M. Andor, again very different in tone from the poetry per se. In this task, and by residing with Noel and Charlie, I completely lost myself and forgot my depression over the loss of Gloria, or as I styled her sometimes, Gloriana, in honor of Spenser's titular heroine animating *The Faerie Queene*.

The composition of the notes, which I had anticipated as a task I could accomplish with ease, resulted in a major undertaking. However arduous, it turned into a fascinating process, because these notes involved a change in attitude rather different from that inherent in the romanticism that created the poetry. This afforded me much amusement, if not actual humor, the romanticism of the poetry contrasting nicely with the ironic, "anthropological" detachment evident in the notes. As Dr. Andor, I had to maintain a certain rigorous "disjunctiveness" appropriate to that august but charming individual. At first Derleth baulked at the size and length of the overall (and concluding) section, but gradually (bless him!) came to accept it for what I intended. We solved the problem of the financing for the notes by Derleth having them printed in smaller type and in double columns, which somehow made them even more suitable and scholarly. As the book went through the process of physical production, it metamorphosed into something unprecedented and beyond expectation.

I did not fully appreciate what I had achieved with the notes until sensitive readers and friends informed me of it after publication. By the time the book appeared, I had already launched myself on into another career, starting around the 1960s, thanks to my dear and extraordinary friend Marvin R. Hiemstra, whom I had met through dear Howdee Hoeffding from Pacific Palisades. During the time I worked at the 21st Street Baths, I lived briefly, sharing a flat with a friend of a friend, in a house on Bernal Hill, not very far from where Marvin resided with a special partner.

This happened before I met, and fell in love with, Gloria (otherwise Gloriana). Marvin would come over from his residence, and we would meet, repairing to some coffee house down on the north side of Bernal Hill. Although he had an M.A. in English from Iowa State University (he hailed originally from the Dutch-American town of Pella), Marvin showed himself in no manner as an academic snob, but as exceptionally open to recent literary phenomena with which the academic world had not yet caught up. Above all, this meant my beloved California Romantics, like Bierce, Nora May French, Sterling, and C. A. Smith inter alia.

I began with Ashton Smith, who subsumes all the other poets and writers—in several ways, all proportions guarded. I introduced Marvin first to Smith's prose fictions and then to his poetry. Dear Marvin (bless him!) responded more than just favorably (hallelujah!), and so much so that I asked him to write an inclusive, overall statement—to appear in my Smith bibliography—which he did, and which he entitled "Clark Ashton Smith, Cosmic Master Artist," indeed! This remains an unique and magisterial interpretation of C.A.S. and his oeuvre, and the first of its kind. Nothing else has overtopped it since its first appearance in the C.A.S. bibliography.

Sometime before I moved north from L.A., probably via Fritz

Leiber, I met the then young Randal ("Randy") Kirsch Everts, the son of Robert Kirsch, the once lone book reviewer for the *Los Angeles Times,* whose deep and evenhanded reviews well served the newspaper's literary readers. (As the son's last name, or names, reveal, his mother obviously married again.) Sometime during 1968 and the warmer weather, by pre-arrangement via letter and telephone, Randy drove in the late morning to my home at 50 Divisadero, bringing with him one of his best and most welcome *trouvailles* from his researches, to wit, the long-surviving sister of the poet Nora May French, by name Helen French Hunt, then in her seventies or eighties, an elegant and still beautiful woman. Age had not ravished her, but had only made her more elegant. I entertained Helen and Randy, the miracle worker, in the front room of the flat, just off the vestibule or front hall. Our visit lasted several wonderful hours in agreeable and wide-ranging conversation.

Helen turned out to be a highly cultured and very well-informed person who had known, quite well, most of the chief literary and other artists whose names I had come to know while doing the research for my Smith bibliography: George Sterling, the editor Theodore Bonnet, the artist Xavier Martinez ("Marty," as Helen called him)—whose murals and other art still adorn buildings in both Northern and Southern California—and so forth: whom had she *not* known? After we had visited for a good long while, I believe that Randy may have driven us to lunch somewhere, thus extending our social interlude. Randy then drove me back to 50 Divisadero after leaving Helen off at her small but quality hotel downtown. In this way our first memorable meeting concluded.

Independent of Randy, to whom we were both grateful for the introduction, Helen and I soon developed our own friendship, which lasted until Helen's death in 1973. Throughout the time of my marriage to Gloria Kathleen, but especially during my first sojourn in the U.K., because she knew that I functioned on minimal funds (how I did it, I still can't quite figure out!), she would send me small sums of money (unsolicited on my part, but not refused) that served a real need in my life, in my minimal lifestyle. I owe dear Helen a huge debt of gratitude!

Emotionally and otherwise, she represented an enormous treasure, and one that I could not keep only to myself. I had to share her with other friends, but just the right friends, who had the requisite sensitivity, culture, and background. And I did have such friends, to wit, Marvin Hiemstra and his partner Lloyd Neilson, no friends more appropriate. Helen came up to San Francisco once or twice a year, and on one of her sojourns I introduced her to Marvin and Lloyd. Our group resulted in an exceptional combination of simpático temperaments, and we always reveled in our special times together. Sometimes Marvin or Lloyd would drive us all across the Golden Gate Bridge, and over to some special restaurant in Sausalito (north of the City), where we would enjoy some excellent meal. Helen could easily appreciate my own poetry (following as it did in the tradition of the California Romantics, particularly her sister Nora May), but surprisingly, gratifyingly, she could also encompass Marvin's own compact, joyful, often understated, and innovative (non-traditional) Muse as well. Helen had amazing depth and a broad range of aesthetic admiration.

Here I must mention another important friend whom I met or re-met while I resided in San Francisco, and who has remained one of my best and greatest allies ever since. I had first met him in one of the English classes in which I performed, or discoursed on, Edmund Spenser and the California Romantics. This happened at Middle Tennessee State University in Murfreesboro (outside Nashville). Professor Charles Wolfe (another great friend) presided over that class; and when Don Herron came to live in the City to get established there, I put him up in my room (I was spending my nights elsewhere for a while) for several weeks (this I did at Professor Wolfe's own suggestion). I was living at that time in the middle flat of three or four on Clayton Street (once again, an old Victorian), not far from the intersection of Haight and Ashbury.

Of all the creative people whom I have helped or encouraged, Don Herron has turned out as the most successful. I take a certain pride in his multifarious achievements. Following his memoir of George F. Haas, *From the Vaults of Yoh-Vombis* (a pure delight), Don's first major opus, his first book, *A Literary History of San Francisco*, has become a standard item at City Lights Bookstore as published by their press in North Beach. Don, and Don alone, accomplished *The Dark Barbarian*, the first major monograph of interpretative and critical essays on Robert E. Howard, the third of the Three Musketeers (in L. Sprague de Camp's memorable phrase) who made a big name writing for *Weird Tales* and other pulp magazines. Don has followed this pioneering monograph with another outstanding volume of essays on the same R.E.H., *The Barbaric Triumph*. And I have not even mentioned his Dashiell Hammett Tour, which lasts several hours and conducts the tourist all through the downtown, a virtual book "on the hoof" (as it were)! This tour has become a modern classic, presented by Don with infinite style and panache.

Wisely Don earns his living as a taxi driver in and around the City, thus supplementing his earnings from his books and his unique literary tours (he also has a very fine one devoted to Fritz Leiber). I have seen Don through three marriages, first to Mary in San Francisco (by whom he has a daughter Bridget), then to Jeannie in Glen Ellen (by whom he has an adult son), and finally to Christine. I owe Don and Jeannie a huge debt of gratitude for affording me much generous hospitality at the house that he shared with her in enchanted Glen Ellen. These sojourns provided me with a much-needed escape from the metropolitan scene, first San Francisco and then Sacramento.

Sometime relatively soon after I moved into the flat northwest of Castro-Market that I shared with Noel and Charlie, the three of us moved en masse to another and much larger flat, the top one of a big corner building southwest of Haight-Ashbury. This new flat had three or four chambers that could serve as bedrooms. I was living there when August Derleth published *Songs and Sonnets Atlantean* in June

1971. Some false understanding appears to exist about its financing, which I would like to correct. I have seen statements that appear to suggest that the volume represents a vanity-press item, and that I paid Derleth to have it published. Nothing could be further from the truth.

First of all, I could not have afforded it, given the limited income on which I have always managed to survive. He accepted the book for publication during the winter or spring of 1971. Augie had already planned to issue it in a kind of hardcover edition produced in England, but I had my heart set on a regular Arkham House release. I somehow convinced him to bring it out printed on the usual Winnebago Eggshell paper and bound in the accustomed Holliston Black Novelex cloth. I had already commissioned the cover art from artist friend Gordon R. Barnett (I had met him during one of my brief periods of residence in Denver, thus away from San Francisco)—a strategic item that Gordon skillfully created according to the basic idea I had long nurtured, involving a piece of heraldry (my own invention) inspired by Plato's Atlantis Mythos, deriving from Poseidon and his scepter-trident-staff.

I had shown Gordon my own sketches of the basic idea for both the cover and the piece of heraldry, that is, the crown and trident, or a trident topping, or placed upon, a conical structure issuing out of the crown. The cover features a crown and trident as it appears inside, or "against," the circle of the sun that sits almost on the water, and thus framed between the waves on the bottom and the clouds at the top. The sun is either descending or ascending, and thus it hovers in interpretation between sunset and sunrise, an ambiguity intended by me, but not very obvious. One does bank on perceptive readers.

It cost Derleth $4000 to produce the edition (2000 copies, like those produced by A. M. Robertson for George Sterling's poetry collections), not a small sum around 1970 to bring out a book in a limited edition from a small specialist publishing house. I had meanwhile done a lot of extra work to earn enough money so that I could make some kind of significant contribution to help Augie with some of the expense he was incurring on my behalf, that is, on behalf of my very own first book. That only seemed fair. When I say that I commissioned the cover art, I mean that I paid for it myself. Again one less expense for Derleth, who seemed wary at first about using the art that I had commissioned (for only a few hundred dollars or less, perhaps only a hundred and fifty), fearing that Gordon's nicely stylized lettering might prove unreadable. Eventually Augie came to accept everything I had so keenly prepared and anticipated. In a sense he allowed me to write my very own ticket, but not without some real struggle on my part.

Hardly had I received my own copies (quite a few, several hundred at least, bought for about the cost of production, as kindly permitted me by Augie) when the news came from Augie's assistant Roderic Meng that *the* Mr. Arkham House himself had passed on in the hospital from massive heart failure. He had become my friend starting in 1954, when I first wrote to Arkham House. Our friendship, begun and maintained largely through letters, had also included several significant personal encounters, first in L.A. and then later in the Bay Area, during several of his lightning trips from Sauk City. At such times Meng would take over the driving, as he did in and around Sauk City and Wisconsin. I had also spent not quite a week in April 1965 at Place of Hawks, his house just on the edge of Sauk City. Quite coincidentally, quite by circumstance, my first book became thus the last book published by Arkham House under the immediate personal sponsorship of Derleth himself.

By another strange coincidence I had received my copies in time for the Westercon, the West Coast Science Fiction Convention, held that year as usual at or near the Fourth of July, and moreover at the San Francisco Airport. A friend in his car drove me down to the airport with a bunch of my books, and moseying around I found a vendor who readily agreed to sell the copies I had brought with me. The vendor was none other than Bob Brown, a friend of none other than George F. Haas, and Bob knew my connection to C.A.S. Bob earned quite a bit of money for me, and thus began a fine friendship that has lasted up to and through today.

The whole series of events had left me reeling from a curious mixture of emotions, chiefly elation at the actual publication of my first book, but also grief at the death, at the loss, of such a cherished and benevolent friend, no less than my very first publisher. When he died, Augie had another book in the works, the long-promised and equally long-delayed publication of Ashton Smith's omnibus anthology of *Selected Poems*. This had originally started life as *The Hashish-Eater and Other Poems* in the mid-1940s and was finished in MS. at the end of that decade. Mailed to Derleth in 1949, it would end up about the same size as *Other Dimensions*, and would appear in November 1971, late in the same year as my own book.

Since I had secured a microfilm of the MS. a few years before, I also helped with Smith's volume, proofing the sheets at Meng's request; but I could have done better. Too many typos had escaped my vigilance. Still, the important thing remained that it had in fact made its appearance, even if it had to wait twenty-two years. I passed through Sauk City, going east to west, and met with Roderic Meng, who showed me Derleth's grave with the special monument that Augie had wanted. He also thanked me again, but this time in person, for the help that I had given him on the C.A.S. *Selected Poems*. Truly Meng had served as Augie's right-hand man. We stayed in touch for a while after we re-met at Place of Hawks, but I never saw Roderic again. Later I learned that he had eventually left Arkham House and Sauk City.

Although I continued to receive some small royalties from Arkham House, my own book and Ashton Smith's volume marked the end of my working relationship with Derleth's unique press until 1979, when it published *The Black Book of Clark Ashton Smith* (in the transcription and edition of Rah Hoffman and myself) under the direction of acting editor James Turner. Meanwhile, starting around 1970 or somewhat earlier, I pursued my supplementary career as a poet-performer, instigated in particular by my desire to demonstrate something of Spenser's essence by dramatizing selected excerpts from his transcendent epic *The Faerie Queene*, chiefly parts of "The House of Pride" (Cantos IV and V of Book I), and above all the first half of Canto I of Book I. The latter turned into my most viable dramatization, because it forms a complete narrative or episode with a beginning, a middle, and an end—something comparatively rare in Spenser's epic, where he is constantly changing from one narrative to another as the good or great storyteller that he remains, to keep the narrative suspense going. This creates a somewhat kaleidoscopic effect. Later I did a two-hour dramatization (with intermission, of course) of Cantos XI and XII, those that end Book I.

Much later, after I had moved to Sacramento, I gave a special dramatization of the complete "Mutabilitie Cantos" (VI and VII), the sole surviving fragment of Book VII, and under the legend of Constancy. It takes a couple of hours to perform this dramatization. What made the Spenser dramatizations special? I memorized all the material, a considerable feat, as I have always done for performances of my own work and that by other poets. That way, dressed in an apt Elizabethan costume, I can more effectively project what I need to enact. I have now performed easily more than one hundred times, and overall have won the approbation of audiences from California to Colorado to Chicago and to colleges near or inland of the Atlantic Seaboard, not to mention throughout parts of England. I also realized that my poetry performances would call attention to myself and to my own first book, which served as the original impetus to begin performing.

Appropriately enough, I began under the auspices of Marvin H. Hiemstra, who then was teaching three grades of English at Grace Cathedral School for Boys, adjacent to the big splendid church itself, at the summit of Nob Hill. As I recall, I received payment for performing from Spenser's epic in grades 6, 7, and 8, thus three days in succession atop Nob Hill, nothing more suitably San Francisco than such a locale. The kids appeared to like me. I soon put together almost an hour that I could perform almost anywhere in the public spaces improvised in any convenient libraries, in the recital halls of music schools, in medium-sized auditoriums—any place at all, and in classrooms in any school, adapting it to the time allowed for each class, generally a little under an hour.

Nonetheless, given the nature of the material that I found suitable to perform (that is, to my own taste, and in terms of my own ability), usually traditional in form but not necessarily in content, and still with an intellectual element that might preclude appreciation from a general audience, I determined that I should target colleges and universities as the most suitable market. Acting as my own agent and working with friends and allies across the U.S., I managed to get engagements (or gigs) in many schools of higher learning, sometimes an hour or less in classrooms, sometimes full-fledged gigs in regular auditoriums. Costume or half-costume really added to an effective performance. Luckily for me and my chosen material, I have a big voice that can project clearly and articulately without amplification, that is, provided that the audience remains focussed and otherwise quiet.

In addition, good or great poetry cast in traditional form has certain built-in advantages denied to non-traditional poetry: it has in large measure music, magic, and a certain succinct quality, a certain tightness, lacking in much non-traditional verse. The latter does not lend itself to memorization, much of it so sterile, prosaic, and anthropocentric that it becomes with too much ease hermetically sealed upon itself, narrowly autobiographical, and often radically deprived of universality, externality, and otherworldliness, all prime requisites for me. Much modern poetry, non-traditional and in open form, does not readily accommodate myth, legend, the fantastic, or the weird. It does accommodate and celebrate urban angst, not to mention alienation, with particular flair. Even Baudelaire, as modern and metropolitan as any poet of the twentieth or twenty-first century, allows for extraordinary music and also a certain unexpected magic. But then Baudelaire does not resemble any other poet, well, not quite.

As a poet-performer I have wended my way from San Francisco to Denver to Chicago to Nashville and Murfreesboro to New York to Dartmouth near New Bedford to Andover (and other places in the Northeast of the U.S.), and not to overlook Sacramento, and then all the way back to the City. I knew from the start that as an unknown poet performing my own poetry I scarcely had the ghost of a chance, but that by adding the "unknown" but celebrated Edmund Spenser to my repertoire, I had an infinitely better chance at performing in colleges and universities. My gamble or gambit paid off, and although I did not enrich myself (I may have enriched a good number of academic venues, however), I did bring the "sacred word, " I did pass the "sacred flame," to unsuspecting but ultimately approving audiences in many parts of the Anglophone world whether American or British.

Plus, I did break even, not an insignificant accomplishment, considering the handicaps under which I labored at that period—an unknown poet performing unknown or little-known poetry, without much money, but with boundless enthusiasm, and with some vocal and histrionic skill—that is, at that period before the emergence of the Neo-Formalists, like Dana Gioia, Timothy Steele, David Mason, and so forth. Today their mere existence (they also happen to be superior poets) gives me an enjoyable feeling of fraternity, solidarity, and consolation. Still, but not as much as when I started, I feel very much like Don Quixote fighting windmills, and at other times like his poor bewildered assistant Sancho Panza!

I doubt that I could have gotten my poetry act off the ground, starting anywhere else except in San Francisco, so rich in possibility was the emotional atmosphere in the City during the Hippie Period, and even after. Thus the last half of my decade in San Francisco passed quickly with frequent sojourns elsewhere, expanding my potential audience via such little ways and means as I possessed. I cannot conceivably cover all the events, acquaintances, and friends that came to the fore while I resided in the Bay Area. The Hippie Period resulted in a magical time for me and many other people. However, all good or great things come to an end. By June 1975 I had resided not quite a full decade in San Francisco, even allowing for sojourns elsewhere.

I was running out of steam, I had once again lost my sense of direction (metaphorically speaking), I needed a change, and the inland area in and around Sacramento (not so very far away) fulfilled that need. As a result of the performances I had given at some of the colleges and universities in Davis and Sacramento, I had established several beachheads there (again metaphorically speaking), not to mention a few solid friendships, especially with Bill Boddy (then primarily a commercial artist, today a fine artist with his own gallery in Salida, Colorado) and his then partner Terry Chambers. Once again I moved, and this time I made the Big Move from the City to the state capital, to an outlying faubourg, the once upscale Oak Park—and once again hauling all the boxes with my books. It turned out to be a very good choice for me.

Chapter X. Sacramento and Beyond

After the tumult and ferment of San Francisco during the later 1960s and early 1970s, the state capital did indeed seem to me like a refuge, a much-needed oasis, if not "balm in Gilead" in fact! I would live there indefinitely, or so it would appear. The residence in Sacramento (a happening place but not overly so) provided me with a great good milieu that I very much needed in time and space. This oasis would last quite a long period; it gave me quite a capacious "window" that had become essential, if not quintessential, for my survival on many different levels. The schools of higher learning where I had performed in the region make an impressive list. In arranging these gigs, a special friend in the Sacramento area had played an important role: the Amerindian Jim Thomas, who interested quite a few friends of his and fellow teachers in my rather original poetry-performances. I owe a special debt to Jim for all his help.

In the general Sacramento area I first performed at U.C. Davis (Gloria's brother had set up the gig with dear Celeste Turner Wright, herself an accomplished poet in traditional forms, and head of the English Department at Davis for many years), and I had arranged a rather demanding program that lasted two hours with intermission, that is, demanding for both the performer and the audience, the first hour consisting of Spenser (excerpts from Cantos I, IV, and V of Book I), and the second hour consisting of the California Romantics, ending with myself as *the* last and nominally modern representative. Despite its length the program won the plaudits of the large audience that consisted of several English classes along with their professors, the classes probably somewhat coerced to attend!

The next engagement, or series of engagements all on the same day (set up by Jim Thomas), resulted in quite a big surprise for me and the new audience(s). Jim had arranged not only a public hour at noon but also several classes both before and after the main event.

This all took place at so-called Sac. State, now known as California State University at Sacramento. On the spot I improvised a basic lecture in which I expatiated on the life and lore of Edmund Spenser, as well as of the California Romantics, and recited with fervor and theatrical panache short poems (or short excerpts) from each of them, including the sardonic Bierce. I repeated the same lecture at each class but varied the contents a little from class to class, emphasizing one poet in one class, and then someone else in another. I did this because (as I noticed) Jim and several other persons followed me from class to class, and I desired to give them the benefit of the variety. The lectures appeared to go over quite well.

But these classes all paled next to the public hour (between 12:00 and 1:00 P.M.) arranged by Lord Jim for the Playwright's Theatre, a kind of theatre in the round (actually a square), but with unforgiving acoustics, the structure featuring cement, steel, and glass. Luckily the audience remained quiet and attentive during my performance, and my solo voice (sans amplification) filled the space and then some. First, I performed the first half of Canto I of Book I from *The Faerie Queene* (once again I featured Spenser as the star poet); this occupied the first half-hour. Then I performed "Duandon," a magical-musical-mystery *tour de force* (narrative) by George Sterling; this occupied the second half-hour.

I had not seen the theatre in the round (or square) in advance, and so I had to adapt myself and the material to the novel ambiance at once on the spot, not the easiest thing to do. I kept moving around in a kind of small circle so that I could face the audience, or different segments of the audience, at all times, relating the material to them on a rotating basis. How did the audience respond overall? Gratifyingly, with thunderous clamor and loud applause mixed in with hoots and hollers of approbation. Since that time, I have never had a larger or a better audience! Their enthusiasm matched that of the stalwart performer!

Coming so early during my career as a poet-performer, I am afraid it rather spoiled me. I have never found another audience like that one, ever! I had brought a bunch of my books with me and sold quite a few, signing them to the individual students and their teachers, whether after the public hour or after the individual classes. The classes in which I lectured after the public hour turned out even better than those beforehand. Some other group or groups of performers that had preceded me from San Francisco, albeit very different, had in a sense prepared the way for my own unique style of voice and movement. The reaction that they, the San Francisco Cockettes in particular, left behind, could only whet the audience's expectation for my performance, and in a sense enhance it.

Later I performed at other colleges (as arranged by other friends) in the area, such as American River College, repeating the same pattern, a public hour along with individual classes. The pattern served me well, no matter at what school I performed, whether in the U.S. or in the U.K. Several very positive developments ensued as the result of the initial performances in Davis and Sacramento. I made some wonderful new friendships, first with Celeste Turner Wright at U.C. Davis (I did English classes for her off and on over a period of years), and then above all others with another English professor, Kathryn Hohlwein, at Sac. State. Not only did I do classes or lectures for her, that is, under her sponsorship, but for several years on end she hired me to perform at graduation parties (for English majors) that she put on at her lovely house and property on DeVille Court, at the end of the school year.

According to my capacity as my own agent, to arrange engagements at colleges and universities, I continued as a poet-performer for at least the following ten or twelve years. This included a major sojourn during the winter and spring of 1972 in England, where I managed to get some ten or twelve gigs, which at least paid for my expenses to go to the U.K. and back. That sufficed, and I sold the copies of my first book (not that many) that I had brought with me, or that I might have sent ahead of me by ship (much cheaper than airmail) to my friend Ian Law to hold for my arrival. The academic engagements that I managed to obtain extended all the way from London in the southeast to Loughborough (pronounced LUF-boro) near Birmingham in the north to Exeter in the southwest.

Only because a kind of counterculture magazine, *Time Out in London*, ran a short piece for free on my behalf (the magazine regularly did this for a lot of performers and artists) did I succeed in getting the gigs that I did in fact, and generally well received. I had wisely sent the notice to the magazine in advance. I made my headquarters, established my base, wherever I could, first and foremost at New Ash Green, south of London in Kent, and first at the home of Ian and Eileen Law. Ian, of course, had remained my true and stalwart friend-correspondent since the memorable summer of 1961, when he had spent several memorable evenings with Rah and myself in Westwood. However, Ian and Eileen had three growing children on the premises, and I had to make do in whatever space I could, on the sofa, on a little mattress on the floor (under the dining room table), and so forth, something less than ideal. (Ahem!)

Ian thereupon negotiated with some neighbors and close friends to put me up for a while (actually a good long while) at their two-story place. They had an extra bedroom upstairs, and there I lodged. Furthermore, they kindly shared their meals with me, as had Ian and Eileen, all very generous of everyone in regard to the "foreigner" from California. Ian introduced me to Jack and Audrey Hesketh, who became in turn my great and good friends, especially Jack, an architect. Jack had a fascination for all things African, and therefore the downstairs of the house contained all manner of African items, masks, shields, spears, carvings, etc. It certainly made for a picturesque ambiance. Starting in childhood, he had also collected quite a few novels by H. Rider Haggard, many of them with an echt-African background. All this continuity made eminent sense, African-inspired fiction and genuine African paraphernalia. Since I had already read some of Haggard's novels (but sometime after those by E. R. Burroughs), as well as the writings of Arthur Machen (a special bond), I could well enjoy and share Jack's interest in Africa.

More than that, when Jack and Audrey learned of my noble quest, or enterprise, on behalf of Edmund Spenser and the California Romantics, whereby I performed bits and pieces of their wonderful poetry, they proved notably sympathetic. One evening they even put on a special dinner in my honor, to which they had invited many special and close friends. At this dinner I recited some apt stanzas from *The Faerie Queene*, the entire Proem of Book II (dealing with unknown or imaginary lands), as well as material by my beloved California Romantics. Incidentally, whenever I recited any poems by any of the latter, they turned out as a genuine revelation, more so than Spenser. (The British do know for sure their own great poets—they study them in school!) One guest at the dinner after I recited "Amithaine" by C. A. Smith became convinced that Amithaine really existed somewhere in France, and I hated to disabuse him. Let people have their myths, is one of my mottoes.

The reader might think it literally quixotic of me (Don Quixote and Sancho Panza remain eternal favorites with me, whether individually or as a pair) that I should have performed Spenser for the English on their own turf, rather like bringing coals to Newcastle. But they proved notably cordial to my novel experiment, including poetry by myself. Again, let me place great emphasis on this fact: Spenser provided the key with which to open many doors, whether in the U.S. or in the U.K. But in performance I gave priority to Spenser and the California Romantics, tacking on at the end only a few items by myself. I did not use these performances primarily to blow my own horn. Such came at the end of each recital, and modestly so. I played the role of the messenger, but I did have to give some proof of my credentials, including copies of my own first poetry collection. From that memorable evening put on for me by the Heskeths (Audrey had created a scrumptious meal for us all, served along with some excellent wine), I recall the reaction to Smith's gorgeously otherworldly "Amithaine" from one of our dinner companions, as just mentioned.

How disappointed he became when I explained that the castle existed only in our collective mental space! Gratifying as it was for me as the performer, I found it even more so for the manes of Ashton Smith, who never traveled very far from Northern California (he could not afford to do so), never mind to his father's ancestral terrain in England. I find it both significant and gratifying that the British have taken C.A.S. under their wing as one of their own, whether as poet or as fictioneer, bringing a depth to their understanding of his oeuvre denied to many folk in the U.S. Cosmic justice, indeed!

Upon my departure from the U.K., after my first "Spenserian" sojourn there, the real culmination of that quest came for me when en route back to the U.S. I took a little side trip to Ireland, a week in the western or southwestern part of the island, as I had hoped and planned. I had earned enough money not only to cover my travel and working expenses but to afford this extra week in the Emerald Isle. I flew to Shannon Airport, and then took a bus from there to or near Buttevant, where I stayed overnight at some unpretentious but cozy tavern-inn. And I hiked and/or hitchhiked to the ruins of Kilcolman Castle, now mostly an ivy-covered tower. There, within what was once a larger enclosed property (a working farm, or a farm-estate), Spenser had lived for much of his Irish residency, when he had employment as a kind of British civil servant.

There, over a number of days, I visited the ruins and paid my devoirs to the manes of the departed Spenser. Like many before me, I found the moist and verdant Irish countryside more than enchanting—I found it inspiring and the Irish people themselves fascinating, friendly, and accommodating. I had achieved my pilgrimage. I bussed back to Shannon, and from there I flew back to the U.S. After an extended sojourn in the Midwest (mostly in Minnesota and the Twin Cities) I eventually returned to Northern California and San Francisco, where I continued to live until I moved to Sacramento in June 1975.

Of all the places where I have performed in the U.S., two stand out in retrospect, my performance at the Harvard Club in New York

City and my multiple visits and engagements in Tennessee, at Vanderbilt University in Nashville (sometimes known as the Harvard of the South), and at Middle Tennessee State University in Murfreesboro, thanks above all to my friendships with the librarian John Charles Moran II (who then lived in Nashville but worked in Murfreesboro at M.T.S.U.), no less than with Professor Charles Wolfe in Murfreesboro (alas, now deceased), who taught English at the university. Professor Wolfe recognized the greatness and unique value of C.A.S. long before others outside California did because of the volumes edited by Lin Carter. All this helped form a strong bond not just between Wolfe and me, but especially between J. C. Moran and me, not to mention the impetus that my performances gave him to create and sustain a splendid special and specialist magazine for a decade (1977-86), *The Romantist*, the term deriving from F. Marion Crawford as a salient romanceer, along with Conan Doyle and Rider Haggard.

In fact, as an act of love and admiration, John-Charles founded the magazine around the work and figure of the notable Romantist himself, one of the best-selling novelists of the later nineteenth century; and I must add, far more entertaining than Henry James, who considered Crawford's novels to be "bad art," a verdict or opinion with which I profoundly disagree. Crawford remains a great storyteller who keeps everything clear, and propelling forward the different narrative threads. I think that something of professional envy figures in James's pronouncement, given Crawford's extraordinary popularity, which a less popular author might resent. Despite the bad opinion that James had of Crawford's fictional art, that did not deter the greater author from refusing Crawford's lavish hospitality on at least one occasion as a pampered guest at the Villa Crawford near Sorrento on the Bay of Naples.

I have spent many notable sojourns in Nashville and Murfreesboro under the sponsorship of Señor Juan-Carlos Morán! Many benedictions on this remarkable human and humane being! To this day he remains one of my very best friends, one with whom I have had many fruitful discussions about art and literature.

Once I moved to Sacramento, I did not, I could not, sever all professional connections with San Francisco, that is, apart from social ties, simply because, until I built up a new network of jobs in the state capital, I could not afford to do so. I depended on certain steady and well-paying customers in the City by the Golden Gate. I needed the money to survive. But this dependence did not prove a burden in any way, because it enabled me to see Fritz Leiber and Margo Skinner on a more or less regular basis. When his wife of many years, Jonquil, died in the late 1960s, Fritz asked us to rescue him from the emotional and physical morass in which he was wallowing. The "us" involved Margo, Gloria Kathleen, and myself (we had just married). Gloria could drive, and she drove well and carefully. Fritz would pay for all the expenses incurred while driving down and then returning. Gloria arranged for the time off in case it exceeded the weekend that we had arranged. We borrowed or leased a station wagon or a four-door sedan. The trip there and back turned into a kind of honeymoon for Gloria and me. Furthermore, it was Christmas 1969, but the traffic to Venice and back (where Fritz resided at the time) did not turn out that bad. Fritz appeared very grateful for our sympathetic company.

Later Fritz, able to maneuver on his own, returned to Venice to oversee the packing and moving of his possessions to San Francisco. He moved into a small apartment not far from Margo's in the same building, a former hotel where the owners had converted the regular hotel rooms (all with bathrooms) into tiny apartments. Although he had to put some of his possessions into storage, Fritz soon adapted to life in San Francisco, a far more urban area than much of L.A. He became one of the City's notable literary lights during the remaining decades of his life. In the combined genre of science fiction and fantasy no high-ranking prize or award exists that Fritz has not won, and more than once—all prizes extremely well deserved. Simply as a human being, Fritz ranks as a prince among those fortunate enough to know him as an intimate friend and comrade. He remains a truly great figure.

Once settled in Sacramento, I found that I could adjust very well to the dismal weather there in winter, the ground or tule fog, and the seemingly eternal overcast, whereby one feels as if enclosed in one enormous room that rarely varies from gray. I could keep busy and bide my time until the glorious warmth or heat of summertime, which exceeded that season's usual boundaries by lasting from April or May until October or November. I would live in Sacramento from mid-1975 until Rah requested that I move in with him down in Westchester on L.A.'s Westside in 1998 as companion and eventually as caretaker or caregiver. The almost quarter of a century that I passed in Sacramento turned into a very good time in my life. Removed from the amorous and clamorous distractions of the City, I prospered as both person and writer.

In the state capital I accomplished quite a lot, above all the extended history of ballet during much of the nineteenth century—as based upon the life (beginning in 1803) and career of Cesare Pugni terminating at his death in 1870—thus from 1818 or 1820 until 1870, and then extending beyond that to 1906, and yet to 1921, with the production of the Petipa-Tchaikovsky opus *La Belle au bois dormant* in London as *The Sleeping Princess* at the Alhambra Theatre by Diaghilev and his Ballets Russes. Beyond that date the monograph (more than 5,000 typescript pages) deals with aesthetic and critical issues on through the 1990s and the early twenty-first century. I began this history around 1980 and finished it around 1999 or 2000. Without planning it that way, I had inadvertently constructed it on the scale of *The Decline and Fall of the Roman Empire* by Edward Gibbon. Taking advantage of hired researchers (above all, Patrizia Salvi through the Conservatory of Music in Milan, Italy), I achieved much of the final research on a major scale for my own opus just before I commenced the actual writing or composition of it, as well as during that essential phase of creation, often just ahead of the actual scrivening.

I designated the opus with great care as *The Case of the Light Fantastic Toe: The Romantic Ballet and Signor Maestro Cesare Pugni*. As already stated, I began the composition in Sacramento around 1980 and completed it around 2000 during the early part of my residence in Westchester (north of LAX, L.A.'s principal airport) with Rah. Apart from taking care of the house and the day-to-day provisioning of the larder (via the nearby little supermarket), I did little else except write, edit, and proof in order to finish up the enormous monograph.

During my long residence in Sacramento, from 1975 on into the late 1990s, I also accomplished much else, including a day-to-day business (even if only part-time) whose earnings enabled me to live and write, a not unimportant matter, or "detail"—detail, indeed! Cleaning house as a fine or fastidious house cleaner for middle-class or upper middle-class customers not only gained me my living but also provided me with regular exercise, beyond what I did at a gym or at home, where I used my own body weight plus a few barbells and so forth. During this overall period I would often visit Rah at his precise invitation several times a year. While Rah did not function in dirt and squalor, he had no one to come in and help him with the housecleaning; he did basically clean and maintain the kitchen and bathroom, those essentials for healthy living.

Nonetheless, dirt and/or dust accumulate, and since I was visiting so often (we discussed this between us), we agreed that I might as well put the time to good use by cleaning and touching up the house. This discussion and agreement happened in the course of my earliest (extended) visits, which usually lasted several weeks, and sometimes around the holidays. The cleaning itself did not require very much time, and to make it easier, I spread it out over several days. (Of course, Rah paid me, and well, at his insistence.) Thus I alternated my existence between my occasional "Spenserian" tours (again acting as my own agent or via the personal agency of acquaintances and friends) and my life and writing in Sacramento, not to forget my sojourns with Rah and other close friends.

At some point, after several years of agreeable habitation with Bill Boddy and Terry Chambers, I tired of the distance between Oak Park and the downtown area, or rather mid-town area, where many of my Sacramento friends lived, and from where I could walk to their houses, as well as to my local cleaning jobs. I had made as well as deepened my friendship with a number of strategic individuals who became quite important to me during much of my long residence in Sacramento, to wit, John Sherratt and Jack (Richard) Richardson, who lived in a three-bedroom flat above Tom's Printing on J Street near 25th Street (part of the Mid-City region). John and Jack often had a third roommate living with them, but at the time when I was tiring of Oak Park, they did not. We discussed this among us three, and they agreed to let me move in; and Tom, who ran the printing business on the ground floor, and the landlord, also approved.

I liked the new neighborhood much better than the one in Oak Park (due to its more convenient location), although Bill, Terry, and I had all gotten along harmoniously. I now resided close to Sutter's Fort, various picturesque churches, a big shopping area highlighted by a gigantic supermarket, a Safeway, that had supplanted the gorgeous Alhambra Theatre (a movie palace from the 1920s or 1930s), which had to yield, alas, to demolition, despite great efforts to preserve it. In addition, from my new home, I could easily walk to downtown Sacramento with its older shops, not to mention the often gorgeous older state buildings (the State Library, the State Capitol, etc.), which I have always admired and utilized when convenient. The capital of California turned into, and has remained, a great good place for me.

Once I landed in Mid-City near Sutter's Fort, I was able to sever my ties to San Francisco in terms of house-cleaning jobs. I had finally built up a sufficient clientele to sustain my lifestyle, and from Mid-City I had easy access to all my jobs mostly downtown or not at all far away. By working only three or four days a week, I could spend about half my time in writing. From c. 1975 to c. 2000 I managed to accomplish a variety of small-to-medium-sized book projects, but I devoted my main energies (whether research or writing) to the ballet history project involving the life and career of Cesare Pugni.

I count myself quite fortunate that, whether I resided in San Francisco or Sacramento, I had clients who respected my writing and my poetry-performances independently of whether or not they approved of the subject matter, or found it suitably popular. I should mention some of the more outstanding customers who employed me, all of them remarkable people in their own right. First, Marsha Raleigh, a vital, vigorous woman who taught basic subjects to children at home throughout the City, all under the umbrella of the San Francisco School District. Gene Raleigh (born Rifkin, but his family changed the name) worked as one of the two Public Utilities Commission information officers in the state, one in the south, and one in the north (that is, Gene himself). They had two children, a daughter and a son. The daughter still survives (and very well, with husband, house, children, etc.), but the son died some little time back, worn out by exhausting travail as a carpenter (despite the tough genetic stock as Russian Jews on both sides). Marsha maintained a beautifully managed home, whereby she kept her sanity, as well as mine own!—and through her I gained many other valuable and valued customers, all of whom kept me alive.

Another special friend, David Morgus (more friend than client), also turned me on to other clients, especially his boss, Mr. Boyd, who employed Mr. Morgus in his business re-doing interior spaces with fastidiousness for well-heeled customers (including Nob Hill, Pacific Heights, the Marina District) across the 69 or 70 square miles of San Francisco City and County combined. David, sweet but ironic, and Boyd, sweet and enthusiastic, made a great pair. When I resided on several occasions in the Haight-Ashbury District, David (who generally resided in some apartment in those modest highrises around Buena Vista Park) would invite me over for dinner along with wine and some good smoking, ahem! How many times did he thus invite me for marvellous meals! In addition, David himself had evolved into a magnificent artist whose canvases turned out as rigorously disciplined as himself. I passed many wonderful discussions and evenings with David, second only to these that I shared with Fritz Leiber. Another bond joined us: we both knew Jesse Allen and loved his art equally well. When I began performing as a poet-performer, David and Jesse along with other artist-friends (for example, Louis and Cynthia Goldstone) made a point to attend my poetic exhibitions, whether public or private, above all, those at the downtown public library, as well as at some branch libraries. Again, Spenser opened many doors for me!

Once I got established in Sacramento, first in Oak Park and then in Mid-City, I began to gain more and more cleaning jobs. This happened as it did because, on one of my return trips from the City, I met a charming and unique individual by the name of Geoffrey ("Geoff") Wong, a lawyer, with a deep voice and practiced graciousness that few could resist. We chatted for a while, and when I explained why I was traveling back and forth between the two big cities, and that I would love to get more jobs in the state capital, Geoff responded at once that he knew several people who could use my services, including himself. Wow, how unexpected, and what a rush! Then through him and his fellow lawyers I met various people who became some of my best friends: first, legal secretary Shirley Paulson and her friend at work and away from work, another legal secretary, Gerda Hoefert-Kennedy, the latter in particular turning into one of my "most bestest" friends of all times, dear Gerdalein. (Hoorah!) But as I continued to live in Sacramento, independently of Geoff (whose friendship still endures), I began to gain other clients, and this led to other interbranching clientele and friendships.

Through John Sherratt, I gained other but only occasional clients like his mother, who provided me not just with interesting work (not too hard) but with lunch and companionship, and who regaled me with stories of her younger life, along with those of her sister, who had lived with John and his mother for much of his aunt's life. His father had died in Canada, after which his mother had immigrated to Sacramento. Thus John grew up as raised by his mother, but always with his aunt present. Chief among the other clients and friends whom I met through John, I count Michael ("Halvie") Halverson and his lovely wife Renée. With them I have shared some special adventures indeed. One time we transported a marvelous meal (made by Halvie and Renée) all the way from Sacramento to Jesse Allen's domicile on Point Reyes Peninsula, to the west of Tomales Bay, and to the east of Mount Vision. When I would visit there by myself, the peninsula revealed itself as a great place for exploration and discovery. Another adventure that I shared with the Halversons involved going to San Francisco to see an excellent production and performance of one of my least favorite ballets, qua ballets, *The Nutcracker*, despite its magnificent score by Tchaikovsky.

Then through the Halversons I met their neighbors, Tim and Linda McKenna, who soon passed from the status of house-cleaning customers to that of special friends indeed. I feel closer to the McKennas than I do to most of my blood relatives, not so strange after all in view of the fact that I rarely see my genetic relatives, who mostly live in the Northeast of the U.S. For both the Halversons and the McKennas I have often house-guarded, as I have for Geoff Wong as well as for Tac Craven and his wife Pat Wong (one of Geoff's own sisters), also housecleaning clients once upon a time, a good long time.

Another customer, or group of customers, also via John Sherratt, the Reynolds family looms large, very much so, not just housecleaning but house-guarding. First, I worked for their son Robin Rowe Reynolds III (now retired from State of California service), who for many years worked at restoring a distinctive, large, two-story family dwelling, at G and 20th Streets (on the north side of G), post-Victorian, belonging to the "elephant column" period, a very spacious and comfortable style of domestic abode. Even after he moved to other locations with other spouses, Robin continued to hire me as house-cleaner. I have never had a better, kinder, more generous patron, nor a more brilliant and well-informed friend. While at G and 20th, when I cleaned for him once a mooneth, Robin would leave for me (in addition to the house-cleaning payment) a sum sufficient to purchase a large luxurious deli sandwich from a smorgasbord kind of cafeteria nearby on J Street, Sam's Hofbrau (alas, long since gone like the others in the same chain). But dear Robin existed, and still exists, in a class by himself, and not just because of his kindness and generosity to me. But also because with him I could share my now lifelong fascination for, and obsession with, the California Romantics (Sterling, C. A. Smith, N. M. French, Bierce, etc.)—now *that* is special, having him recognize along with myself (as the literary historian) these particular poets and writers as the California classics that they have become during my own lifetime.

Last or next in time after R.R.R. raised to the third power, but not least in appreciation, come Robin's parents, both house-cleaning and house-guarding clients as well as close and special friends, particularly when they resided on San Antonio Way, a lovely, medium-sized, two-story dwelling with swimming pool in the back yard, the latter truly appreciated in Sacramento's long annual season of warmth (or real heat) from May or June through October. I have been swimming most of my life (since around the age of ten, or maybe eleven)—indeed, I can swim like a fish underwater, as others have noted and informed me—and how great to immerse myself in fresh water at any time of the day or night!—like descending (not too deep) into a wide and shady well in the middle of a blazingly hot desert of sand! How great, how refreshing, how restorative! Even when Robin's parents moved to a large apartment on Cathedral Heights (not far from the National Cathedral) in Washington, D.C., they permitted me to stay overnight with Robin's mother, one of my favorite people, while I did research for my Pugni-centered ballet history/monograph at the Library of Congress (the older, opulent, turn-of-the-century structure). The research took several weeks (primarily for the early part of the long Russian section, in this case, 1847/48 to 1858), and I never enjoyed better hospitality than what I did via the auspices of Robin's mother, blessings on both her and Robin III himself.

It happened at this time that I achieved the primary research for the long Russian section of my historical monograph, 1847/48 until 1903 or somewhat later, an extremely important part of the narrative, usually inaccessible for obvious reasons to non-Russophones. This primary research occurred among the Tsarist-period newspapers and other periodicals, a vital source of immediate reaction to new productions. As it was, I had just enough Russian to be able to identify what I needed. Later, for a little while, I used a few hired researchers, and finally (for the major period in my own life as the writer-compiler) I used the long-suffering staff at the "L. C." itself, but only at spaced-out intervals. I would ask them to find me specific reviews for specific premières, mostly at the Maryinsky Theatre in St. Petersburg, usually just in advance of the specific production that I was actively describing at the given time. My first priority lay with the productions (the dance dramas) of Jules Perrot, 1848-58 (his active period), which I was able to research myself directly. But then came the secondary, prolonged, and perhaps just as important priority involving the extended "intendantship" of Marius Petipa as ballet-master (the principal one from 1870 until the early twentieth century, but his active period runs from 1862 to 1903 or 1906). Petipa preserved the best elements of the Romantic Ballet (say, c. 1831/32-50, maybe longer) up to the decade preceding Diaghilev's Ballets Russes (beginning in 1909 with the first season at Paris—Petipa himself died in mid-1910).

The ambiance where I managed to conduct all this preliminary research, at the old "L. C.," contrasted nicely with the spacious apartment of Robin's parents during the several weeks I pursued the research itself. After working for the State of California during much of his life, Robin's father, Robin Rowe Reynolds II, held an important job working for the World Bank in the federal capital. This job took him often to Pakistan and India, among other parts of that region, those parts dominated by the Mohammedan religion. Fortunately these business trips took place long before war began to plague that sector of the planet here and there, and now and then. Although I rarely saw them again in Sacramento until Robin Senior finally retired and the Reynolds returned to the state capital to live out their final years there, I always enjoyed their reassuring presence whenever I could.

From the time of my major research accomplished at the "L. C." until 1998 (when I left Sacramento to live with Rah), I spent almost all my time, apart from my part-time business, in writing and putting together the actual text of my magnum opus during the major part of the 1980s and 1990s. As already recorded, I did manage to work on other writing projects c. 1980-98 while still residing in Sacramento, but they turned out so much smaller that I could still succeed in completing them, and having them published, all the while continuing to work on my magnum opus. In particular, my Ashton Smith bibliography had finally, but finally, made its appearance in 1978, although the repercussions from that book continued on into the early 1980s. I had other good reasons for moving back to L.A., and moving in with Rah than just his overt request to do so.

In May or June of 1998 I received a phone call from Paul Dingwell and Susan Lovett, who had married sometime previously. After an accident sustained while riding his bicycle (not fatal but serious enough, requiring several spinal surgeries to correct and improve), Paul had moved in with Rah at Paul's request, Paul already having divorced his first wife, Jeannon, and thus leading once again a single man's life. Susan as my longterm friend went back to the hippie days in San Francisco, to the later 1960s, but had already divorced her first husband, Michael Lovett. Both natives of Porterville on the eastern side of the southern half of California's great central valley, Michael and Susan as teenage sweethearts had married after high school and had moved to the City as the then "happening" milieu.

I met the Lovetts while I resided at 50 Divisadero and they resided on Oak Street right at the eastern end of the Panhandle extending eastward out of Golden Gate Park. The Lovetts and I became firm friends; and even after their divorce Susan and I stayed in touch. She had moved to Sierra Madre but worked in downtown L.A. before she found suitable employment in Sierra Madre, working for a spiritual center under the direction of Rosalind Labruyère. Born in Westchester, Paul had lived there all his life; and he had known Rah since Paul's teenage years. Despite the difference in their age (Paul was younger than Susan by about fourteen years), I figured that the two might make good friends (Paul had become somewhat isolated at Rah's), and so I introduced them while Paul still resided with Rah. Well, one thing led to another, Paul and Susan fell in love, they married, and Paul moved to Sierra Madre to live and work alongside Susan. In fact, he had been spending much of his time with her there before they married.

Meanwhile Rah had made Paul his heir, and although he had formerly preferred to live by himself (as he had often stated to his closest friends, including me), he had found after living with Paul (certainly an animated and enthusiastic housemate, withal quite pleasant) that now he preferred to live with some agreeable companion. Rah discussed the matter with Paul and Susan, but above all with another close and longterm friend, the bibliophile and bookseller David Benesty, who then suggested myself as someone whom Rah knew very well, and with whom he could live in harmony. Rah agreed and informed Paul and Susan of his decision. But as it turned out, Rah had had me in mind all along.

Hence the unexpected phone call from Paul and Susan in May or June of 1998. I had arranged to come down to Rah's during another visit when incidentally I would clean his house for him again. Paul and Susan informed me that Rah during my visit would ask me to move in with him, and that I should prepare myself so that I could make my decision in advance. The idea hit me with the force of a lightning bolt, that is, metaphorically and emotionally speaking. I had no problem reaching a decision, and instantly: a giant yes! I had not prepared for my old age at all, or very little. The move to L.A. would solve my existential dilemma as if made to order. All that I would have to do was to wait for Rah to ask me. I had been feeling something close to panic!

The visit and the house-cleaning went swimmingly as usual, and just a few days before I was to return to Sacramento, Rah popped the big question. Would I mind sacrificing (huh?) my life in Sacramento and move down to Westchester to live with him? As recompense, I would receive my room and board, and a small monthly stipend. Rah would also arrange it so that I could write checks for needed household expenses, which he would sign. Paul and Susan handled, or oversaw, Rah's personal finances, and they did so with competence and honesty. I feigned a certain mild surprise but expressed a certain gratification as well. I said that I probably would agree to his proposition, but I wanted to sleep on it, and that I would let him know the next day. However, we both knew sans any further discussion that I would answer in the affirmative. What a huge relief did I feel flood over me! How deeply and very well did I sleep that night!

The next day, about midmorning, I gave Rah my decision in the affirmative. I would need a month or so to terminate my part-time business, to find a new house-cleaner for my customers, and otherwise to wind up my affairs in Sacramento. It would take me most of July to do all this, in addition to giving all my customers a month's notice, and as soon as possible. I also had to box up all my books, files, and other possessions (very little apart from clothing). My great and good friend Ron Hilger (better than a son to me—we had now known each other as very close friends since about 1988 or so) arranged with his employer R.G.B. to take several days off and move me and my gear down to L.A., using one of the company's vans. What a saint! He ended up moving me and my gear a total of six or eight times.

Everything went as planned, and sometime early in August, thanks to Rah and Ron, I found myself ensconced with all my stuff in Rah's comfortable domicile. Because I had, since the mid-1970s, already spent so much time in his house, the place could only feel like home, and moreover it was as if I were returning home, which in one sense I was. Rah had positioned against a bookshelf near the front door a placard that seemed to give me a particular greeting when I returned from up north. It displayed a sentence that was an obvious reversal of a well-known line from some old movie in which Bette Davis exclaims upon entering a dilapidated building: "This place is a dump." Only Rah's placard said something more amusing: "This dump is a place." Although no palace, Rah's residence clearly ranked infinitely higher than any dump!

Chapter XI. Westchester and Back

Actually I had brought down with me to Rah's only half of my books, including my various dictionaries, some large, some small, some in English, and others in the Romance languages, and two pocketbooks with essential vocabulary in Russian and German. But I could also use any of Rah's dictionaries, a *Webster's Unabridged*, plus others in Russian, German, and Latin. The other half of my books I stored "for the duration" (of my residence with Rah) with Rinaldo (Ron Hilger) and Michelle (as great a friend to me as Ron) at their new property at the end of Cab CalloWay northwest of their former home at Lake of the Pines, the latter lying about halfway between Auburn and Grass Valley.

Taking care to keep them dry, Rinaldo stored my boxes of books in a new large shed, quite sturdy, that he had made out of two smaller but still viable sheds that had stood on the property at Lake of the Pines. These he removed with the permission of his in-laws. Ron and Michelle had rented the house and property from her parents for several years. The parents had moved to, and were living in, a new place in Santa Cruz, north of Monterey. The parents were selling their property at Lake of the Pines, the direct cause of why Ron and Michelle had moved themselves. Having worked in house construction as both a carpenter and a "tape and paste" man, Ron was and is always able to turn his professional skills to his own domestic advantage when required.

Meanwhile I could let my mind rest at ease about the boxes and other stuff that I had left behind with Ron and Michelle. Apart from the large double bed that Paul had left behind in the southwest bedroom (which he had formerly occupied) and two bureaus, I had the vacated chamber to use as I saw fit. Rah had the northwest bedroom, and the good-sized bathroom separated the bedrooms, all these on the west side. Rah's medium-sized house faced south onto Firebrand Street. Otherwise I had already cleared out, and thoroughly cleaned, my new bedroom. I bought several small bookcases at yard sales in the general neighborhood; and Susan and Paul kindly brought over from Sierra Madre for my own use (really my possession, as it developed) several extra bookcases that Susan had but did not need. The large double bed already in place had two cabinets on either side that could serve as bookcases (for extra-large tomes), as well as a shelf on the headboard that ran between the cabinets. Both bedrooms had large wide closets with built-in shelves on one side (plus ample storage space above the closets proper).

Between the closet and the door into my room from the hallway there stood a tall bureau or chest of drawers. I had plenty of space for my clothes, my Spenser costume and appurtenances, as well as all my books, that is, those that I had selected to accompany me from Sacramento. I got to work at once, unpacking and then placing all my stuff in the suitable locations, the clothes first in the closet and the bureaus, and then the books, arranging them nicely per size or subject matter. I wisely kept all the boxes (already identified as to the contents on the outside of them), and stored them on high, atop the cabinets and bookcases in the garage, which serves for storage in many homes in lieu of the once common, ancestral attic. All through the fifteen years during which I resided with Rah, the boxes remained in perfect shape.

Since I was "living in," and cleaned as I went along, I rarely had to do special cleaning, and usually set aside only one day per month to attend to the kitchen and bathroom, as well as to touch up (or touch down) areas that otherwise simply sat there collecting dust, the floors collecting the inevitable dust mice, or dust kitties, that would gather under beds, at the bottom of closets, and in unsuspected corners. I have always enjoyed cleaning, so straightforward and hands-on, without ridiculous theorizing and non-physical contact. Cleaning has always furnished me with a good reason to move, to exercise—and it has kept me young far beyond the usual allotment of conventional youth in terms of duration.

Meanwhile I had the constant comfort and consolation of Rah's delicious company and ever inventive drollery. I have never watched much television, but not through any disdain or superiority. I preferred other things to do—reading, writing, and staying physically active. Rah had the television on much of the time, day or night; and so, while I lived with him, I watched more television than I have ever done in mine entire life. What a big surprise I experienced!—at how good much of it came out, mirabile dictu! Not only the news, but even some of the ongoing series, never mind the special stuff, Oi vey Maria!

I found some of the special dramas and movies made expressly for TV fascinating and even overwhelming. And what can I say concerning the documentaries, beginning with *Victory at Sea* (with the superb music of Richard Rodgers and Russell Bennett!) continuing with *Cosmos* (with the irrepressible Carl Sagan) and then the new series with Neil Degrasse Tyson! Not to mention the magisterial documentary series created by Ken Burns, above all on the Civil War! And much earlier, what about the revival of the *Our Gang* series (made in the 1930s) as *The Little Rascals* (in the 1950s), with their inimitable characters as enacted by their child actors! I had never watched them in my early childhood (even though it ran parallel with the series for a while), but experiencing them as a young adult in my evenings while I attended U.C.L.A. proved a delightfully enriching education.

To a supreme degree Rah and I shared a similar, almost exactly the same, love of language. Nor were we restricted only to English. Rah had once taken a course of conversational French at Beverly Hills High School, in the auditorium of which I had attended more than one concert with my boss Henry Knowlton of Homespun House. One in particular I recall: an evening with Elizabeth Schwarzkopf, who sang a two-hour program (with intermission, of course) of German lieder and French art songs, and impeccably so. Even without French art songs or French literature Rah learned far more than just conversation thanks to his better-than-average intuitional grasp of English and French side by side and interlinked.

Rah and I both loved puns and similar verbal play, and we would indulge in such banter in several styles and languages. A stickler for good usage in whatever language we employed, he possessed an excellent accent in all the languages he studied—Latin, French, and German. Not for nothing had he descended from ancestors emigrating into the Midwest from Alsace-Lorraine, or Elsass-Lothringen, with its mixed heritage of German and French. While his keen musician's ear aided him in his grasp of spoken idioms, his keen intelligence, his native brilliance, enabled him to grasp their essence and to plumb their depth and range intuitively. Coming to a language cold, the student does need the teacher as guide, first for pronunciation; and once that is gained and mastered, the rest is up to the student.

But, but, but—I must not forget the supreme quintessence, linguistical, that first drew us together, and that continued to keep us together in a special understanding. Not just mere (mere?) wordplay, but the love of language in its purity of style and expressiveness (yes, its elaboration) that we found in writers like Lovecraft, Ashton Smith, R. E. Howard, H. S. Whitehead, and others in the modern ranks of the modern masters of fantasy and science fiction. Moreover, Rah knew several of these masters as close friends, whether in L.A.S.F.S. ("LASS-fiss," the Los Angeles Science Fantasy Society) or in the commissary at MGM—these included Ray Bradbury and Charles Beaumont, as well as (unrelated to modern f. and s. f.) luminaries like Adolphe Menjou (always impeccably dressed) or that magnificent composer of movie music, Miklos Rozsa. Whereas I as a Johnny-Come-Lately discovered the best *Weird Tales* writers via August Derleth and Arkham House, Rah had first discovered them as an early teenager in the 1930s when a quarter (which represented a lot of money back then) would purchase a monthly issue of *Weird Tales* from off the magazine racks in the drugstores no less than the cigar stores. He also purchased, when his meager funds permitted it, copies of Hugo Gernsback's "scientifiction" magazines *Wonder Stories* and *Thrilling Wonder Stories*.

How natively brilliant Rah must have turned out as a kid of only ten or twelve to register the luxuriant style of H.P.L., C.A.S., and R.E.H. with their outré prose rhythms, their uncommon erudition, and their sheer lexicographical abundance and richness! How different from the sterile, prosaic, and anthropocentric writings of people like Ernest Hemingway, F. Scott Fitzgerald, and James T. Farrell!—even if all these last-cited scriveners have their specific and respective moments of deep psychological brilliance and linguistic triumph. Rah also read as a teenager (and earlier) the delightful juvenile series by Leo Edwards (Edward Edson Lee), lightly tinged with plausible fantasy, such as Jerry Todd and Poppy Ott, with their inimitable caricature-like illustrations by Bert Salg. From the discussions of our preference for imaginative literature, as contrasted with so-called realism whatever that might be, I recall Rah saying (in reference to some realistic fiction) in lighthearted deprecation, "That has too much reality for me. Too much realism. That spoils it for me." Meaning, of course, unleavened or made less weighty by the sovereign alkahest of imagination and humor, which can often lighten too much portentous realism.

In the late 1930s Rah and his mother, Hazel, emigrated from Des Moines, Iowa, to L.A., and Rah joined L.A.S.F.S., where he discovered fellow (sibling?) acolytes like Ray Bradbury and Paul Freehafer, the brilliant young mathematician who worked on the first theoretical and practical atom bomb. As kindred spirits Paul and Rah became very close friends; and when Paul realized that he had congenital heart failure (per medical advice), he bade his best friends farewell and returned home somewhere in the eastern U.S. to die. After Paul's death his mother gave Rah her son's collection of pulp magazines including *Weird Tales*, *Wonder Stories*, *Thrilling Wonder Stories*, and other pulp magazines, thus adding them to whatever issues that Rah had already collected as a teenager in the 1930s as well as somewhat later.

In pursuit of their admiration of Ashton Smith, a group of aficionados from L.A.S.F.S. drove up from L.A. to visit, and to pay their respects to, "the Bard of Auburn" in the winter of 1940-41. The group included both Freehafer and Hoffman, and they had apprised C.A.S. in advance of their visit, who, as they approached Smith's cabin after parking their automobile and following his directions, was approaching them from his home, or cabin, in the midst of deciduous and evergreen trees, or as described by Forrie Ackerman in one of his happy turns of phrase, from Smith's "umbrageous abode." Smith was carrying not only a pile of empty hard-liquor bottles but also a placard with his full name printed on it, which he was to put in place to guide the aficionados to his cabin. Instead, because they all met on the path to Smith's cabin, the placard served to identify C.A.S. himself in an immediately personal way! When the group noticed the pile of bottles that he was carrying, Smith hastened to assure them that it represented something accumulated over a real period of time, and not as the result of one night's imbibing!

Later, not drafted into the military (the U.S. Army) during World War II until 1943, Rah studied music at the University of Southern California, with such master teacher-composers as Miklos Rozsa (originally from Hungary, and colleague and friend of Béla Bartók), whom he knew at MGM in the mid-1950s and later. On occasion Rozsa would invite Rah and other bright, promising students to some social gathering at the house that Rozsa and spouse shared, a house that Rah described as very "Mittel Europa" with towers, turrets, and rather dark interior, rather like the dwellings manifested in the horror films of the 1930s and 1940s. Also, as customary for music teachers and students, Rah would help Rozsa with some ongoing project. Rozsa ranked with Bernard Herrmann as one of the most brilliant composer-conductors furnishing music for feature films, Rozsa at MGM and Herrmann at 20th Century-Fox. Rah found it quite agreeable and instructive to work for Rozsa this way whether at U.S.C. or in Rozsa's atmospheric home.

A few years later, after World War II had completed its weary and wearying course (not to mention atrocious, destructive, and wasteful), Rah returned to U.S.C. and continued studying counterpoint and composition under Rozsa and other teachers. Eventually Rah graduated with a B.A. in music and found gainful employment working for various employers who had nothing to do with music. Eventually a close friend with connections found Rah an opening position as apprentice (film-cutting) editor at MGM in December 1955, sometime soon after the death of Rah's mother, with whom he had resided near U.S.C. since they had both settled in L.A. While at MGM Rah met many music professionals, not to mention non-music ones as well. I believe that he met Dick Kynon through L.A.S.F.S., and then, among a myriad of others (some via Forrie Ackerman), Rah met yours autobiographically here, one Donald Sidney-Fryer, in May 1961. I had already met Fritz and Jonquil Leiber in February of that same year. A few months later, after Ashton Smith's death in mid-August, Rah would meet his widow Carol Jones Dorman (Smith) in September, and when she left the L.A. area, she left Smith's commonplace book, or his "black book," with Rah. This set up the conditions for deciphering and transcribing the literary material in the notebook by Rah and myself. In one sense everything fell neatly into place for this transaction. It simply remained a question of arranging it all in time and space.

Almost at once, when we met, Rah and I realized our kinship spiritual and emotional because of our deep interest in music, meaning above all classical music. We discovered at once that we shared a very strong interest in certain great composers, not necessarily all belonging to the great Austro-German symphonic tradition. Among modern masters in that tradition Rah appreciated Paul Hindemith more, but Arnold Schoenberg less; and I, composers like Franz Schmidt, Max Reger, and Josef Marx, not to mention the odd bird out, like Josef Matthias Hauer. Rah also had a real respect and affection for the exceptional modern composer-songwriters of Broadway, Tin Pan Alley, and Hollywood, which I came to share over time, although I had already realized the worth of many composer-arrangers creating music for Hollywood feature films, composers like Cole Porter, Irving Berlin, Richard Rodgers, Miklos Rozsa, Bernard Herrmann, Max Steiner, and so forth, too many to mention. On the other hand I knew, and appreciated, the music of the composers belonging to the French theatrical tradition of grand opera and opéra-comique such as Grétry, Méhul, Cherubini, Boïeldieu, Hérold, Auber, Adolphe Adam, Meyerbeer, and so forth.

Above all else we loved the music of the Russian composers, Tchaikovsky, Rimsky-Korsakov, Glinka, Borodin, Stravinsky, Prokofiev, Shostakovich, and Khachaturian. Again on the other hand I also appreciated certain Russian composers whose music Rah did not know but which fascinated me, such as Arensky, Glazunov, and Tcherepnin, no less than the foreign-born master musicians who came to Russia to work in the Russian musical theatre (from the eighteenth to the nineteenth century and later). In particular, I had a long-standing interest in certain minor masters, foreign-born, who worked in Russia for a very long time at the principal musical theatres (the old Bolshoi and the new Maryinsky at St. Petersburg, and the Bolshoi in Moscow). These composers functioned in Russia as respected professionals, even if now deprecated as hacks, the famous and later infamous Cesare Pugni, Ludwig Minkus, and Riccardo Drigo. To return to more recent times, and to Rah, he had come to know personally many well-known and little-known music people (composers and arrangers) who worked on the same films and TV programs as had Rah himself, all during the period he worked as film and TV editor at various Hollywood studios, and then finally as music and special effects editor for Ed Norton's post-production sound editing.

Beyond the special cult that we reserved for Ashton Smith as poet, fictioneer, and all-around man of letters, our love of Tchaikovsky's music cemented our friendship. Rah, and Rah alone, allowed me to hear for the first time via his hi-fi set many compositions (in recorded form) by the great Russian composer of which I had only known the names: the long and uniquely powerful Manfred Symphony, the first three regular symphonies, the four orchestral suites (minus the *Nut-*

cracker Suite) that are one with Tchaikovsky's three great scores for the ballet theatre of his time, the concertos for violin and piano (not counting the well-known first piano concerto), and other miscellaneous music, including his often enchanting pieces for solo piano.

Both Rah and I cooked, or could cook, on occasion, but we gradually gave it up for the convenience of the microwave and frozen foods. Thus for some fifteen years our life together proceeded apace with much enjoyment and enrichment for both of us, its tranquil course broken only by minor issues like dental and/or medical appointments (for both of us), or (for myself) major issues like occasional trips to Northern California, above all to Sacramento or San Francisco, or really big issues like extended trips abroad, lasting at least four weeks, and sometimes six, for which I either had saved my shekels patiently or funded by some advance on a MS. that I managed to craft together. Living with Rah in Westchester also enabled me to travel the short distance across town to U.C.L.A. so that I could use, and perambulate amid, the fabulous libraries that the university had gathered and maintains. I also used the first-rate dental clinic and school in the medical center at U.C.L.A.

Since I had no computer, I produced the typescripts the old-fashioned way, first in longhand, and then in typescript, sometimes rehandling certain sections a number of times before I could get them right. However, as time has gone on, my intellectual focus has improved when I write, to the point where one longhand version, followed by one typescript achieved at once, now generally suffices. On occasion I might add a needed insert, or subject a given passage or page to multiple drafts. My facility with verse has also become a little faster, and otherwise improved, even if in one sense a poet does not improve and merely changes from one period of development to another. All decently factured poetry, whether traditional or non-traditional, requires the same hard work and relentless attention, indeed often endless tinkering.

In my scrivened endeavors, because I have no computer and have not yet learned to operate one, several people have aided me in transforming an old-fashioned typescript into an e-text. First, Adam Lopez, who edited and transferred the very long MS. of my ballet history into computerized form. Then, my good great friend Alan Gullette (in Oakland), who has transferred all my other MSS. likewise into the same form. To both of these individuals I owe an enormous debt. I hereby acknowledge my indebtedness to these friends with humility and profound recognizance. Learning how to operate a computer (which many friends have assured me does not constitute an impossible task) will form the next step in my own personal evolution.

Starting only a few years agone, I began making several extended trips abroad, all apart from my earlier trips to England, Wales, France, and Austria during the 1970s. Then recently I began focussing on more exotic destinations rather than European ones: first, six weeks in Southeast Asia during March and April 2011 (two weeks in Cambodia and four weeks in Thailand, starting and ending in Bangkok, but most of the time on Koh Samui, the tourist island, with my friend Stan Gayuski); second, three weeks in Egypt during February 2013 (I had planned for four, but that might yet happen at some non-remote future time); third, a six-week return to Southeast Asia (a week in Bangkok, a week on Koh Samui, two weeks in Cambodia, and two final weeks in Bangkok) from mid-June to July 2014; fourth, and most recent, El Salvador in Central America during October 2014.

At other and earlier times I have traveled through Mexico and parts of Central America, such as Guatemala, Honduras, and Yucatán. Some of my travels I have written up in travel journals that I have maintained as I move from place to place. From the journals I have then written up regular reports, but not necessarily in the style of travel articles like those in travel magazines or the travel sections of Sunday newspapers. I did not write up my return trip in Southeast Asia (too much a repeat of my first one), nor have I done so for the recent journey through much of El Salvador, more a trip of discovery and exploration in regard to a hacienda in which I have invested along with two other friends (one, an expatriate artist from Kenya; the other, a native Salvadoreño), with a view to residing there during the winter months. As I age, I relish cold weather less and less.

Even if I did not write up my return trip to Southeast Asia (mid-June to July 2014), I do have one poignant moment from it that I would like to record. I had scheduled two final weeks in Bangkok (the two last weeks in July) for dental work, only to discover that, apart from a regular cleaning, I did not need any other work done at that time. Or so the chosen dentist reassured me. Big surprise! Accordingly I found other matters to occupy my final days in Thailand's capital and environs. I returned from the dental area (half a mile or so east of where I was lodging) along the main thoroughfare before heading south along the side street to the wonderful boutique Swan Hotel. The latter stands just north of the new, rather Frank Gehry-esque French Embassy. As usual I walked in the shade along the north side of the main thoroughfare. I had almost reached the side street leading to my hotel when I noticed an elderly woman sitting to one side and evidently requesting alms. Most people chose to ignore her.

In a flash I asked myself, "Who is this woman? Whose lover, whose wife, whose mother, whose grandmother? Why is she here alone, begging alms? Where is her family, where are her friends?" so touched was I that I almost began to weep in sympathy, and automatically I gave her what few Thai coins I happened to have on me. I returned to my chamber in the hotel when I had a sudden bright idea. I possessed little cash, but I remembered a 20-baht bill that I had among my luggage. I retrieved it, and going back to that poor old woman, I gave it to her. She smiled and thanked me. Without words I thanked her for "being there," and respectfully I directed a Buddhist hand-prayer gesture toward her, to thank her for allowing me to bestow this charity on her. I only regret that I did not have more ready cash to give her.

I have already recorded this moment in my report on my Egypt sojourn (the three weeks during February 2013), but I wish to revisit that moment here. It occurred soon after I had embarked on my Nile trip by flat-bottomed boat between Luxor and Aswan. It happened late morning, while I sat in a chair beneath an awning on the top deck: actually the roof covering the chief level, that is, the main deck with the individual chambers for the passengers. I had by this time visited the Great Pyramids, the Serapeum at Saqqara, and so forth, not to mention the inspiringly grandiose temples at Luxor and Karnak.

It had begun to sink into my head that, lo and behold! I had at long last attained my long-cherished ambition, nay, my dream, to visit modern Egypt with all her marvelous antiquities, from a world that had existed long before Rome, Macedonia, Greece, Persia, Assyria, Babylonia, and all those other empires. This moment of realization became so very intense that I seemed to remain in my body while my higher consciousness appeared to levitate out of and above my corporeal frame. The moment did not linger long, but while it happened, it seemed to last forever. How to explain such moments? One cannot—one can only record them.

In an especial aside here, I should mention that I carefully prepared for all, or most of, my trips, by reading extensively concerning the given countries that I visited, whether reviewing materials first read years agone or absorbing completely new materials more recently published, especially the Lonely Planet guidebooks, which have worked the best for me.

In certain respects, as I have intimated earlier, the fifteen years that I passed with Rah in Westchester turned unexpectedly into the single happiest period in my life, and certainly the most productive, during which I accomplished quite a few scrivening projects, some of them long anticipated and planned, too long, perhaps. During February 2013 I was traveling through Egypt and had completed almost three weeks when word came via Abdou, my travel agent and friend in Cairo, that Rah had just had an accident: he had fallen and broken his hip, had had it surgically repaired in the hospital, and was recuperating in some convalescent home not far from his house. Then, some further word came via the same source: Rah had passed on in the rehabilitation center. I completed my week in and around Aswan, including a day trip by plane to Abu Simbel and back, but had to forego my one to three weeks planned for the oasis towns, which I hope to prosecute at some future time soon. Quite apart from Ancient Egypt—that is, what remains from that period two thousand years or so buried in the past—Islamic or modern Egypt has its own fascinations. Whatever their problems, or rather despite them, the people themselves remain extraordinary and marvelous, let me state that at once!

Thus it was that with extremely mixed emotions I returned to L.A., to Westchester, to Rah's house, to find therein the container of his ashes (Rah had wanted his body cremated without a funeral). How strange it seemed to return to his house without him there anymore! I had already expressed my grief off and on while in Egypt, and would continue to express it off and on once I had come back home. Thank Goddess, but Steven Reschetar down the street to the west had taken care of everything in mine absence, visiting and comforting Rah in the hospital and at the rehab center, taking care of the body, having it cremated. And he had accomplished all this in an exemplary manner. I must give him all due credit.

As things had worked out, I had now become the sole heir. Just several years before Rah's own death Paul Dingwell as the only and original heir had died, at the early age of forty-nine, at almost exactly the same age as his father, when the latter died. After Paul's early death, at my suggestion Rah had made both Susan Lovett (as Paul's widow) and myself the joint heirs, in order that, in a sense, Rah would have a close friend to care for him, whichever one of us (Susan or myself) died first. When Susan died just a few years later after Paul, I became the only heir. Therefore it became incumbent on me to settle the estate and empty out the house. Once that had happened, I could return to Northern California, as I had long since planned, to reside once more in Sacramento.

With the invaluable aid of a real-estate agent and friend, Joanna

Park, who lived in the neighborhood, I settled the estate. With the immediate assistance of Terenzo (Terence McVicker) for several days, the rare-book dealer in Glendale—and the great and good friend of both Rah and myself during quite a few years—I proceeded to empty out the house, no easy or quickly done task, as I soon discovered. It took me more than three months to accomplish it, from March until June of 2013. Other people helped me, particularly the Hispanic, Carlos, whom we discovered while he drove by in his pickup one morning, looking for scrap metal. We had some (not a lot), which we happily gave him. We were working out of the garage, Rah's chief storage area, with the garage door upraised to take advantage of the light and air. Once Terenzo had left to resume his own life and work in Glendale, dear and amiable Carlos with his pickup became my chief collaborator in removing stuff of no great value out of the garage to the nearest city dump. Anything of value that Carlos fancied, he could keep, including appliances and kitchenware, such as pots, pans, dishes, etc. I also paid him a daily fee, plus the daily fee to take the discarded materials to whatever nearby city dump he was using. I would also give him a handsome bonus, once all the work had reached its end.

Rah still had a very large collection of 12-inch long-playing records, placed on specially built shelves in the hallway connecting the bedrooms. Per Terenzo's arrangements a very pleasant middle-aged couple who owned a fine bookstore in Glendale came over with a large van and spent several hours or more removing the LPs from the hallway and stowing them inside the van. I had gone away to run some errands and came back to help them but rather minimally, I am afraid. Many other books remained, not to mention a huge collection of cassettes and compact discs, mostly classical music, but some film scores and Broadway shows.

I could hardly make a choice from the many books that remained, never mind the extensive collection of cassettes and CDs. With my older-man ambivalence and indecision, it turned out to be simpler just to get rid of them all. I made arrangements with the owners of an excellent used bookstore in Culver City, Robert Klein and Larry Meyers, where David Benesty, a longterm and close friend to Rah, had worked for many years. Robert and Larry came over, looked at the collections, and bought them on the spot. Soon thereafter either they or someone else arrived to collect books, cassettes, CDs, and so forth, and then to transport them to the bookstore for sale. That took care of all those particular items.

Meanwhile, and before the business with Klein and Meyers, and before I really got going with Terenzo and Carlos, I invited several close friends over, one by one, and gave them each the materials that Rah wanted them specifically to have: the music scores and reference books (I took one or two) went to the pianist as well as stage and studio musician Roger Steinman; the cookbooks went to someone else (I forget the name); and so it went, each special collection to a special collector. Forget not: Rah had spent much of his life and resources as a serious collector, and had earmarked each particular collection for some special collector-friend. This all took place as Rah had wished (nothing written, but I remembered exactly what he wanted), and then I could concentrate on the real task, getting rid of almost everything else. I had put aside for Rinaldo (for whenever he could come down) one whole bookcase just to the right of Rah's big king-size bed, the particular bookcase raised up high, and containing five or six well-packed shelves, representing the cream of Rah's book collecting, which included books (many of them first editions) by Lord Dunsany, Lovecraft, Ashton Smith, and what have you. When Rinaldo could finally come down to L.A., he could pick out whatever he wished, or could simply take them all, with the exception of the titles by Ashton Smith.

I had become so busy and so fatigued with emptying out the house that I mercifully could forget or postpone my full grief over Rah's death. Because I have discussed it so minimally, I do not want the reader to think that it had not impacted me. It did indeed impact me. How vividly I recall the moment, about 7:00 P.M., at the hotel in Aswan, when the local agent for my travel arrangements in and around

Aswan (including Abu Simbel), a small handsome younger man with moustache, knocked quietly on the door of my room. Without any idea as to who would come to my door at that time, I opened it, saw who it was, and let him in. He had some important news to tell me, but waited until we had both seated ourselves. Then he announced that he had just gotten some further news from Abdou in Cairo: Rah had just died in the rehab center, which he had entered after his surgery to repair his hip. Truth to tell, I had had a premonition of his death during a dream I had experienced a night or so previous, a dream in which I received the news of his death, by a strange coincidence. Although my waking mind had not dwelt on the first news from L.A. about his accident, my subconscious was grappling with it.

Finally we had completed the huge task of emptying out the house. I was leaving the washer and dryer in the back-door vestibule, plus the fine Baldwin upright piano in the living room, for the new owners, a charming and very attractive young couple; and they seemed happy to accept washer, dryer, and piano. All that remained was for Rinaldo and me to fill the enclosed back of the small truck he had hired with my two bureaus (inherited from Rah), my few possessions (clothing and the like), and my many boxes of books. Ron had already picked out the books he wanted for his own library. I was retaining the special shelf and more of nothing but the books by and about Ashton Smith, because I had almost none, or very little. I was also retaining all the bookcases in my bedroom, plus those in the garage that Rah had had especially constructed. Later I would have the three or four tall ones cut in half, and then rebuilt as separate bookcases, easier to handle. We packed everything we were transporting to the new domicile in Sacramento, the new place that I was renting, and that I had already selected and leased for six or eight months, during a quick trip by Amtrak to the state capital expressly for that purpose. Having helped me move down from Sacramento to Rah's in Westchester, Rinaldo now helped me move back.

I had outlived Paul, Susan, and Rah; I had survived to return to reside in Sacramento. Without my asking him, Ron had volunteered once again to help me move. Ron and Michelle had asked me about Rah's little-driven and essentially brand-new four-door sedan, for the use of their daughter Lindsey Anna. Since they had both assisted me over many years, I sold it to them for one dollar only, as a way of expressing my gratitude to them for all their help to me during several decades. Ron had already made a solo trip by air to Westchester, to drive the sedan back to Northern California. We had made everything ready, and at long last we drove off.

As we proceeded on our long drive north from Westchester to Sacramento, I would on occasion heave a huge sigh, shed a few tears, and wipe my eyes. I would rather that Rah had not passed on, and that we had continued our life together. But there was no going back. My second major period of residence had reached its term, and I had more or less once more finished with L.A. Although I moved into a little-house apartment in Sacramento in June 2013, settled in with all my books aptly placed out upon the shelves—including the other half of my library that Ron had stored for fifteen years inside the big sturdy shed at his house, and that Ron returned to me in Sacramento—and otherwise resumed my residence in the state capital, I had not yet quite finished with L.A. because of medical reasons.

While residing with Rah, I had had all my dental work done at U.C.L.A.'s excellent, state-of-the-art dental clinic, also a school for dentists that gave instruction in both the medical and oral-dental requisites. I had visited the clinic every six months for examination and any dental work deemed necessary, most of it routine, with the exception of one major procedure that had become unavoidable. In the autumn of 1956 after I left the Marine Corps, I had had two bridges installed left and right among the back teeth of my lower jaw. The bridges had served me well, very well; they had lasted me for more than half a century, the proof of excellent work by the dentist who had installed them at his office in Santa Monica on the north side of Wilshire Boulevard near Third Street. The students at

U.C.L.A.'s dental clinic now removed them; they were finally showing signs of decay as revealed by X-rays and oral examination. The new team at U.C.L.A. now installed excellent new bridges that I still have, of course. Even with little or no pain dental work always turns into an ordeal for the patient. No help for it!

Meanwhile, early on while residing with Rah, I had joined the Kaiser Permanente hospital-medical system (which has given me superb attention and care), and I have used the hospital facilities at Kaiser West L.A. off and on ever since I joined. They have saved my life now twice at least, in regard to my colon, including three surgeries and quite a few colonoscopies (as mandated every six months). In the spring of 2008 my personal doctor, Hyman Milstein, during a routine exam noticed blood in my stool. A colonoscopy revealed a large tumor, which the renowned abdominal specialist surgeon Dr. Adil Farooqui expertly removed on 9 June 2008 in the course of an extended laparoscopic procedure. As Dr. Farooqui remarked to me following what had resulted in a very challenging operation for him (as he intimated), he had probably given me about eight extra years at least to continue living. That statement gave me pause! I recovered from the tumorectomy in record time and continued to have colonoscopies every six months.

Then a certain persistent polyp (not easy to remove because embedded inside the intestinal wall of the colon), which a regular gastroenterologist could not remove despite repeated attempts, required again the surgical expertise of the same Dr. Farooqui. Before I moved back up north, he and I in consultation set up the surgery in April 2013 for the following September. For various reasons the new surgery did not take place at that time, but on 6 December, with the second and last surgery taking place on 21 January 2014. In order for the first surgery (done near the mouth of the anus) to heal properly, I had to have a temporary colostomy to stop the regular use of the lower intestine, thus involving the use of a temporary bag, which the surgeon removed. He then reattached the alimentary canal to the lower intestine on 21 January. He effected both surgeries, the one in early

December and the one in late January, by means of the same laparoscopic method, always a challenging procedure for the surgeon. Again, as in the case of all my surgeries, I recovered from the effects of the most recent one in record time. However, the awkward consequences for the functioning of my lower intestine still remain with me, and are still taking place, alas!

Each of my last two surgeries required an initial period of basic recuperation (just from the effects of the operations) of about two weeks, which for obvious reasons I could not conduct at my new home in Sacramento. I had had all three surgeries done by the same expert specialist for the obvious reason of professional continuity, that is, of proven expertise, and what is more, as proven to me, the patient involved. Enough said! I had arranged with my special friends, the McVickers, to conduct each initial convalescence with them *en famille* following the surgeries in December and January. In each case Terence came over expressly from Glendale to pick me up and take me back to their house. I must express here my deep appreciation for their kindness and generosity. You certainly discover who your real friends are when you must have a temporary medical-related refuge! The atmosphere of cheerfulness that reigns in the McVicker household also helped a lot for me to recover.

In each case I recuperated well enough to take the Amtrak system of bus and train back to my little house in Sacramento. As I have often said to my closest friends, I prefer the Amtrak system because it results in greater convenience in getting off and on the train than does an aeroplane in an aeroport, with all the complicated security measures (however necessary), not to mention the airlines' preference for the passengers to arrive an hour and a half (at least an hour) before the given flight. Relative to my recovery from the latest operation, I had hardly begun living at my new address in the state capital in June 2013 when I rediscovered that I did not like living by myself, particularly after my fifteen years with Rah. So, in a sense, I had already set up a "complication" in my life. Should this have come as a surprise to me?

Looking back over my adult life, I realized that I have always lived with selected others, whether roommate, housemate, or lover. As an elder, I would rather live with a housemate than with a lover or any marriage partner, the latter often leading to complications and expenses that one cannot anticipate and sometimes cannot handle successfully.

Another serious medical problem that I almost forgot to mention, and not minor at all unless handled at once, even if comparatively routine today thanks to the advances of medical science! Between my tumorectomy of June 2008 on the one hand and the colon-involved surgeries of 2013-14 on the other hand, but closer to the latter in time, I noticed a mild discomfort in the region of my appendix (that is, the lower right-hand side of the lower abdomen). At first I thought that it indicated some slight problem with my regular digestion, but the discomfort persisted. Appendicitis? I became concerned, told Rah about the problem one evening, and the next morning went by bus from Westchester to Kaiser West L.A. I registered myself at once in the emergency room.

The medical people handled me at once, gave me a colonic evacuation by machine, and otherwise prepped me for an emergency appendectomy. I don't recall even going under the anaesthetic administered by needle (that is, through the drug-channeling lifeline, or I.V.); the next thing I knew, I was waking up in the recovery room from the temporary drug-induced oblivion. After a few days they discharged me from the hospital, and a friend brought me back to Rah's. Interestingly enough, the very next morning, who should be checking on the recent surgical patients, not the doctor who had operated on me, but Dr. Farooqui himself, whose presence as always gave me comfort and reassurance! As usual, but even faster this time, I spent the week in bed writing a narrative in verse, as I recovered completely from the appendectomy. Within two weeks I could accomplish my full complement of exercises, including the usual fast walking, but (of course) proceeding with great care at first.

Some people exhibit, or feign, dismay or boredom when their

friends confront them with even a brief account ("Did I tell you about my operation?") of a recent surgery undergone from which they have quite recovered. First, a real friend will ask questions and/or manifest genuine interest and/or concern about the medical problems of other friends. That goes without saying. Then, too, it represents information about a medical ordeal that the real friend might need to endure at some future time, and the information could come in handy. Having undergone several surgeries now, but only late in life, I had endured no serious medical problems earlier on, not even tonsillitis/tonsillectomy in childhood. Whether undergone by friends or by myself who have survived the given operations, we remain astonished by, and profoundly grateful to, the efficacy of modern medicine and medical science (especially as compared to former times!), as well as to the whole community of doctors, nurses, and hospitals that administer them.

Once I had gone past the surgeries of 2013-14, I had made arrangements with longtime friend James (Eldon) Patterson to move into the old farmhouse on Gambah Drive, off Bell Road, in the countryside of North Auburn, just several miles west of the shopping center at Highway 49 and Bell Road. James readily agreed to have me live with him in the same house but in the two attic chambers above him, the east chamber above the kitchen and the west chamber above his winter bedroom. But I would need to rent the space separately from the landlord, David Anello, who lived on the property but in a separate abode, and who happily agreed to my proposition. I arranged all this well in advance of the first surgery early in December. Meanwhile I hired an expert carpenter friend, Derek Shepherd, to cut the three or four tall bookcases from Rah's garage in half, and to convert them into separate pieces of furniture much lower so that they would fit into the new spaces as configured by the lower walls resulting from the A-frame roof (nicely waterproofed). Once again I boxed up my books while Derek effected the needed conversion. We did all this in middle to late November of 2013, and we moved bookcases and boxes of books into the attic chambers around Thanksgiving, the chambers that I had already cleaned and nicely prepared.

Thus I did all the heavy lifting with Derek in advance of my actual move, which would not take place until late February, nominally scheduled for the 23rd, depending on my condition after the second surgery, and how much and how fast I would have recuperated from it. I had already long since given notice to the real estate office that handled the little rental units around the court where I had been residing. Thus, as soon as I had recovered, I could move myself and my few remaining possessions out of the former rental unit with no trouble or complication. Everything went as planned, and by late February I had ensconced myself in my new chambers. Almost immediately I went to work unpacking my boxes of books yet again, and to place them all out on the bookshelves yet again, also including all my files, folders, and envelopes. Just as I planned and measured, everything managed to fit in perfectly against the walls of their new surroundings. Thus, with everything settled into the new home, including myself, I could get back to my regular work, writing and editing, as soon as possible.

I have remained in place now since that last February, that of 2014—well, more or less—apart from mid-June through July in Southeast Asia, and then late September through late October of 2014 in El Salvador. In spite of my best planning I still find myself in place, mostly in Northern California, during this winter of 2014-15, when I would rather be sojourning someplace in Southeast Asia, perhaps Koh Samui or Chiang Mai in Thailand, or even Bangkok, the major port of entry for most people flying in from the Far East, the Pacific in general, and the U.S.

Chapter XII. Catching Up

Although I have now laid out, more or less in chronological order—in the course of this autobiography—the major people, events, movements, and periods of my life to date (February 2015), I have missed mentioning certain events and places with certain persons. My first and main concern remains the one with which I began: to record those major persons and events that have impinged or impacted most strongly on my life. Yet inadvertently I have overlooked some important events or people. Just recording my life's mainstream has proven enough of a challenge, if not in fact quite a challenge, above all at eighty! Even if I can still recall much of my life in detail, the exact chronological placement of certain items has eluded me here and there. Thus this final chapter exists only to catch up with those things that I have failed otherwise to record. But I cannot complete this chapter until I revisit all the preceding chapters. *Ainsi soit-il!* So be it!

Since late grammar school or early high school, when I first heard excerpts from Tchaikovsky's music for *Swan Lake*, this particular ballet has fascinated and even obsessed me. The ballet itself has long since become a standard item in the repertoire of many or most ballet companies worldwide, whether Act II alone or the entire ballet. As demonstrated by later recordings of the complete original Moscow score in four acts, the first complete recording by the Minneapolis Symphony, conducted by Antal Dorati, an experienced ballet conductor, manifested a different ballet from the standard one with choreography by Marius Petipa and Lev Ivanov. In a certain sense it revealed, paradoxically enough, an unknown ballet with a different sequence of numbers and a certain small amount of unused or new music—an unknown ballet in terms of the composer's original theatrical concept.

However, since the mid-twentieth century, while retaining the now standard choreography by Petipa and Ivanov, different ballet masters in different productions (at least in Russia) have reinstated the original sequence of musical numbers. If the music originally served as the reason for the ballet's revival in the mid-1890s, as ordered by the director of the Imperial Theatres, based in St. Petersburg, I. A. Vsevelozhsky, then a curious dichotomy exists between the original Moscow score (1877) and the now standard stage version first performed at St. Petersburg in 1895. A big mystery: why did Petipa as chief ballet master at the Maryinsky Theatre not use the original Moscow score as extant? The original Moscow scenario does not reveal certain aspects of the drama that the music does.

A fact not at all incidental to a discussion of Tchaikovsky and the ballet theatre of his time: from early in life the composer loved opera and ballet, with a partiality for story ballets, dance dramas of a fantastic nature (the Romantic Ballet par excellence). While at school as a teenager in St. Petersburg, roughly 1850–60, he witnessed the dance dramas (many of a fantastic nature) by genius ballet-master Jules Perrot, who revived in augmented form his successful ballets created in Western Europe, and who also created new major productions in the Tsarist capital. By virtue of this exposure to ballet early in his life Tchaikovsky became quite a sophisticated balletomane.

In 1953, at the Bolshoi Theatre in Moscow—something unprecedented of great importance—Vladimir Bourmeister effected a new production of *Swan Lake* with the music in its original order of individual numbers, and thus (apparently) retaining but simply reordering the sequence of choreography by Petipa and Ivanov, which certainly still works just as well in this reordered sequence. I can only guess what the new ballet-master did with the problematic *Pas de six* in Act III. This dance has only five, not six, official variations, but per the character of the music in one of the variations something dramatic and outrageous takes place. The Baron von Rothbart and his daughter Odile, both embodiments of evil, have just arrived before the *Pas de six*. Odile resembles in dress and body Odette, the Swan Queen. With only five official variations, where does then exist the sixth, as identified by the title of the overall dance? It would seem that Odile as the sixth and unexpected would-be bride interrupts, or invades, the solo dance of the nominal would-be bride to whom the variation legitimately belongs.

The original published scenario gives no clue here, only the music does, which seems to hold the key to the dance drama purposed by Tchaikovsky. If in a sense Odile triumphs over the nominal would-be bride, then the coda to the overall *Pas de six* captures the brilliance of the triumph achieved by Von Rothbart's evil daughter over all the five leading would-be brides. Since Prince Siegfried takes part in the extended waltz of the would-be brides, Tchaikovsky might have intended that he should also participate in the coda, thus implying that his choice will fall on Odile, who the prince innocently thinks is Odette, the Swan Queen. The five characteristic (national) dances that follow serve to delay with extended suspense the startling revelation in the dramatic finale. Do these dances indicate official embassies from their respective principalities?—as follows: Hungarian dance (czardas), Russian dance (representing Moscovy), Spanish dance (bolero), Neapolitan dance (tarantella), and Polish dance (mazurka).

The simplification of the scenario done by Modeste Tchaikovsky for the 1895 production of *Swan Lake* in the Tsarist capital represents a marked improvement over the original published one, and could be the result of some exchange between Modeste and his brother, the composer. Also, we do not know if, at some point after the successful première of *The Sleeping Beauty*, Petipa and Tchaikovsky might not have discussed the possibility of Petipa himself producing the composer's first ballet. Historically we know from his letter to Rimsky-Korsakov that Tchaikovsky had long wanted to try his hand at this type of music. And we know that Tchaikovsky managed to finagle a commission for a ballet, *Swan Lake* in this case, and we know that he created the score without a ballet-master, quite unusual for the period. Beghichev as the suitable official in charge at the Bolshoi Theatre in Moscow obliged him with the commission, and as experienced theatre professionals both Geltser and he oversaw the ballet anent the scenario and the music, advising the composer as to the practicality of the composer's own conception. When a suitable ballet-master showed up on the scene, one Wenzel Reisinger, his choreography left much to be desired, starting in 1877, but two later productions in the 1880s by Joseph Hansen, which the composer might well have seen, ranked much higher on the critical scale. Hansen functioned as a better professional than Reisinger.

When *Swan Lake* had its première in Moscow in 1877, the ballet-master as a professional courtesy received the credit for both scenario and choreography, but, as revealed by Modeste Tchaikovsky, Messrs. Beghichev and Geltser deserve the credit for the scenario, a credit only partially true, because we know that the composer based his conception on a "house ballet" that he created for the children of some close relatives at their home, for which he evidently improvised the music on the piano. This is all plausible aside from being historically attested. But the concept, as apparently nurtured since the 1850s or 1860s, went very deep in the composer's creative psyche. From all this it would appear that Tchaikovsky himself created the scenario, that he laid out the individual numbers according to his own original idea, and that, aided and abetted by Beghichev and Geltser, he did all this in anticipation of working with whatever ballet-master would come along from inside or outside Russia to fulfill the composer's choreographico-dramatic scheme.

I should state and emphasize here that the intensive and longterm study of the scenarios for dramatic ballets (from the late eighteenth on into the mid-twentieth century), as presented in Beaumont's *Complete Book of Ballets*, has helped me to shape my own individual sense of the dramatic, in terms of what works and what does not work in the theatre. Such study finds reflection here and there in my own writing.

Reviewing my military service in the Marine Corps and the big move from Opa-locka, from northwest Miami, to El Toro, near Santa

Ana, Southern California, I must make a major correction. We did not cover that distance in an airplane all in one day; although possible, not probable. We stayed overnight at some base on the outskirts of Dallas, a big beautiful town, which I have never really seen, but have only overflown. If we arrived in the early afternoon of 5 September 1955 as indeed we did, and at Toro, then that means we would have left Opa-locka on the early morning of 4 September. I remember clearly the relief I felt when we finally touched down, as well as the keen dismay I registered—after lush, tropical Miami—to find myself in what seemed like a dun-colored, barren desert. The ambiance truly appeared to my first perception as "The Abomination of Desolation." But I adjusted pretty fast, as I consoled myself with the thought: here I was at long last in exotic, far-off California. Looking around me at the dismal countryside, with so little vegetation, I received my first lesson in geology, in the starkness of unadorned landscape, of naked hills and ravines. At first glance this exotic, far-off California looked like nothing more than some alien planet.

The whole saga of the first decade or so when I resided in Northern California, from the mid-1960s to the mid-1970s, perceived in retrospect some forty years later, seems now like a curious and kaleidoscopic dream, but it did transpire in everyday reality. In particular I remember certain special events with certain special friends, most of whom have transcended back to the Other Side.

Not long after I first met them, that is, while they resided in their compact apartment on the north side of Oak Street, just barely still at the eastern end of the Panhandle emerging from Golden Gate Park, Mike and Susan Lovett phoned me mid-morning. With a small group of friends (including the irrepressible Vern from Laverne Avenue in Mill Valley, who would later marry Gloria and myself), they were driving up into Marin County from the City in some vehicle or other (probably a station wagon), to go swimming in some "swimming hole" among the Marin Hills (somewhere south of Mill Valley).

Would I like to go with them? I answered with an emphatic yes. I just happened to have the day off, away from the 21st Street Baths, and was free for the nonce. We discussed the outing briefly. We would probably pass no more than a few hours over at the swimming hole, plus the half hour to get there and the half hour to get back. We would probably return to San Francisco by early or middle afternoon at the latest. Fine!

Rather exceptionally it just happened that both the City and Marin County were undergoing at the same time a rare interlude of real warmth. I dressed casually, T-shirt, shorts (down to the knees), and some kind of sneakers with low socks. I brought my shoulder bag with me with the essentials (just on the odd chance that I might need them): wallet, some cash, a long-sleeved shirt of some kind, and so forth. Per the Boy Scouts, *semper paratus: always prepared* (well, more or less), like a good kid for whatever contingency might arrive. Mike and Susan came by the flat at 50 Divisadero and collected me. Off we went!

Thanks to the warmth and nice clear air, the day promised an ideal occasion for a delightful outing. Once past the Golden Gate Bridge, we drove and moseyed along some back road among the Marin Hills. Guided by Vern (truly a modern hippie Puck out of *A Midsummer Night's Dream*), who had already used the swimming hole—he knew the terrain, in fact he instigated the entire outing—we parked and then walked in. The swimming hole turned out to be a no longer used reservoir of drinking water, a man-made lake, and larger than I had anticipated. Almost everyone was swimming in the nude, and I joined them, not being bashful at all about nudity, especially after the Cub Scouts, the Boy Scouts, and the Marine Corps. I took my clothes off under a tree a little distance away from the water and placed them on my shoulder bag, leaving my stuff there under the tree. No need to worry about theft via these mostly upper middle-class kids.

I entered the water (comfortable temperature, refreshing, but not cold), swam around a bit, and then emerged back onto the land. Mike and Suzie with the others in our party—they still had their clothes on and had not yet gone swimming—were walking around here and there, and I joined them while they talked and joked. That was it for me, and I returned to the tree where I had left my shoulder bag with my clothes, preparing to get dressed. No one was in a hurry, but I did want to return to the City. Something not apparent to Vern (even if he did not live far away), but it seems that an explosive situation had been building up over several weeks that would erupt that very day. To our chagrin, especially mine, we found out somewhat later what this involved. The residents, whose fancy homes lay along the back road leading to the man-made lake, had become somewhat disturbed, if not angry, at all the teenage kids (mostly underage) going back and forth between the parked cars and the reservoir, making a mess and a ruckus as kids sometimes innocently do. The residents had become fed up with the whole situation, and these taxpayers (ahem!) had complained to the local (county) police.

The day that we visited the reservoir just happened to be the day for which the police had planned a raid. They had surrounded the immediate area quietly, surveying the scene. If anyone had noticed them, it did not result in any alert among the swimmers or loungers. At a certain signal suddenly the police made us aware of their presence, and they proceeded to arrest most of the people around the reservoir, but almost none of the adults, including Mike, Suzie, Vern, and a few others in our group. They had not yet undressed or entered the water. The police arrested me, because of my nudity, technically for "indecent exposure." They let me put my clothes back on, keep my shoulder bag for the nonce, and handcuffed me. They then walked us all back along the back road to where they had parked several big police vans, and packed us in. We first went to some local police station, where they booked me for my misdemeanor. But after delivering a stern warning about the mess the kids had been making and bothering the local residents, they let the kids go, who after all had only acted as kids will. However, me the criminal adult they took next to the county seat at San Rafael, to the old porticoed county courthouse (probably since replaced by a more modern structure) with the jail underneath it.

There they incarcerated me for a brief while before they brought me into the public courtroom. Feeling rather strange as dressed in my rather casual attire, I stood before the judge, who read and reviewed the charge against me, that of indecent exposure, nothing more than a misdemeanor. I asked the public defender if I could speak with the judge. Yes, I could, and I briefly explained that on my day off I had left San Francisco with some friends for an innocent outing at a swimming hole in the Marin Hills. The judge realized that obviously I was not a hardened criminal, but nonetheless I had broken the law. He fined me $25, to which he added $10 as the court fee, making a grand total of $35. Perhaps the sum does not seem like so much today, but back around 1970 it had much greater value. I did not have $35 in cash on me (I had no checking account then), nor did any of my friends with whom I had gone on our ill-fated excursion. (Thanks a lot, Vern!) They followed me from place to place in their station wagon. I thanked them for their concern and loyalty, but told them to go home. I would get out of jail somehow, but could not do so until someone paid the fine and court fee for me.

The police, of course, allowed me to make a few phone calls, to locate a friend who would come and pay what I owed and get my release. I phoned a few close friends to explain my dilemma. Sympathetic, they would like to have helped me, but were having some serious problems of their own at the moment, which prevented them from rescuing me right then and there. My former lover Bob Crook over in Oakland fell into that category. He could not help me, a bitter disappointment. Finally, nearing desperation, I phoned Marvin Hiemstra. He could not come over to Marin that afternoon, but would do so the next morning. Huge relief! Wow, what a friend! You do find out who your real friends are when you find yourself in a predicament such as I did that day. I had also requested Marvin to phone my bosses at the baths, to explain my situation—that I could not appear for work the next morning (so they could make other arrangements for the cleaning), but would in fact appear for work the morning after that. Marvin did make the call, and my bosses assured him that they had no problem with my dilemma. All three of them were rather amused by it, and certainly sympathetic.

Well, what a fine kettle of fish! A day of leisure, and what had promised to be one of fresh-air fun had resulted instead in an unexpected sojourn in the calaboose! I felt chagrined, disgusted, embarrassed, and plain stupid. I felt relieved, however, that the weather had become unusually warm, because otherwise I would have found it kind of chilly, garbed as I was in light casual attire. I shall say this per the unexpected sojourn in jail. You never can tell in advance just whom you will find with you as jailmates. I met some hip and simpático younger men in jail, in a literal sense mostly hippies, most of them arrested on minor charges, and mostly related to marijuana. They all appeared middle class, well educated, and well informed. We had some great and edifying conversations.

The supper, as well as the breakfast the next morning, consisted of one or more baloney sandwiches, and on white bread (horrors!), with which we drank glasses of regular tap water. The food staved off the pangs of hunger, and that was all. I had otherwise eaten nothing during that day of days except my usual small but substantial breakfast at home, and thus I had worked up a good hunger. Oddly enough, I slept okay that night in jail. Marvin showed up around midmorning and paid the fine and court fee for me. Thanks to him, and only him, I walked out of the jail as a free man! How good, how great, it felt!

Marvin then drove us back to the City and thus restored me to my usual haunts and habits, many benedictions upon him! As soon as I arrived back at home, at 50 Divisadero, I phoned my bosses at the baths. Unfazed, they had made other arrangements for the cleaning on that day and thanked me for the consideration I had shown in letting them know what had happened. (Well, I did not want to lose my job!) All had turned out well after all. Phew! As soon as possible, as soon as my meager funds allowed (within a few weeks), I paid Marvin back what I owed him for the fine and court fee. But I shall always owe Marvin a huge debt of gratitude for coming to my rescue when no one else could or would. I felt almost ecstatic to have come back home, living in my usual digs, and eating my usual chow. Such was my one and only serious and inadvertent encounter with the law. I vowed that I would never again put myself in a position to fall into the clutches of "the Man." And I have kept that vow.

I have already mentioned Fritz Leiber as a great thinker, a great writer, a great critic, and a great friend, indeed as a prince among friends, a friend nonpareil. But I must mention something very special about him before I forget and it goes unrecorded. And it is not his big feet (as noted by several commentators), which, although they were that, rated as no more than proportionate to his height, six feet four inches. Even though noticeably tall, he did not seem big or bulky, because he was not big-boned, nor broad nor massive in the shoulders. He possessed a very well-developed cranium, an extremely large and noble forehead, which (if a little larger) might have made him resemble those early depictions of what some artists thought Martians might look like, the illustrations in popular magazines of the late nineteenth and early twentieth centuries.

Fritz had great social skills, which (as the actor he had been) he deployed mostly to reassure those whom he engaged in serious conversation. When listening to others and their sometimes outré stories or opinions, he displayed great social tact—I personally benefited from this myself many times, when I would confront him with the most outlandish ideas and concepts. Nothing ever seemed totally alien to him if emanating from a fellow human. (Not for nothing had he studied fencing, chess, and philosophy.) When he listened (and he was an exceptional listener), or when he delivered some thoughtful response, Fritz made a certain characteristic gesture that always impressed or inspired. He would put his right hand to his extra-large forehead and hold it there (as if shielding his eyes from a too brilliant light), and state with deliberation, "I think I know what you mean."

I swear that, had he had a serious conversation with someone like Charles Manson, who might have been explaining why he had committed those infamous murders, or had caused others to commit them, Fritz would gamely have tried to understand and would have reacted to Manson's revelations with the same thoughtful gesture. During the entire forty years or more that I knew him, Fritz remained the same profoundly thoughtful person, as perceived by others, that he was innately.

In the same manner as Fritz, the Goldstones—Louis, or Lou, and Cynthia, and not to forget Lou's lovely and gracious mother, Florence Farrell—stand out in memory, as they did in life, as eminently sane, decent, and humane. In fact, I met them, inadvertently, through Fritz, and none other. Plagued by alcoholism during much of his life in the same fashion as his wife Jonquil, Fritz had fallen off the wagon on one occasion and had admitted himself (he sensed when he needed to ask for help) into a small, private but excellent hospital (one that specialized in alcoholic problems) somewhere in the central northern section of San Francisco. Gloria and I, married by then (this was about 1970), went to visit him at the Sullivan Garden Hospital, not far south of the old (Art Deco) Sears Roebuck building. Fritz already had another longterm friend visiting him, but she was leaving, or almost so, when we entered Fritz's private room. This friend was Cynthia Goldstone, quite a handsome and cheerful woman, and as I soon discovered, a remarkable artist. We introduced ourselves, talked a little, and then Cynthia excused herself and said goodbye. Later, when she encountered Gloria on the Muni, they exchanged addresses and phone numbers.

At some point not long thereafter, we arranged a visit and supper with the Goldstones at their flat just south of the Mission Dolores, with the impressive Catholic basilica to one side (on the north) of the picturesque old Mission structure and its enclosed garden-cum-cemetery. (The closest intersection is Dolores and 14th Streets.) We passed a beautiful evening in the simpático atmosphere of the Goldstones' apartment. Both before and after my divorce from Gloria, I cultivated my friendship with the Goldstones, truly remarkable friends and artists, if ever such existed. Cynthia worked as a secretary in downtown San Francisco, while Lou stayed at home as the househusband, taking care of the apartment, often making the meals or preparing items for the meals, which meant in their case the evening meals, a time of relaxation often with wine, some good vintage made in California.

Lou handled many or most of the chores in the kitchen and the flat, that is, when he was not painting, but he painted more often than not. Although he had worked for many years as a staff artist or illustrator (such an artist in a technical sense must be highly trained and highly competent) for the *San Francisco Chronicle*—I believe that he grew to dislike executing necessarily conventional depictions of people and places, however well paying his occupation—Lou ended his days creating abstract paintings (not à la Jackson Pollock, I hasten to add), highly disciplined, with such shapes and graduated hues of almost the same color that they seemed almost mathematically determined in their carefully calculated gradations.

Both Lou and Cynthia had long specialized as quite serious readers of fantasy and science fiction, particularly as once purveyed by *Weird Tales*, *Wonder Stories*, and the other pulp magazines of the 1930s and 1940s (meaning the fiction of Lovecraft, Ashton Smith, Henry S. Whitehead, R. E. Howard, Manly Wade Wellman, H. Bedford-Jones, and Ray Bradbury), not to leave unmentioned the new digest-style magazines of imaginative fiction, including the best one of this type, the aptly titled *Magazine of Fantasy and Science Fiction* (edited for an extended time first by Anthony Boucher and then by Avram Davidson), and not to overlook *Galaxy*, *Astounding*, *Analog*, etc. Less influenced in their art by the fantasy and science fiction that they read and assimilated, Lou and Cynthia *naturally* came by what I can only term their science-fiction perspective, which I certainly shared, starting early on during my military service, and somehow hovering always around Plato's Atlantis Mythos.

Cynthia's art—her sketches and paintings—resembles nobody else's creativity, sometimes representational, sometimes not, but always deliciously quirky, thus uniquely her own. More than Lou's, her art reflected the mind and sensibility of someone who possessed an innate and natural affinity for, and an orientation toward, the depth and breadth of modern science fiction and science fantasy, but not in the sense of Tolkien, that Milton of modern prose epics. As part of this orientation, the Goldstones had long functioned as vegetarians (an ethical choice) and prepared highly nutritive and satisfying vegetarian meals, including their own form of dahl, that Indic specialty, and in their case made from lentils. As vegetarians, Lou and Cynthia adhered to no doctrinaire régime, but would also prepare meat, including the occasional steak, for Lou's non-vegetarian mother, Florence, who lived with son and daughter-in-law, and who always impressed me as a warm and charming white-haired lady of considerable beauty.

What I remember above all about the Goldstones beyond their friendship, their marvelous art, and their social gatherings, which they hosted superbly, is their humanity. Above all else they exemplified, in the broadest and most inclusive sense, the humanities. This humanity came into special play at their gatherings. On several occasions, when I would return from some extended absence elsewhere in the U.S. or abroad in the U.K., the Goldstones would stage, in my honor (deeply appreciated and overtly acknowledged) some special event to which they would invite their most simpático friends, including various artists and other local luminaries in the genre of fantasy and science fiction residing in the Bay Area, such as Fritz Leiber, Margo Skinner, David Morgus, writer-editor Avram Davidson (a very dear man), and super-prolific science fiction author par excellence Robert Silverberg. Gatherings like these, well supplied with drink and food, assuredly made for an especially cordial, if not heartwarming, welcome back home to San Francisco!

Whenever I was present in the City, even after I moved to Sacramento, I would attend a rare exhibit by Lou, or quite a few of the exhibits mounted by Cynthia with the help of her nephew, also a remarkable artist (as well as an art teacher), at some women's club in the Mission District. These exhibits always turned into something special, and I can never forget the first such exhibit that aunt and nephew mounted there to display the full depth, charm, and range of Cynthia's art, vibrant with unexpected colors and combinations of shapes and patterns, a thing of beauty and unexpected joy. This exhibit featured quite a bit of novel and recent art, including small pieces of a whimsical nature framed by extra-large matting, which emphasized the whimsy. I had entered the viewing areas and had not yet greeted Cynthia because she was conversing with other fans and friends. So, while I patiently waited to talk with her in my own turn (we had exchanged glances and silently acknowledged each other with a smile), I began to inspect and contemplate her art on display, beautifully and sensitively mounted.

I had hardly begun when what I witnessed and consequently felt simply overwhelmed me with such an intense sensation of delight, wonder, and gratitude that I started involuntarily to weep (no other art has ever done that to me since)—I almost began sobbing—at this unexpected revelation of the pure beauty that Cynthia's craft as an artist had created in me. Just as this moment when tears were cascading down my cheeks, Cynthia came up to me and began to ask me what I thought and felt about the exhibit, but stopped when she saw my condition of abject and wonderful surrender. Then she said, "Oh, Donald," and paused. We embraced. I could hardly talk, so overwhelmed had I become. In turn she became emotional and overwhelmed herself by my spontaneous reaction, extremely gratifying to her as an artist. She confided that she had never had anyone else respond to her art so vibrantly. All that I could express, as I sought to recover, all that my voice could half whisper, half croak, was "Thank you, dear Cynthia, from the bottom of my heart." I remained in a rapture of wonder-struck observation for quite a few minutes and went up to Cynthia, thanked her again, we embraced, and I departed.

She had already given me as a gift a delightful small painting of Puss in Boots (he wears boots and a fancy hat with feather), and later she did another piece of art, for the cover of *Songs and Sonnets Atlantean: The Third Series* (Phosphor Lantern Press, 2005), the actual cover design by another special friend, Lance Alexander, thus adroitly incorporating Cynthia's art. Within a circle suggesting a ship's porthole, Cynthia has placed a lovingly realized seahorse against a patterned, multicolored background suggesting sea growth. Again she did it as a gift and refused any payment. What can I say?!

Whenever I would give some public poetry performance as at the downtown San Francisco Public Library or at one of its branches, not only would the Goldstones make a point of attending but would make sure that some of their best friends knew of it so that they could attend in their own turn. What can one state in appreciation of such magnificent friends as those? Beyond fantasy and science fiction, both Lou and Cynthia had a keen literary sense as well as a cultivated sense of poetry, and above all when cast in traditional form, and innovatively so, due to the increased possibility of music and magic. When my first series of *Songs and Sonnets Atlantean* made its local arrival and appearance, I went over from where I was living in the Haight-Ashbury to their flat, to deliver to the Goldstones their own advance-ordered copy, signed to them, of course. When I returned a few days later at Lou's express invitation (it was in the late morning), Lou confessed that he had stayed up all night to read and assimilate the book in its entirety. Wow, such an honor!

Lou and Cynthia appreciated the poetry, qua poetry, but not less the introduction and notes, the latter with their different orientation and sensibility, their subtle sense of humor. Surely, perfect or ideal readers! Often, when I would go visit Cynthia by herself (after Lou had died), she would read aloud, and supremely well, some exquisite narrative by Edna St. Vincent Millay (a favorite with Fritz and Jonquil Leiber, as well as myself), especially "The Harp Weaver." Cynthia made it all the more special because she possessed a tonally beautiful voice, nuanced and expressive, unlike the often strident voices of so many American women. Although the Goldstones have now both transcended back to the Other Side, their essence, their warmth, and their love live on in my heart.

Last, but not least, of all the extraordinary friends I made literally by means of San Francisco, there now comes along a person whom I have mentioned only indirectly, and not by name, but whose name is Craig Anderson (also professionally known as Calvin Anderson), originally from the Seattle-Tacoma region in Washington State. I do not know his current whereabouts, nor even if he is still alive. I probably met him before I moved to the City (that happened in the winter of 1965-66), during one of my weekend visits at the Embarcadero Y.M.C.A. At that time Craig, a science major of some type, worked as a graduate student at the University of Colorado in Boulder. Oddly, although we found each other attractive, a sexual exchange between us never quite worked out. We tried several times, but an urgent chemistry or alchemy was missing. However, and perhaps better, we developed a special friendship that we could share on many levels and in different areas of interest.

Although a graduate student in Boulder, Craig resided in Denver, in a big, solid, painted brick, two-story family house or mansion that he rented with several other housemates to share and minimize expenses. Likewise they shared the kitchen duties, cleaning, etc. Craig invited me to come visit him, or live with him and the others, at some point, whenever. I had no desire to move from Northern California right then and there—living in Auburn, I was already planning to move to San Francisco herself soon—but said that I would at least like to come and visit. We shook hands on that and exchanged home addresses and phone numbers.

As I did, Craig had a sophisticated appreciation of the handsome, well-formed, and muscular male physique (and other particulars), as captured and revealed by the art of photography. It appeared to be an art that he had already practised as a non-professional, and that as a professional he would pursue later on, specializing in the Afro-American physique as it had evolved. At some point I became disillusioned with the City for a while, or simply wanted, or thought that I needed, a change of locale. Craig and I exchanged letters and phone calls, and we arranged that I would visit with him in Denver for several weeks or more, possibly with the prospect of settling down there, at least for a while, if I liked it. I was not exactly an utter stranger to Denver, since I had passed through it, or stayed overnight there, with Bob Crook back in the middle and late 1950s, but I recollected very little about it.

Accordingly I took the then ever reliable and economic Greyhound bus during the early summer to Denver, where Craig met me with his car and brought me to the big family house, where he and housemates resided. The mansion was located in an old neighborhood of similar houses, some quite handsome, some in better shape than others. After San Francisco's old, wooden, and rather fragile Victorian houses, these big family structures impressed and rather amazed me. Craig's place (where they all pitched in on the rent) stood just north of Washington Park, where a tradition of staging musicals in the summer had long taken root. Craig resided not far from Old Town to the west, and not far from the downtown area with the handsome and imposing state buildings.

The state capitol building rather resembles the Capitol in Washington, D.C. How many beautiful imitations has the federal Capitol inspired! A truly beautiful city, Denver has many trees and parks like Indianapolis, Minneapolis, and Sacramento. These and many other cities across the U.S. benefited from the City Beautiful movement that came about in the late nineteenth and early twentieth centuries. Even if just as many people had just as much cupidity back then as now, they also had much more idealism and altruism that was manifested in activities like the City Beautiful and other community-enhancing movements. How far we seem today from such inspiring idealism!—although we do seem to have far more official charities.

However long I would end up sojourning in Denver, I knew that I would enjoy living in such a lovely metropolis. Not far away, but appealingly smaller, Boulder did not take a back seat to the state capital, and seemed even lovelier as college or university towns (fortunately non-industrial) often do. I would go back and forth between Denver and Boulder many times, driving with Craig in his car, and also driving with him up into the Rockies on occasion. I had no sooner settled in as much as I could when I became somewhat homesick for San Francisco. Meanwhile I was looking for part-time or full-time work, and as part of my contribution to the house I took over the cleaning and certain kitchen chores, but not the cooking, however, even if I did make an occasional casserole that everyone seemed to like.

As it was taking place, that season just happened to turn into the Summer of Love in San Francisco (1967), and Scott McKenzie, with a rare beautiful voice, released an especially beautiful song that opened "If you're going to San Francisco, be sure to wear some flowers in your hair." Scott, and none other, sang this haunting song created by his friend John Phillips, the leader of the folk rock group, the Mamas and the Papas. In regard to love or sex I found enough in and around Denver, even if I could find much more in the City. However, that was not what caught my attention, because I had never had any problem attracting sexual partners wherever I went or lived for a while. I forget exactly where I was standing or working in Craig's house (probably the kitchen), when I first heard and really noticed the song.

I found myself almost alone, but one other housemate had turned on his radio nearby, and I could hear it quite well. The song has an unusually beautiful and well-developed melody that, along with the words, creates a relaxed but still powerful incantation of longing and nostalgia. At least it did so for me. Emotionally it hit me precisely where I lived, where my affective center lay. I began weeping, almost sobbing, and that very moment decided me to return to the City, which I did via "the Dog" (that is, the Greyhound) once more, and as soon as possible. However, I had not yet finished with Denver: I would return later and reside for some three months under the roof of Craig's house.

Craig conducted his graduate studies at Boulder during the later 1960s for three or four years, and I came back to live with Craig and housemates, but this time not in the summer, rather in the autumn and winter. Once again I had a welcome respite from San Francisco, and this time I got me a job almost at once, as a gym instructor at a weightlifting place in fancy Cherry Creek not far from Craig's part of Denver. While working there I met a variety of people, including a father and sons who owned a packing house that processed beef cattle. I had always wanted to visit a slaughterhouse to see just what the process involved, even if I am not a great meat eater at all (except in a certain restricted sense), and have always preferred fish fresh or packaged in some form. The people in New England, including those in New Bedford, indeed know how to prepare and cook fish, well and simply.

I arranged with the people who owned the packing house to visit the place. They picked me up and afterward returned me back home. I perceived in every detail and phase just what slaughtering large quadrupeds for meat entailed. Although it did not turn me into a pure vegetarian, the process is for a fact quite intense and gross. I had prepared myself in regard to the visual aspect, but had forgotten my sense of smell—worse, and overwhelming!—an odor compounded of what smelled like urine and pure shit, mixed in with heavy animal fear. Deprived of nutriment for forty-eight hours, they do not feel like their normal selves. One by one they enter the inside of the slaughter space through that certain door, and then a heavy hammer hits them directly in the head, killing them at once before they are enchained, lifted up, and torn asunder via the machinery quite efficiently, with various parts of the bodies segregated and whirled aloft from place to place. What a kaleidoscope of skulls, halves of hides and bodies, urine, shit, and blood—blood everywhere, plus water, as the workers constantly hose down the body parts and the pavement underneath. Without water the packing houses could not function, period.

The owners noticed that I had changed color while watching the spectacle, but especially inhaling the heady brew of odors. They suggested that I step outside for fresh air to recover. This I did, and once restored and re-balanced, I finished my inspection of the process—enough! Now I understood, and understand, why beef, cooking and cooked, smells and tastes the way it does. That night, by an odd coincidence (in fact I was the one who did the cooking, once I returned home), we had roast beef cooked as usual in the oven of our own stove—and it still tasted as delicious as usual! However, I need never visit any slaughterhouse again anywhere, amen.

Another person whom I met via the gym at Cherry Creek, and with whom I enjoyed an intimate and longterm friendship, looms more importantly today than the father and sons who then owned the packing house. Russell Nakata!—an unusual and empathic individual, verily, who worked as the deacon at some grand Episcopalian cathedral in downtown Denver. We got together several times for meals in restaurants and other socializing before I went back to San Francisco, where he continued to call on me when I resumed living in the City. We had hit it off at once, equaling each other in enthusiasm, outgoingness, and so forth. We had much in common, but whatever it involved in the course of our exchanges, we brought equal amounts of adventure and fun so as to make everything much lighter, and more enjoyable.

While I still resided in Denver, Russ gave me privately a grand tour of the very large Gothic structure whose religion he served. I had anticipated that religious details would obtrude upon our friendship, once I told him that I had grown up as a Roman Catholic, albeit attending public schools. But no problems came up, just the opposite, because Episcopalians and Catholics have much in common in ritual and belief. Moreover, dear Russ maintained quite an enlightened attitude concerning rock-bottom Christian belief. He simply regarded it as "the Tradition" without carrying it any further than that. Russell would never have condemned any heretics to burning at the stake or to any torture. Sharing large areas of profound affinity between us—he realized and shared the strategic importance of high culture—we always had a wonderful time whenever we met and visited, and wherever, Denver or San Francisco. I miss dear Russ and his enthusiasm since he left us and transcended back to the Other Side.

Once he had completed his graduate studies, Craig moved to San Francisco (as he had long intended), where apparently he got a job at once teaching science at the high school level, but he seems not to have pursued that for hardly any time at all. In short order he leased a big three-story family mansion in Pacific Heights (on or near Gough Street), got established in it, and soon filled it with simpático housemates to share the rent and other expenses, in the same manner as he had in Denver. He also established a fine photographic-art business (he had turned himself into a photographic artist) called Sierra Domino, specializing in the Afro-American physique. This latter-day Bob Mizer did quite well in his specialty, and he prospered. He continued living at the big family house for many years, and helped many people, aspiring models and bodybuilders, including myself. In return for his help I cleaned the house on occasion, and later according to a specific schedule.

During the early 1970s Craig funded my first sojourn in England and Wales, my first Spenserian tour there. Upon my return, and after my big move to Sacramento, I still owed him the money for the three-month trip to the U.K. (late winter and early spring 1972). Since Craig had no burning need for the money as ready cash, I made a deal with him to pay it back by cleaning the public rooms, including the bathrooms, in the house (not the individual housemates' chambers, except his own, of course), once a month for eight months or more, but I continued beyond the payment of my debt to him. The arrangement gave me added remuneration and the chance to continue my sojourns in the Bay Area, where I often stayed overnight at Craig's house, in one of the extra bedrooms. With the passage of time I eventually severed my money-earning ties to the City, and we ceased communicating. I remain indebted to Craig Anderson for something far beyond mere money.

As a codicil to my residence in Denver under Craig's aegis—how clearly I can see him, tall, slender, with his great smile, with his fund of great good will, with his inclination toward helping others—I should mention my friendship with Gordon R. Barnett, artist, sculptor, whatever, a friendship that has continued and grown over the years since the latter 1960s. He moved from Denver to the Seattle-Tacoma region quite some little time agone, and now lives on Vashon Island west of Seattle and accessible by ferry boat. Like Jesse Allen, Gordon remains one of the very few artists, qua artists (pictorial and otherwise), who has not only managed to keep afloat as an artist per se (Bill Boddy furnishes another example), but has actually prospered, bespeaking astute intelligence and the ability to find his own artistic niche, to persevere in it, and then to prosper within it, not always an easy task.

Surviving as an artist (without wealthy parents to support one, ahem), even under the best of circumstances, never becomes easy (or but rarely)—it takes guts, tenacity, and sheer determination, never mind the difficulties the artist might encounter on occasion in a technical sense, within the chosen art and/or arts. The cover art that Gordon created for me for the first series of *Songs and Sonnets Atlantean* has assuredly served me splendidly, not just for that volume but for the entire trilogy, *The Atlantis Fragments*, as well as for the background narrative of all my Atlantean books, meaning the novel also extrapolated with great care from Plato's Atlantis Mythos. I am profoundly indebted as well to artist-designer Lance Alexander for adapting Gordon's cover art to the needs of both the trilogy and the novel.

Among my closest friends, even if we do not visit and communicate often, I must mention Arnold Z. Gamble and spouse Erin O'Toole. Erin survives as a commercial artist who also does fine art on the side, mostly landscapes of remarkable facture somewhat in the tradition (and worthily so) of the early American artist George Inness. Arnie creates fine handmade guitars and on occasion, by special commission, other plucked instruments like lute or mandolin. He also does repairs and restorations, and he himself ranks as an exceptional guitarist of classical guitar and lute music. Beyond the natural sympathy and affinity that artists often feel for each other, Erin and Arnie provide genial and excellent companionship not just to each other but also to their lucky friends. I should know because I resided with them for an extended period of time, occupying what was then an extra bedroom when their daughter moved out to conduct her own young adult life elsewhere. Thanks to them I enjoyed a very pleasant residence at their charming cottage in Sacramento.

(A little aside here on the "Z" in Arnie's full name. When he went into the obligatory military service, he had no middle name; his parents had not given him one. Accordingly he supplied the "Z," to stand in for middle name and/or initial. Curious, but in British usage "z" pronounces as "zed," which does make some kind of name, like "Ned.")

When I decided that I needed a lute to accompany some of the poems that I maintain in my (memorized) repertoire of performance poetry (after having had many friends and acquaintances urge me to take up lute or classical guitar for this purpose), I went to Arnie for the special instrument that I required (after much research on my part), because I knew that Arnie could think outside the ordinary confines of his luthier's craft and art. Before he began, we had many long discussions about what I wanted and needed. The process of making lutes turns out to be quite exacting. The luthier must first make out of wood a solid lute-body form, to take the wide strips of thin rosewood (or whatever wood the client or the maker might require) that the luthier nicely fits over the form. These long pieces of wood, together with the soundboard, determine the tone of the lute of whatever type or size needed.

What Arnie finally made for me resulted in an innovative chitarrone (pronounced KEE-tuh-RROH-nay) with fourteen single strings—for the top seven or eight courses, we decided on classical guitar strings, easier to buy—tuned overall to E (but with the third string tuned to F# rather than the usual G), but otherwise using special German-made bass strings to accommodate the lower (bass) courses. I have employed this bass lute on occasion for some of my poetry recitals (or concerts), that is, when I can transport it with some ease to the given engagement, via someone driving me there. (Bill Boddy made the sturdy case expressly to accommodate the bass lute, also an exacting task.) I also use a small but quite effective amplifier so that the audience can hear the sounds that I make as vividly as I can hear them. The bass lute has an unusually beautiful tone and does not sound quite like the regular lutes or bass lutes, the latter always a different sound. Even if I cannot rank as a natural musician, the lute does indeed go very well with my poetry act whenever I can use it.

Even if I present it almost at the tail end of things, I must mention here my longterm and ongoing admiration of William Hope Hodgson (1877-1918) as one of the most unprecedented among the modern masters or the weird and fantastic tale, whether embodied in the form of short stories or (rather exceptionally) full-fledged novels, four in all. When Arkham House under the astute management of August Derleth, the owner-editor, published in 1946 the fine omnibus of supernatural (or "weird-scientific") fiction *The House on the Borderland and Other Novels*, it represented something very special indeed, and quite beyond its impressive size, at almost 640 pages, and at 40 lines per page, in small but yet legible type.

The publication marked not only the finale of a very long campaign conducted by H. C. Koenig on behalf of Hodgson, but above all the resurgence back into public view of the major works of a genuinely unique poet and writer, almost in the manner of some hitherto unknown or forgotten scrolls, retrieved by some arcane method from some now submarine libraries of ancient Atlantis.

I first read the omnibus volume in Southern California, while I resided with Bob Crook in our little house at the end of Monument Street in Pacific Palisades—this reading took place during the first half of the 1960s. The omnibus volume made a very deep impression on me, including the two novels dealing with nautical things, particularly since I come from a general New England background. In my case it began during my early teens, when our father bought his first (12-foot) catboat (with a single sail, no jib), which I believe we called a beetle, and which we tried out in the harbor of South Dartmouth, or Padanaram, venturing forth from the Padanaram Yacht Club, almost as soon as he had purchased it. Of course, navigating in a small sailboat does not resemble very closely traveling in a clipper or whaling ship, but it does introduce one to the elements of sailing in the most basic way. I recall how, during that first time out in the boat, late in the day, our father, still getting the hang of things, sailed too close to the bridge north of the yacht club, getting stuck against one of the arches, until somebody going over the bridge pushed the mast away from the structure, with our father reversing course at once. Dad felt a little embarrassed, but we all cheered him on, spouse Ernestine and we two sons.

However, we never encountered (I give thanks!) any monsters of the sea such as Hodgson describes! The unique manner in which Hodgson creates and sustains an otherworldly and often vehemently frightening atmosphere (one of suspense fraught with dread, as emanating from the ocean) remains without any true parallel. The contents of the Arkham House omnibus recapitulated Hodgson's four novels as they appeared chronologically, and uncut: *The Boats of the "Glen Carrig"* (1907), *The House on the Borderland* (1908), *The Ghost Pirates* (1909), and towering above the preceding three, *The Night Land* (1912), a supreme romance if ever such a one existed!—and romance in all definitions. In its own way *The Night Land* remains as much of a challenge as *The Faerie Queene* appears to be for modern readers, in school (college or university) or outside of it.

Various critics, especially H. P. Lovecraft, have reacted negatively to what they regard as Hodgson's uncouth and grotesque attempt at archaic language (as if in one sense all speech and language is not innately archaic!), at an olden style befitting the material being communicated. Whatever the style he chose and for whatever reason, Hodgson had the instinctive genius to write as clearly and simply as possible, given the pressure from the teeming conceptions of his unique imagination. We refer here to *The Boats of the "Glen Carrig"* and *The Night Land*. As one who has read and re-read both of these remarkable prose narratives, all that I can say about this vexed matter of style in succinct compass is this: Hodgson attempts to clothe both novels less in some vague olden style but more in what he considers one suitable to the subject matter, artistically distancing the reader from the reader's everyday mundanity, while keeping the prose as direct and basic as possible, all proportions guarded. And? And it works! That is all that matters. Neither narrative would work without the manner in which Hodgson tells it, any more than *The Faerie Queene* would or could exist without the stanza that Spenser created to bring his vast epic poem into existence.

Now joining Hodgson's previous books, whether assembled and published by himself while alive or by others after his death, a recent omnibus volume, *The Wandering Soul*, brought out by the ever enterprising Tartarus Press in 2005, and exemplarily compiled and introduced by Jane Frank, stands out almost as prominently as the Arkham House volume of 1946, and in size more manageable and readable, at 384 pages, and at not quite 40 lines per page, in small type but not overly small.

Among other advantages, this new omnibus permits the Hodgson aficionado to trace how the writer began scrivening professionally—unpretentiously advertising his school or studio of physical culture (bodybuilding via calisthenics and weightlifting), located in the small industrial city that is Blackburn, Lancashire, some thirty miles northeast of Liverpool as the bird flies. He opened the studio in the autumn of 1899, and it stayed in business at least into 1903.

He also began writing professionally, somewhat later, by preparing the lectures he delivered when he would give his slide shows of his adventures at sea during his teens, these being slides made from the photographs (they still seem quite impressive today) that—as a pioneer photographer working under rather dangerous conditions—he took of the ocean and the ships (let the fact receive emphasis) on which he sailed as a mariner, not as a passenger. Even a full-fledged sailing ship of real size can feel frighteningly small in a storm on the open seas, never mind the added peril when furling or unfurling the sails aloft, high above the deck or above the ocean herself as the ship tosses and pitches from side to side, or dips deep into the water as giant waves bury the deck.

Since he was trying to communicate with the average reader of his period (late Victorian times up to World War I)—a reader probably far more literate or literary than most readers of today—Hodgson instinctively kept what he wrote as clean and simple as he could make it. This lucidity remains utterly apparent, as evidenced by his articles on physical culture no less than the texts of his surviving slide-show lectures on sailing and the sea, on how he managed to take his photos, and to develop them, all the while aboard a sailing ship, with all that such implies in terms of bad weather. The not quite six dozen photos, reproduced very well in this new omnibus, permit us uncommon glimpses and insights into Hodgson's life and career, as well as the family from which he derived.

These photos provide information at once revealing and fascinating. The family photos display Hodgson's closest relatives as healthy and handsome folk, with William himself as the handsomest. The fourteen plates that show Hodgson demonstrating various basic exercises confirm the fact that he functioned as a complete and accomplished professor of physical culture. At five foot five inches (more or less) tall, but sturdy and well-knit withal, he may have found himself subject to bullying from shipmates bigger than himself, superiors or the other mariners—even if people in general wherever he went seemed to have responded very well to his easy and outgoing charm. William was no fool, and he knew how to get along with people, essential for a small guy.

This relative smallness of his is probably what motivated him to develop his body and strength to the extent that he did. He advertised his school of physical culture (among other means) by a series of postcards displaying his well-developed physique in appropriate but tasteful poses. One in particular stands out. This photo focusses on his upper body clad in a tanktop. Clean-shaven, with his hair neatly parted on one side, he stands with his arms folded over his lower chest and upper abdomen, a typical pose (but again tasteful) for the strongmen of his period, including the legendary Eugene Sandow. With regular features, he seems remarkably handsome. (The photo probably displays him in his middle twenties.) According to the standards of antiquity the Greeks and Romans would have called him a beautiful young man, what people today would consider a hunk, and what gay men would find irresistibly cute.

Thus William Hope Hodgson still stands out as a great master of the weird and fantastic story but also claims the unique status, undeniably, as the cutest guy among all the great masters of such fiction! I pronounce this opinion as a lifelong physical culturist myself, trim and muscular at eighty. As a bodybuilder of one period I salute the bodybuilder of an earlier one! Enormous thanks to Jane Frank for her work to bring this novel omnibus into existence: *The Wandering Soul, Glimpses of a Life: A Compendium of Rare and Unpublished Works by William Hope Hodgson*. (I share completely the sentiments expressed by Mike Ashley in his foreword, "The Last Redoubt.") The volume gains an added poignance when the informed reader assimilates the fact that an enemy shell blew this beautiful body apart, this beautiful man, at the age of forty, during World War I. What a waste!

During the time since I first manifested in my current incarnation in this dimension that we all share, that is, since 8 September 1934, the human population has grown from around two billion to more than seven, and now promises to increase to more than nine by 2050. In other words, it has more than tripled in some eighty years. As noted earlier, I first became aware of the subject (or the "problem") back in the winter of 1941-42, when, in the fourth grade at the elementary level of education, our class studied geography with Miss O'Malley at Mount Pleasant Grammar School in New Bedford. I noticed how many towns and cities existed on the maps that we used, little dots and squares, which indicated communities big and small. I recall asking the teacher with some concern about the food grown for all these communities, how was it supplied, and was it adequate. Miss O'Malley reassured me that I need not worry, that everyone at least in the U.S. had enough to eat, and so forth. That became my introduction to the ratio between food supply and human population.

I did not think about human population again (in critical terms) until some thirteen years later. I was fulfilling my military obligation in the Marine Corps. While glancing through some magazines at the base library in Opa-locka in the summer of 1955 (before the big move to El Toro), I came upon a recent issue of *Scientific American*. I leafed through the issue in question, reading here and there, when I came upon an article by Julian Huxley (brother to the better-known Aldous), "World Population." The subject arrested my attention, and I read the entire article slowly and thoughtfully. And then I re-read it. Sobering, rather frightening, and more than alarming! And I have never forgotten it, nor the dire vistas it opened up for me. The piece became a clarion wake-up call for any thinking person with the requisite prescience (pre-science?) and sensitivity.

Virtually everything predicted by Julian Huxley has come true. As the sheer bulk of human flesh has increased, that of all the other species has diminished, except for those we farm as meat for human consumption. Also as foreseen, much of the civilized world (how civilized, we might question) has become more and more like a police state, and I do not refer here necessarily to China and Russia, even if they might seem to furnish ideal examples, but the police state has long since been happening in parts of Africa and Latin America. It is also happening in the good old U.S.A., ever so slowly and insidiously. Humans individually seem to expect that society at large can expand indefinitely to absorb them. They do not seem to grasp how they impact the world collectively, never mind the ratio between food production and human numbers. Other factors exist to thicken the soup, often quite irrational, such as religion.

It recently took a bright young woman of my acquaintance of twenty-three to give me the courage to ask in capsule form on these pages, "Too many people?"—she used the phrase when we were discussing human population, only she did not use it interrogatively. And it brought me right up against the Great Taboo, that is, against speaking in utter seriousness about the negative consequences of an infinitely expanded or expanding human presence, that there might be too many of us. In the last several years I have been traveling around the world, twice to Southeast Asia and once to Egypt, in some respects the center of the Muslim Arab-language world. Quite incidentally I noticed how many young men had no employment, nor could find it in spite of academic degrees and professional training. Without a job they could not get married and continue with the expected normal adult life. This is also gradually becoming a problem in the U.S., but not yet to the extent that it has become in the Third World.

I am not predicting or anticipating some Great Catastrophe or Great Cataclysm in the manner of Plato's Atlantis. No, but what I can anticipate rationally is the gradual but unavoidable decline in the quality of life, and not just in the Third World. Their problems will change into our problems, as desperate people will seek increasingly to find a refuge here in the U.S. from the prevailing chaos, poverty, and general misery. We have already destroyed, degraded, and transformed much of the known and unknown world, not only the land but the oceans just as much, which we have always used as dumps and sewers. It seems to be standard procedure. And quite frankly I do not see how we can avoid the negative consequences of our uncontrollable human procreation en masse—unless, of course, we could start populating other planets of our solar system after making them suitable for our species—if such were possible in terms of logistics and expense. William Hope Hodgson's *Night Land* might descend and engulf us a little faster than what we can foresee. It might be closer than what we think.

As a corollary to the greater number of human beings today, there seems to exist a correspondingly larger number of gay people. (By gay we mean all homosexual individuals whether male or female.) Do the relative proportions of gay to non-gay hold the same as they do formerly, or the larger number of gay people indicate that more of them exist than in previous times? Have their numbers grown exponentially? Or anent what seems like their exponential increase, could this actually indicate that more gay people exist today than yesterday? Or, more to the point, could it indicate that more people today simply have the courage to declare themselves to be gay? The recent declaration of their gayness by many high-profile people would appear to support this possibility, or the possibility that many people are naturally bisexual, as they have discovered themselves to be down through the ages, from Graeco-Roman or Egyptian antiquity onwards. Self-preservation comes before self-declaration, as people always learn under repressive régimes political or social.

Or is this phenomenon of evidently more homosexuals just one of the ways in which Mother Nature attempts to curb or control the ever-increasing numbers of people in many parts of the planet? A question worth pondering. People of the same sex do not procreate, although they can arrange to become parents via various modes other than direct procreation. This has become a fact, and is not a fantasy. Not all of us wish to become parents via our own capacity to procreate.

At eighty I can perceive, as I perceived earlier, that I personally never wanted to become a parent either directly or by adoption. Circumstances have allowed me to add perhaps a few grace notes here and there. I have no regrets as a poet, scholar, and specialist writer. What I have managed to do suffices for me. Immortality of any kind remains rare, if not (strictly speaking) impossible. For me the advantages of gayness have far outweighed any disadvantages, as I came to experience them in the pre-AIDS world of the U.S. As I wended my way along the course of life, my passionate sexual nature manifested itself early onward, from eight or so, from the first experience with a beautiful older (teenage) male. That led to the discovery of solo sex or masturbation, which I could also practice with buddies of my own age. This pattern, thus established as early as neurally or socially possible, has remained a constant for me from eight to eighteen to eighty.

From eight to eighteen I indulged in every form of sexuality (except anal intercourse) with whatever buddies came to hand. I rigorously avoided women (not that sexual intercourse with them ever proves easy, apart from the physical aspect) for obvious reasons: sex with women, carried to the logical extreme (beyond petting), usually ends in pregnancy, marriage, and a life sentence with children and wage-slavery, or (if you will) a death sentence. No freedom openly to explore as well as to discover not just sexuality but all of life, including all non-human life. I felt that I could never trust any woman to function other than what she would manifest naturally, except perhaps a female prostitute. (Male prostitutes have their charm and utility as well.) I mention female prostitutes with honor and respect. They have professional honesty and understand healthy males quite well, even if I have never had to purchase the services of any prostitute male or female. In each and every case they waived payment.

Thus my adolescence went very well, if not fantastically, in regard to sexual expression. During my military service I avoided sex almost completely until I linked up with Bob Mizer and then Bob Crook. The latter kept me safe and sound, protectively anchored for much of the decade of 1955-65. After that decade I moved north, first to Auburn and then to San Francisco, where I discovered and reveled to the maximum in the sexual paradise that the City provided for the passionate same-sex male. Later, during the Hippie Period (c. 1965-75), in addition to sex with guys, sex with girls became a reality for me, thanks to the birth control pill, as awesome an invention as any in human history.

Then, fatal encounter, I discovered that sex with women could prove a supreme pleasure, and once I found that out, I realized that eventually I would have to avoid it again if at all possible. A supreme pleasure, dependent on a female Other, could only spell madness or disaster for me. I returned to males, whom I had known since the age of eight. They spelled safety and more abundant fun, even if accompanied by sexually transmitted maladies, gonorrhea, syphilis, crab lice, regular lice, and what have you. Promiscuity leads to medical "discoveries" (ahem!) for the engaged individual! If that is the price for catting around with males or females, well, it hain't so bad because of modern medical treatment. People are not going to experiment?

As I realized in more ways than one (even if it took a long time for me to make the realization), retrenchment by moving inland from San Francisco to Sacramento had turned into an absolute necessity in terms of survival, difficult at first, but it became a little easier as time went on. I still availed myself on occasion of the fleshpots of the City, but local possibilities opened up for me just walking on the city streets of the state capital, and not via the divine institution of any gay baths like those in San Francisco.

I wish to express my gratitude to the cosmos at large (blessedly indifferent otherwise) for affording me the opportunity to glut my sexual appetites to the maximum. I also wish to say thank you to the many beautiful men and women who have graced me with their beauty, their lust, and their reciprocated pleasure. I realize that I have scarcely mentioned many of them by name, or assumed name, never mind expatiating on their individual charms and what we did together. Perhaps I could also write a small book, detailing many of them, a sort of register. Perhaps I could also write a companion volume, *Ways and Means of Deeply Pleasing Lovers of Varying Ethnicities and Preferences*. Avoiding monotony would prove the main challenge in either volume.

Much else exists for which I might thank the cosmos, not least that I acted responsibly within my own terms, and that I did not add another person to the overall human population.

Looking back over this chapter, essentially an addendum, I see that, despite my best intentions, I still have not mentioned many salient friends who have played quite an important part in my life, but mostly since I moved inland from San Francisco to Auburn and Sacramento. In Oakland Jack and Adelle Foley rank very high on the list of my best friends in the Bay Area, next to them Alan Gullette and Julie Hodge, closely followed in San Francisco by Nancy J. Peters and Philip Lamantia (deceased). I must also mention my special circle of friends in the Chicago area headed by Lou Irmo and Randy Broecker. Perhaps I could include these people, plus my unrecorded lovers, all in some further volume of autobiography.

Afterword

I decided to write my autobiography while I could still do so, while I still possessed enough mental acuity, while I could still summon my memories with relative ease, and while my recollections could still square with external reality. This extended memoir could very well turn out as my last book, or at least one of any real size. Mentation and recollection have become harder with age (even if only in the last year or so), which luckily for me has just caught up with the autobiographer at eighty. Physically I remain atypical for my time of life, muscular, trim, flexible, and so forth. Regular exercise (not requiring a gym, but featuring calisthenics and a few light weights), rapid walking (and often, as always), and sensible diet with small portions of food (and with some alcoholic beverages): such a regimen has made me healthy, well balanced, and relatively sane.

In addition to staying in excellent shape (apart from the ongoing colon problems, over which I can exert only minimal control), I have attained a certain contentment. (May all this not sound smug, smart-ass, or self-satisfied!) Despite the odds, whether external circumstances or my own personal problems and limitations, I have succeeded in my ambition (conceived in adolescence) of having a life and career as an old-fashioned man of letters, as contrasted, say, with a steadily producing and prolific fictioneer specializing in adventure novels or family histories or fantasy trilogies.

This goal I have largely achieved first as a poet, second as a scholar and literary historian, and third (linked with the last-cited) as a literary and general culture critic. My discovery (via Arkham House in the middle and latter 1950s) of the three chief poets and fictioneers who had made the most significant contributions to *Weird Tales*, once again, the Three Musketeers, in L. Sprague de Camp's happy choice of phrase—H. P. Lovecraft in the 1920s and 1930s, Clark Ashton Smith and Robert E. Howard mostly in the 1930s—proved strategic in gradually making me first into a scholar (and critic-historian) and then into a poet seriously employing myth, or "mythoglyphics."

As I slowly woke up to the importance of Ashton Smith as a great and unique poet (not to leave unheralded, as a fictioneer), I realized that the worth of his output—as well as that of the other writers associated with him and his orbit, Ambrose Bierce, George Sterling, and Nora May French, along with a few other figures—demanded some basic literary and bibliographic investigation, and critical appraisal. This led to a series of pioneering essays (since gathered in collected form), and the editing of three volumes (1965, 1970, 1971) of hitherto ungathered materials by Ashton Smith, culminating in *Emperor of Dreams: A Clark Ashton Smith Bibliography* (Donald M. Grant, 1978). The Three Musketeers of *Weird Tales* have now become solidly established internationally in English and other languages, Lovecraft and Howard much more so than Ashton Smith, but even *he* now has a definite place in the acknowledged literary landscape. The greater recognition that has at last accrued to Smith and his output more than justifies my own pioneering (foundational) research and related scholarship.

It is of some real interest and purpose to speculate what might have happened, in terms of earlier recognition and acclaim, had any one of these three writers had a volume of his fiction brought out by a major New York publisher during the 1930s. There did exist at least one writer during the 1930s and 1940s who made an unprecedented success with weird or fantastic, romantic or exotic writing, as remarkable in its manner as the fairy tales of Hans Christian Andersen. This exceptional scrivener wrote under the name of Isak Dinesen (Karen Dinesen Blixen, 1885-1962).

In one of her letters from her coffee plantation in Kenya to her family in Denmark (*Letters from Africa, 1916-1931*, University of Chicago Press, 1981), while discussing art and literature in the 1920s (although what she states applies just as much to the 1930s and 1940s, if not even more so), Dinesen points out the great hunger, the great need, among people (as understood in the international world of culture, that is, of higher culture) for fantasy, for the free play of imagination, and (in a certain sense) romance or romanticism.

The undoubted success of this unique author and her own type of fantastic and romantic tales, no less than her own memoirs, bear witness to this hunger, this need, and what it requires to satisfy it in a distinctive and original way. It does explain to some degree the distinguished and unusual success that Dinesen (in the tradition of H. C. Andersen) enjoyed with readers and critics alike: first with *Seven Gothic Tales* (1934, 1935), second with *Out of Africa* (1937, 1938), third with *Winter's Tales* (1942), fourth with *Last Tales* (1957), fifth with *Shadows on the Grass*, her second and last book of African memoirs (1960, 1961), and sixth with *Anecdotes of Destiny* (1958) and *Ehrengard* (1963), and then with both of them in one volume as *Anecdotes of Destiny and Ehrengard* (1985). The fact that the Book-of-the-Month Club chose at least three of her volumes for their special distribution and endorsement—*Seven Gothic Tales*, *Out of Africa*, and *Winter's Tales*—helped to make Dinesen's particular success all the more spectacular, given first the idiosyncratic nature of her writing and imagination, and given second the taste and temper of the times in the U.S., very different from our post-Tolkien *Zeitgeist*.

As the 1930s approached their end, Ashton Smith entertained thoughts of gathering together all his *Tales of Zothique* (his title) in a quality hardcover edition published by a major New York house. He rationally surmised that, if suitably presented as a handsome book (possible illustrated), such a collection might sell well enough, might rate favorable comparison with the fiction of Lord Dunsany and James Branch Cabell, and might score with both readers and critics, at least those with a yen for pretty strong stuff. Even today this appears as a sensible expectation. If Cabell could score with his mediaeval tales of Poictesme, why could not Smith do likewise with his tales of Zothique, and should that volume do well enough, why could he not have followed it up with his mediaeval tales of Averoigne?

Possibly Lovecraft and R. E. Howard might have entertained such hopes themselves, that is, of hardcover editions of their idiosyncratic fiction, as published by a major New York house; but neither lived long enough to see such hopes actually realized, both dying in the middle 1930s.

In any event, August Derleth and Donald Wandrei came to the rescue of the Three Musketeers of *Weird Tales* by setting up a small publishing firm, to wit, Arkham House, specifically for the purpose of bringing out their work in book form, and then by doing just that, thus giving these and other deserving authors greater permanence in terms of their best fantastic fiction. Although these poets and writers have in fact established themselves posthumously (thanks to the cults that discerning and faithful aficionados have built around their works), their early volumes from Arkham House did not receive the acclaim and accolades from the mainstream literary critics of the 1940s and 1950s that had greeted the volumes of Isak Dinesen during the 1930s and 1940s, even if the Three Musketeers were purveying a sense and style of romance and fantasy, however different in kind, that turned out as distinctive and original in their own manner as those embodied in the oeuvre of Karen Dinesen Blixen.

Let me return to myself inter alia still as an Ashton Smith disciple. To have served as a man of letters (in a sense such as Arthur Machen would have understood), to have done pioneering scholarship for the promulgation of great literature as created by great writers (even when little-known and unrecognized), and to have produced an acknowledged and respected corpus of original poetry—all this, accomplished as a labor of love (despite some financial recompense), seems to me to represent something of more than passing value, particularly in an age more than ever dominated by those twin gods, Mammon and Moloch.

In summing up, let me say that I have written and achieved to the best of such native capacity as I have, that I have husbanded and employed with great care my small stock of invention and innovation, but most of all, that I have kept faith with myself and my vocation as poet, scholar, historian, and critic. All this might not seem like so much, but in my own perspective, all things considered, and all proportions guarded, it rates as enough.

–DONALD SIDNEY-FRYER

Auburn, California,
27 February 2015

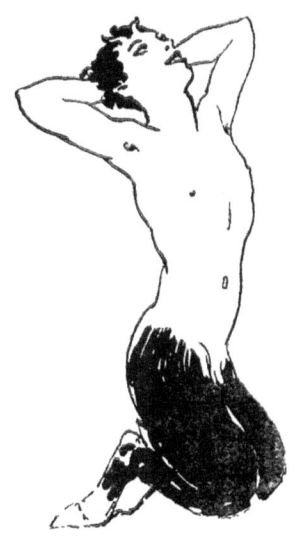

Odds & Ends

An Exotic Miscellany

Poems in Verse and Poems in Prose

DEDICATED

to RICHARD L. TIERNEY,
fellow poet and craftsman,
with deep respect and admiration.

Contents

A Spectral Realm Nearby 285
Solomon Kane Surveys the Vestiges of Empire 301
To Do Gone Like the Doe 302
Villanelle 303
"Authentic Irishman for Hire" 304
Almost As If 306
Pohnpei and Kosrae, Micronesia 307
Hawaii, the Big Island 308
Pool Sweep, Hollywood Hills 311
Just a Thought 322
A Bit of Doggerel 323
A Rendezvous with Poedelaire 325
    Preliminary Note 327
    Correspondences 329
    The Enemy 330
    Bad Luck 331
    Anterior Life 332
    "I Love You the Same" 333
    De Profundis Clamavi 334
    Duellum 335
    "I Give You These Verses" 336
    "What Will You Say Tonight?" 337
    The Cats 338
    The Broken Bell 339
    Spleen 340
    Destruction 341
    Epigraph to a Book Condemned 342

Contemplation	343
The Abyss	344
The Complaints of an Icarus	345
Consolation	347
Nenuphar	348
A Third Pilgrimage to Buddha-Land	349
Speech of Love	355
A Far-off Memory of Notre-Dame	356
On Going Past a Curio Shop Deep in Bangrak	358
Fragmentary	359
Baan Shadis, Koh Samui	360
Baan Shadis, the Swimming Pool	362
Quietude	363
Geometry for Picnic Time	364
On Walking All Around the Old Grand Palace in Bangkok	365
Aftermath	366
A Meeting with Rimbaudelaire	367
The Intoxicated Steamboat	369
Goodbye, Brother William	371
The Lighthouse Above the Cemetery	372
Undersea Tableau	373
Notes, *by Dlanod Yendis*	375

Odds and Ends

A Spectral Realm Nearby

Dedicated to Derrick and Anastasia.

The old lodge at the gate still stood shadowed and silent,
But all cleaned up, and refurbished with furniture,
Awaiting the young caretaker couple to come.
The two halves of the gate, pushed back on either hand,
Stood open wide. I had arrived from Sacramento,
In my old battered Cadillac that still was running,
On the renewed, resurfaced road that led amid
The woods and rolling hills, the prelude to the Hall,
The giant manor house with several wings and stories.

What fun to visit these old friends in their new digs,
A British-style estate in Northern California!
Often they had bought my art, and still were buying;
I was curious to see what changes wealth had brought—
Their greater affluence—for them and for their own;
They must have now become, say, multi-millionaires.
At least they had retained their family name of Jones;
If nothing else, they had invited me to visit
Sometime before the three big year's-end holidays;
I had arrived mid-autumn and mid-afternoon.

The stone mass of the house, with chimneys everywhere,
With overhanging roofs, gables at every level,
Loomed high ahead, the main door at the porte-cochère.
There I parked to one side, and went up to the door;
I rang the bell that sounded somewhere deep inside.
The door swung wide; the long-term butler, Dean, stood there.
Both of us bowed, and I did so with real respect:
Dean and I long ago had become easy friends.
"So, Master Alfred Smith, welcome! The family sits
In the drawing room. I'll take your bags to your suite."

The hallway rose two stories tall. I looked in awe
While we proceeded quickly to the drawing room;
After Dean announced me, he took my bags upstairs.
The family rose, we all embraced, then sat us down
As we exchanged the customary salutations,
The father, the mother, the youngest son and daughter:
The maid was serving tea, with sandwiches and cakes.
"I've brought some new paintings. I'll show them to you later.
They're in the trunk." The family all looked up, and smiled.
The father said, "We are quite excited to see them."

The older children, now adults, had flown the coop,
Were doing fine at college or at their professions.
I ventured, "Quite some pile you have erected here;
I was out of the country while you had it built.
A great locale, the foothills of the high Sierras!"
Here Gregory the father frowned, and interposed,
"Correction. We had it dismantled, had it shipped,
And from southwestern Devonshire, and then rebuilt,
Or (rather) reassembled here amid the woods."
I could not hide the shock my face had registered.

"Good God!" I blurted out. "That must have cost a fortune!
I'm sorry, excuse me." The father only smiled,
"That's okay. Yes, it did. It was money well spent.
A great grand-uncle on my mother's side built it
After he made a fortune in the Eighteen Hundreds.
He left it to us, only if we lived in it,
And if we did, then the major part of his wealth.
So what we did, resulted in a legal compromise,
One that the barristers could not forbid at all."
My shock had passed, I raised my hands in wonderment.

Then Anne the gracious mother added, while she smiled,
"You come on the eve of an even greater eve,
The only pagan holiday that still survives:
Tomorrow is the Hallowed Evening of the Dead."
"I had no choice, the single weekend I had free,
The only weekend that I could arrange," I said.
It happened at not quite the halfway mark between
The winter solstice and the autumnal aequinox,
On Saturday, the thirty-first day of October,
Two thousand and fifteen, perhaps auspicious and benign.

Dinner would be at eight, and we would dress for dinner.
I nodded, drank my tea, and went up to my suite,
Guided by Dean: bedroom, bathroom, and dressing room.
I showered, took a nap, and then dressed up for dinner.
Dean had brought up my new paintings from the trunk
Of my beat-up old car, and so I rearranged them
Around the room for easy viewing later on—
The space would serve as well as any other in the house,
More ample as it was than many living rooms:
The work bore witness to my last Cambodian visit.

The canvases were fairly large, five feet by four,
Some smaller, some larger, but all acutely focussed;
I would exhibit them, but during Halloween.
I was hoping that they, the Joneses, might like them,
Though much less fancy that most of my early work.
They did have more imagination, in one way,
But differently centered, maybe more of magick,
As if restoring to reality more marvel,
More of the mystery that lies behind it all,
Behind the veil that our perception might pierce through.

The dinner, overall, went very well, indeed:
Their chef was French, a master of nouvelle cuisine,
And had prepared a toothsome feast: big salmon steaks,
Asparagus, fine wines, with salad and dessert.
We talked, and listened, and we talked yet even more:
We had a lot to talk about since last we met.
I told them of my latest trip to Southeast Asia,
Of Thailand, Myanmar, then at long last Cambodia:
Of Angkor, Angkor Thom, and Angkor Wat—divine!
Last, I invited them to see my art upstairs.

Next day, at breakfast, we discussed the expo further,
And thought it best to have the art on view downstairs.
Dean with help moved it down into the entrance hall,
And there displayed it all per my preferred arrangement,
Where the light proved ideal, not too bright or diffused.
Some friends were coming-by that night for Halloween,
And so we could set up a regular exhibit.
I had the paintings covered up with towels and sheets
Until mid-eventide but after early dinner:
Electric light would work as well as daytime's own.

So dinner came early, at seven, not at eight.
The special friends who came were charming and urbane,
And everyone felt primed for something rather new.
At eight we all trooped out into the entrance hall,
Well and sensitively lit by Dean for the event,
For the two dozen paintings displayed here and there.
Since the entire family had visited Angkor
And other places in Cambodia, I was hoping
That my own "reconstructs" would edify somehow,
Thus building on whatever else that they had learned.

Halloween? We did not celebrate it otherwise,
Apart from this especial preview of my paintings:
One by one, I removed all the covers as I talked.
Look, here was Angkor Thom, and there was Angkor Wat;
Next, Preah Khan, and Phnom Bakheng with spiral trail;
The Terrace of the Elephants; the Baphuon;
The Bayon most of all with its fifty-four towers,
With its two hundred sixteen Buddhas glaring down
From every height and angle—huge kaleidoscope!—
Those calm, impassive smiles that no one can escape.

It seemed distinct from what the family could recall,
Not merely piles of stone, of carven laterite.
I had restored the sites as they had once appeared
In their prime at its height, the center of an empire:
Like day from dark, how different then compared to now!
Hundreds of statues, dazzling-bright, stood everywhere,
Of goldlike bronze or brass, with gold leaf on all parts,
Or thus it seemed. The banners flowered from every height,
Like tongues of green and blue, of amaranth and silver;
Like bees, the local people swarmed in each locale.

Tradespeople, soldiers, builders, foodstand folk, and monks,
With children, chickens, cattle, pigs, and elephants,
With funeral processions, and parades of royalty,
Thus every single spectacle of Khmer-dom!
My paints could not evoke the rich and ripe aromas,
But my art had elsewise brought it all back to life.
My audience perceived the magick I had wrought,
Warmly congratulated me, but kept on looking,
Quite fascinated. I foresaw some future sales,
A consequence that I would find quite satisfying.

Then Anne the gracious hostess-mother soon spoke up,
"I think I speak for everyone who's here tonight,
Dear painter friend, but these must rank among your best.
These paintings represent reality, but more—
Exotic, otherworldly, but still somehow real.
You bring to life a past evanished otherwise,
One even lost perhaps to present-day Khmers."
My audience applauded next, as if on cue,
Expressing "Bravo" and "Bravissimo" at large.
I smiled, and said, "Thank you—you justify my art."

More talk, a final cocktail, and the guests departed;
My hosts and I embraced, and then we went to bed,
Our heads replete with ancient Khmer imagery.
But had we slighted our own pagan holiday?—
By staging and attending our own exhibition?
Or had we added to it in some subtle way?
So I thought as I lay, quiet and calm in bed,
Before I fell asleep with further Khmer dreams:
A devaraja, yes, a god-king, in procession
With ministers, all mounted high on elephants.

The elephants in armor and brocaded hangings:
Here in dream was your fair and fabled "gorgeous East"!
The next day, going down the stairs in the front hall,
I thought that I perceived some white-robed family members
On their way to a swim. As I called out, they disappeared
Into the air. Stunned, I thought, "Could this house have ghosts?
A pride of specters brought on over from Great Britain?"
Meanwhile I'd keep this to myself but on my guard
And on the lookout for other manifestations.
Had my tableaux of old Cambodia stirred them up?

At breakfast, ere we ate, Greg took me to one side:
"Again, congratulations on your latest paintings!
When we woke, Anne and I discussed it. We would like
To buy the full two dozen—we love them that much.
Some we plan to keep, and a few we'll give as gifts;
So, think it over, and we can talk prices later."
I smiled, and I said, "Great!" But then I asked point-blank:
"Greg, is this house haunted?" "Do you mean, by the past?"
"No, I mean, is it haunted by ghosts?" "Yes, it is.
They came with the house, when we shipped it from Great Britain."

"You're kidding?" "No, I'm not. However, you need not
Fear or be concerned. They do no harm, but they help.
We co-exist as one big family more or less."
"I suppose I should feel amazed or stunned or fearful,
But I don't. Let specters be specters, or bygones."
The family found they were enjoying me so much
They begged me to remain until the next weekend.
I agreed since I wished to see more of the ghosts,
No less than to enjoy the family for itself:
We agreed on a very good price for my paintings.

I would leave on Friday to return to Sacramento:
Further than that, I could not stay due to commissions,
Some already with payment, thus needing some action.
But I saw no more of the ghosts until Wednesday night,
Until the night itself of Wodin, as it happened,
When we all had a collective hallucination,
While we seemed to be sleeping, the family and I:
When the East and the West combined to make a new magick,
While we seemed to meet outside in a broad meadow,
Otherwise in Cambodia near some templed pile.

Yes, outside that big house in Northern California,
While at the same time we seemed to exist otherwhere:
As I've said, a mere collective hallucination.
Can such things take place when experienced in common?
I can only report the adventure we shared!
We appeared to be standing with other Cambodians
Along one side at the approach to Angkor Wat,
The main one on the west before crossing the moat,
The approach on the west ever sacred to Vishnu,
The Preserver, the second god of the Trimurti.

The Preserver, one with Brahma and one with Shiva:
The thought flashed through me, and imparted reassurance.
And what did we perceive as we stood to one side?
A repeat of the dreams I had on Halloween:
A devaraja, yes, a god-king, in procession,
With ministers, all mounted high on elephants,
The great beasts in armor and brocaded hangings!
Could this be *the* Suryavarman who built the temple,
Which also served as his own tomb, his mausoleum?
The gorgeousness of the spectacle left us half blind.

The attendants on beast and on ground gripped the staffs
From which unfurled and flowered the banners held aloft
Like tongues, like flames, of green and blue, of amaranth,
Of gold, of gold and silver joined, which is electrum.
And the god-king?—Seemed handsome, strong, and muscular,
And wore aloft a high-spired, gold, pagoda-crown,
While all the half-nude bodies in procession wore
But lightly woven robes of silk with many colors.
Suddenly, down at us, the god-king turned his gaze,
And smiled . . . a warm, serene, and love-inspiring smile.

He seemed a Buddha-prince beneath a bodhi tree,
In this case under some extended gold umbrella.
Then he removed his gaze, to look ahead elsewhere,
While we returned our consciousness into ourselves,
Where we slept in our beds. Was this a dream, a vision?
Had the ghosts in the house combined with Hindu gods
To raise this vision-dream up to another level?
Could one threesome of gods—of Wodin, Thor, and Freya—
Elect to help another trinity of gods?
Could such divine co-operation really happen?

At breakfast the next day we all appeared subdued,
If not preoccupied with something beyond us,
When I spoke up, "I had the strangest dream last night,"
And then began to tell the Joneses of my dream.
They all seemed thunderstruck, amazed despite themselves:
They each confessed that they had each dreamed the same dream!
Now consternation and confusion reigned supreme,
As everyone recalled the prince's Buddha-smile,
As it seemed to recharge each person's inner life,
A genuine epiphany for everyone concerned.

I left on Friday, still bemused like one and all.
The question stayed the same: What could our vision mean?
We talked and talked, but found no answer or solution.
Whether then, whether now, it would remain a mystery,
But was it possible upon the astral plane—
Divine cooperation there, was it commonplace?
Instead of conflict and of combat, as with us?
Perhaps more of us need a place of peace and yearning:
When you have your own links to those other dimensions,
How facile to connect with spectral realms nearby!

What could our dream, our vision, mean or represent?
Were we sometimes allowed to visit our past lives?
Or was it a mere glimpse into another dimension?
What agency or entity has charge of that,
Or any other access into our inner lives?
Or any other indication from that space?
Was it a genuine group memory that we shared?
Should we not be content with what we could perceive?
A moment when a god-king looked into our eyes,
And gave us to imbibe from his own inner life?

Solomon Kane Surveys the Vestiges of Empire

>Dedicated to Gary Gianni
>for his painting of Solomon Kane
>travailling through the desert sands.

With hat to guard against the heat and glare,
With staff and sword, the weapons in his hands,
And with the skirts of his great coat aflare,
He comes, the pilgrim of unholy lands:
He gazes out across the desert sands
To where colossal ruins lapse and sprawl,
Where winds reveal the toil of many hands,
And where those beasts lift up above it all,
Those harpies that with wings extend their grasp, their pall:

He comes here, to unhex that place, to right the wrong,
That harpies fly that should not fly, that shadows crawl,
That monsters clash, with sounds that echo like a gong:

And when he conquers those old frights, he shall once more depart,
To seek out new locales—and foes—that still remain apart.

To Do Gone Like the Doe

Dedicated to Do Gentry, in memoriam.

How long, dear Do, has it been since you left—
Just a few years, or was it yestereve—
When your departing made us all bereft?
Wherever you have gone, would you believe
How much your presence, gone, could make us grieve,
The friends and allies whom you left behind?
Whatever web the days and nights might weave,
Let us not be forgetful of your mind,
And the three special books that you compiled and signed:

Your work remains incisive, elegant, precise—
You are a Virgo, and as one of the same kind,
Myself—I feel it as that mix of fire and ice:

But best of all I love *The Number of Infinity*,
    Counting the syllables upon the face of Time,
    In supple measure, thus freed up, without the rime:
The seconds, minutes, hours—our sacred *modern* trinity.

Villanelle

Translated from the French of Leconte de Lisle.
(A moonless night, during a calm, under the Equator.)

Time, Extension of Space, and Number
Have dropped from the dark firmament
In the sea motionless and somber.

With shroud of silence and of umber,
Night takes back to her element
Time, Extension of Space, and Number.

A speechless weight to disencumber,
The soul through sleep's void makes descent
In the sea motionless and somber.

In and of itself, all sinks—somber—
Remembrance, daydream, sentiment,
Time, Extension of Space, and Number,
In the sea motionless and somber.

"Authentic Irishman for Hire"

Dedicated to James Arthur McVicker, 1926–2012, in memoriam; who left Northern Ireland for America as a young man.

>Authentic Irishman for hire.
>
>Storytelling and singing,
>
>Dancing and carrying on.
>
>Available all hours.
>
>Experienced drinking companion.

(A printed placard mounted in an unglassed picture frame, as left behind by J. A. McVicker as a legacy to his son Terence.)

In spite of all the horror spawned by war,
And by religion as the primal cause,
Which makes us all the fool, that is, the dor,
Something of truth comes out of it that awes,
A something genuine that gives us pause,
Such as "Authentic Irishman for hire."
In spite of all the rules and petty laws,
Something escapes, like grace notes on the lyre,
To link its orbit and its music to some cosmic gyre:

A full-mouthed Irish brogue intones a full-mouthed Irish rune,
To exorcise from Ireland's isle the wrath, the woe, the ire—
Replace them with their opposite—a miracle and boon!

How sweet to dream to exorcise the troubles, hates, and fears—
    With a rune, with a rime, with a dance, with a song—
To add a piece of music to the music of the spheres!
    Never, alas! nor then, nor now, nor yet erelong.

Almost As If

It is almost as if somehow the cosmos grows
A consciousness, thus of itself, but only through
The life in all its forms that it creates and grows:

Not only humankind, that which in its own view
Measures all things, but gives no other life its due,
Reserving for its proper self the first estate:

And as the Measure of All Things, to start anew,
To grasp and guide its life as if ordained by Fate,
To see that which the future holds as through some sanctum's gate:

At best the cosmos is indifferent to humankind,
Which in and of itself remains a mercy that has weight,
However neutrally remote it seems, yet more than kind:

Must humankind engage a god to open up a trail?—
    Past beauty and past bane, through desert mountainscape,
Past ocean shore and forest glade, through darkness and past bale,
    On into paradise and plashing fountainscape?

Pohnpei and Kosrae, Micronesia

Up from the seafloor these twin islands mount,
Kosrae and Pohnpei, miles on miles apart—
These massive seamounts of such grand account:
If Leluh Town holds Kosrae's greatest art,
Then Nan Madol claims Pohnpei's better part,
Twin wonders of the old Pacific world:
Up from the planet's core, up from her heart,
Up from her guts, old Mother Nature hurled
Her white-hot molten rocks, mixed up, and churned, and whirled:

Over millions of years the lava flows compile
To shape each ocean-mount, the lavish greens unfurled
From shore to mountain top, to make a perfect isle:

Free from tsunami and typhoon, removed from their purview,
   Kosrae's Insaru-place and Pohnpei's Nan Madol
   Lie safe behind the shore, behind the ocean-wall.
Outside that shore, that seawall, spreads
                        the sea's dark blue on blue.

Hawaii, the Big Island

I

It came to pass, but only in the final years of his life, that he had arrived on this island, and thus as an inconspicuous elder, a man whom we shall call the Poet, also the Philosopher, perhaps the Metaphysician as well. He came to this big island by means of a curious flying ship all of metal, and thus direct from the mainland far to the east.

The island, mountainous and broad, spreads out in the Pacific Ocean, a body of water so named in 1513 by a Spaniard, Balboa, who had not yet seen that enormous ocean save in a quiescent mood unruffled by wind or tempest. The Poet called the big island by the same name that its inhabitants had called it since time immemorial, that is, as "Ha-VYE-ee."

Coming as he had most recently from a parched and arid land, the Poet found himself amazed, if not astonished, by the abundant rainfall that seemed to descend every day and at almost any hour of the day or night—and no less than by the overwhelmingly lavish verdure that the rainfall nourished, and that extended from precipitous cliffshore to mountain peak. It completely took away his breath, so much so that at times he seemed actually to have trouble breathing, so great did his wonder and marvel increase.

II

Only following his arrival did the Poet, the Philosopher, and the Metaphysician come to realize a basic and overwhelming fact about this mountainous locale. He had often thought about it when contemplating the island from afar by means of atlas and guidebook.

The two gigantic volcanoes Mauna Kea and Mauna Loa dominate the landmass. Mauna Kea has lain quiescent now for some little time, and has evolved thirteen observatories on her summit, which she will soon increase to fourteen, despite the protests of those natives who hold it sacred.

The two volcanoes have thus both lain quiescent for a while, but Mauna Loa could erupt at any time, and spew her lava flows wherever the terrain allows, above all in the saddle area between the two massive summits, and almost anywhere else except the Kona-Kailua coast on the west and the Kohala peninsula to the northwest.

The threat of destruction by these volcanoes thus assures an almost unique phenomenon in terms of the easily accessible and inhabitable parts of planet Earth. It does not permit long-term and serious construction of any buildings by human beings. Here the native goddess Pélé reigns and rules without compromise, and in this way she defeats the alien and monstrous god Mammon, otherwise as relentless as Moloch who devours all that he can.

Pool Sweep, Hollywood Hills

Dedicated to Valerie K. Beatts, in gratitude.

I

Vangelis Grahm, or (otherwise) Evanhelos
Grammatikos, but Van or Vangie to his friends,
Tied to no place, jack of all trades, master of none,
World-wanderer, maybe prodigal son as well—
He had come back, despite his self-imposed exile,
Home to Los Angeles, to house-guard, to dog-sit,
But only for old friends, and for quite a good fee—
Up at their fancy place with pool high in the hills,
With triple swimming-pool in the Hollywood Hills,
Overlooking the L.A. basin to the south.

II

Yes, Vangie had come back, despite his long exile,
Home to Lozangeleez: Smogsville, or Phony's-Ville,
As he had called the place when he was growing up:
Dear old Lozangeleez, Big Time Town, U.S.A,,
Where the Big Buck, and the Big Deal, not the Big Book,
They spoke the best and biggest lingo of them all:
"Big surprise," Van thought of it all, disdainfully,
Although his promised fee had helped to bring him back,
Home to L.A., but more, in time for Hallowe'en,
The dread Samhain, or "SAH-win," of the Keltic world.

III

His old friends had gone off to Europe, here and there,
In autumn for a month, maybe more, on vacation.
The friends, Tom and Jane Smith-Jones (yes, Smith hyphen Jones)
Had left their dogs, more like their kids, in Vangie's care,
A striking pair of sweet and handsome Weimaraners,
Male hunting dogs, and brothers from the selfsame litter,
Completely gray, both sleek like seals, and both the same,
Except that one had blue-gray eyes, the other amber,
The quickest way to tell the dogs apart by sight;
So one was called Amber, and the other one Blue.

IV

Vangelis and the dogs had bonded right away—
No wonder that they soon adored him: he was kind,
And handled them as if they were his kids, or buddies,
As constant companions, night or day, by his side.
He gave them their dog treats on a regular basis,
He took them on long walks two or three times a day,
Along the winding road to the north of the house,
Or on the open space at the top of the hills,
Or sometimes on the summit of Mount Hollywood,
Or even around that old Hollywoodland sign.

V

No wonder that the dogs adored him: he was fun,
And more than matched their own high spirits with his own.
His favored hours of day with the dogs at his side—
The early morning hour when he would sip his coffee,
The early evening hour when he would nurse his cocktail—
He spent on the terrace on the south of the house,
The wide-eaved, supermodern house of glass and stone,
Above the level of the three-part swimming-pool,
In turn above the level with the garden-close,
Both pool and garden fixed to look like nature's own.

VI

But it was that long pool that caught and held the gaze,
Those arbored, pondlike pools that linked up east and west,
That formed the chief appeal of this unique estate.
Just as the house and grounds were kept up without fail,
So did the pools get their own weekly maintenance
When someone came to clean and chlorinate the water.
The first day Vangie swam, he noted that each part
Possessed its own pool sweep, timed to work during daylight.
They seemed like big black bugs with water-spurting tails,
Like little biomechanoidal squids malign,
At which the dogs, when sprayed, would often bark like mad.
How strange at first they seemed, as if they were alive!

VII

It was evening after sunset, the cocktail hour;
On an outdoor chaise longue, or lounge, with solid back,
Van sat on the terrace with the dogs to one side.
He got up, and looked out, first to the three-part pool,
Then to the parklike garden-close, and then beyond.
There he stood, looking south, out on the glittering plain,
L.A. at night, a zillion lines and points of light—
Confused kaleidoscope, it seemed a pure illusion—
Despite his savoir-faire, it took away his breath.
All at once he recalled that it was Hallowe'en!

VIII

Although he came of Greek descent, Vangie well knew
That hallowed evening, sacred to the pagan Kelts,
When the doors opened up from the dead to the living
On that one night alone, a detail overlooked
By modern pranksters in their holiday attire.
He might have gone, by invite, to some neighbor's party,
As some Greek godling, say, Antinous himself—
He was well-built and even elegant enough—
But he had not slept well at all the day before,
And chose instead to make an early night of it.

IX

Vangie had one more drink, and then he went to bed,
As usual the dogs lying down at its foot.
Just to be on the safe side of things he had put
The alarm system on, the biggest concern being
On the north or street side, with garage, of the house.
Below the lowest level, on the south, the land
Just dropped away, but reinforced with concrete footing;
Along the sides high walls delimited the lot,
But otherwise than that, there was no need to worry:
Only a bomb, or hand grenade, could make a breach.

X

Free from external worry, Van went right to sleep.
Sometime before midnight, the dogs had stirred awake,
But then went back to sleep: Van awoke, and lay still.
However, sleep did not return. The night turned warm.
Vangie heard from afar the sound of partying,
Feeble and unobtrusive. He lapsed back to sleep,
But then woke up again, and this time stark awake.
He yawned, and thought, "A midnight swim?" Indeed, why not?
Van got up out of bed. Half-asleep, the dogs roused;
He signalled them to stay, so they fell back asleep.

XI

Leaving the house, he left the sliding glass-door open,
In case the dogs might wake, and want to follow him.
He crossed the terrace-patio, and broached the gate
That led down to the swimming-pool, which lay in darkness.
He closed the gate, but did not latch it, so the dogs
Could follow him, in case they wished. He then went down
The staircase to the first, the eastern, arbored "pond."
He almost switched the pool lights on, but enough light
Came from the city and the moon. Faintly he saw
The pool sweeps lying at the bottom of the water.

XII

In this oasis of nocturnal calm and beauty,
Van quietly lowered himself into the pool,
And plunging deep, he swam from that end to the other;
Coming up twice, and briefly, for a gulp of air.
Way at that western end he rested, then swam back,
Dog-paddling tranquilly back to the eastern end.
Odd, but he could not see the pool sweeps at the bottom,
And as he noticed this, something black touched his foot,
His knee, his back, his neck, before it slithered on.
Odd, the pool sweeps were not supposed to work at night.

XIII

Had Van done something to release them into action?
No matter, no big deal: but he would check it out
As of when he would get himself up from the pool.
He felt relaxed: another lap would do no harm.
Once more Van headed west, once again under water,
But coming up for air more often than before.
Once more a pool sweep slithered past, and then another,
Their hoses attached to the side of their own pools,
Like umbilical cords of infinite extent.
Another slithered past! Just how many were there?

XIV

One arm got tangled in a coil, and then a leg,
And then the other arm, and then the other leg.
Another spiral wrapped itself around his waist,
Another coil around his feet, and then his head.
With all his might Van struggled upward to the surface,
Just managing to gulp some air, to catch his breath,
When all the coils, like tentacles, began to tighten.
Above his head there lifted up a squidlike bulk
That neared as if it would enfold and smother him.
What awful thing was this that had him in its mesh?

XV

Van tried to yell; he had no voice. He thrashed about,
To no effect. He just let go; his end had come.
Right then, like clarion calls, he heard some furious barking
Could that be Blue and Amber, coming to his rescue?
Van could not see them, but he heard some furious plashing.
Could these dogs be the Weimaraners that he knew,
Transformed through love and stress to archdemonic canines
That clambered on the squidlike mass, to bite and rend?
What fierce primaeval scene of carnage did that moonlight
Not manifest to any eyes that might have watched?

XVI

When he regained full consciousness, Van found himself
Out of the water by the pool, with Blue and Amber
Licking his face and ears with sweet enthusiasm.
In gratitude he hugged them both. Faintly he saw
The pool sweeps lying at the bottom of the water.
"What in the hell was that?!" Van exclaimed at the dogs,
But they could only look at him, and wag their tails.
What had that been, in fact? What was it that had happened?
Was it a dream, a vision, an hallucination?
The dogs were soaking wet, and Vangie's welts were real.

XVII

At least there was no blood; it could have been much worse.
With big bath towel he dried himself and then the dogs;
He went up, and back to the house with dogs in tow.
Lost in astonishment, how strange he felt no fear!
If his adventure had been real, what was the purpose?
Was there some lesson here for him in all of this?
He, Vangie, needed to relearn that life was weird?
He thought that he had learned that lesson long ago,
But if he had, what did this new adventure mean?
Yes, life *is* weird, but is it *even* weirder than you think?

Just a Thought

Even if Shakespeare would not have had to have lived,
The English would have had to have invented him,
Such a source he becomes of stuff still not outlived!–
Just like the Bible of King James, that first Lord Jim.
Am I too bold? I go too far out on a limb?
No other source is quoted more than both of these,
A truth of truths, inspiriting, but also grim.
What other scrivener could fight such verities,
Could then deny or yet compete with such celebrities?

Forget it, do not even think about it, do not go there.
It ends up as but improprieties and inebrieties,
Thus a thing accomplished, gone and finished, bleak and bare.

In the court of literature, with none to help or heal,
To this there can exist no lawsuit, recourse, or appeal.

A Bit of Doggerel

Oh, for a burst of lyric poetry,
Exuberant, impassioned, with a wow!—
Not set in dim anteriority,
Nor yet in vague futurity, but now!—
In dark modernity, that sacred cow,
That golden calf, the start and end of time,
The future's far antiquity, right now!—
But more, a fevered antic pantomime,
Beyond accord, beyond the likelihood to chime!

The poet holds the archetypes to realize,
A paradise and paradox of paradigm,
With keen and fervent sense atremble with surmise:

Let the poet bring form and order into life,
To calm the chaos and the madness and the strife!

A Rendezvous with Poedelaire

Seventeen Translations from the French

Dedicated to Judd Hubert

Preliminary Note

The following translations from *Les Fleurs du mal*, by Charles Pierre Baudelaire (1821-1867), I frankly purpose as experimental, and experimental only. I have attempted to write them in what I term "liberated alexandrines" (except when cast in octosyllables), on occasion in iambic hexameter, but generally in no particular measure. However liberated on occasion, I have usually respected the syllabical count—usually twelve, but in a few instances thirteen or fourteen, so as to do justice to what Baudelaire is actually saying in French—that is, as my task, in more or less close English equivalence. In general Baudelaire has himself served me as my direct guide not just in terms of sense, tone, and style but especially in that of his original rhetoric. The line itself and the syllabical count per se dominate the discipline of the translation process in the present case.

I purpose the reference to Baudelaire as Poedelaire (and also that of Rimbaud as Rimbaudelaire) in a merely playful and affectionate way, but still always with respect. Even if the American poet exerted no influence on Baudelaire in his poetry, Edgar Allan Poe (1809-1849) must have had some kind of authority over Baudelaire, given the considerable time, energy, and sheer industry that the latter had to expend to make his magisterial translations into French of Poe's output in prose. Baudelaire it was who solidly established Poe's European reputation.

—D. SIDNEY-FRYER

Correspondences

Nature is a temple in which the living pillars
Permit sometimes words in confusion to come forth;
Man passes there through these forests of breathing symbols
Which observe him with eyes like those of his own family.

Like prolonged echoes that at a distance are blended
Within a shadow-filled and profound unity,
Vast as the night is vast, and vast as is the light,
Perfumes, colors, and sounds respond to one another.

There are perfumes as fresh as is the flesh of children,
Sweet as are the oboes, and green as is the prairie,
And there are others, rich, corrupt, and all-triumphant,

Possessing the expansion of infinite things,
Like amber, and like musk, and like myrrh, and like incense,
Which sing the raptures of the soul and of the senses.

The Enemy

My youth was not much more than a darkness-filled storm,
Enlightened here and there by a few brilliant suns;
The thunder and the rain have so ravaged it that
In my garden remain not many vermeil fruits.

It is there I have touched the autumn of ideas,
So that I am forced to use the spade and the rakes
To gather once again the inundated lands,
Where the water digs holes as capacious as tombs.

And who knows whether the blossoms that I conceive
Shall find in this earth, washed like the shore by the sea,
The mystic nourishment that would create their force?

O dolor! O dolor! how Time devours our life,
And the dark Enemy, who keeps eating the heart,
Increases and strengthens from the blood that we lose!

Bad Luck

(*Le Guignon*)

To lift up a burden so heavy,
 Sisyphus, we would need your courage!
Though we have the heart for the work,
How long is Art, how brief is Time!

Far from the renowned sepultures,
Toward an isolated graveyard,
My heart, just like a muffled drum,
Goes beating some funereal march.

—Many a gem-stone sleeps enshrouded
In the shadows and oblivion,
Far from pickaxes and from drills;

Many a flower pours out with regret
Its perfume sweet as is a secret
Lost amid profound solitudes.

Anterior Life

A long time have I dwelt beneath vast porticoes
Which ocean suns have touched up with a thousand fires,
And which their columns high, straight and majestical,
Have made to look, at night, like grottoes of basalt.

The surges, rolling back the heavens' images,
Have blended in a way solemn and mystical
The chords, all-powerful, of their own lavish music
With the flames of the sunset mirrored in my sight.

It is there I have dwelt in voluptuous calm,
In the midst of the blue, of the waves, of the splendor,
And of the naked slaves, all imbued with perfumes,

Who have refreshed my face with fans made out of palm,
Whose one and only care was this, to fathom deep
The secret weight of grief that makes me languish still.

"I Love You the Same"

*(Baudelaire probably addressed this kind
of abbreviated sonnet to Jeanne Duval,
his live-in lover of more than fifteen years.)*

I love you the same as the firmament of night,
O you urn of sadness, O you great silent woman,
I love you, my fair one, the more you flee from me,
The more you appear, O ornament of my nights,
Ironically to accumulate the leagues
Which divide mine embrace from the vast space of blue.

I go to the attack, I climb to the assault,
As after their feast the worms climb over the corpse,
And I cherish, O beast implacable and cruel,
Even that coldness which makes you more beautiful!

De Profundis Clamavi

("Out of the depths have I cried to thee," Psalm 130.)

I implore thy pity, Thou, the unique one whom I love.
From deep in the dark gulf into which my heart fell:
A mournful universe with horizon of lead,
And where horror and where blasphemy swim in the night.

A sun without warmth hovers above for six months,
And the other six months the night obscures the earth;
A country more barren than any polar land;
—Without beasts, without streams, without green, without woods!

There is no horror in the world that could surpass
The frozen cruelty of that sun all of ice,
Or that enormous night so like that of old Chaos;

I envy the fate of the lowest animals
Who can plunge themselves on into a torpid sleep,
So slow the skein of time is it to come undone!

Duellum

(For Leo Grin, *duellum* as the older Latin word for *bellum*.)

Two warriors have rushed up, the one against the other;
Their weapons blaze the air with lightnings and with blood.
These feints, these clinks and clanks of steel, remain the clash
Of youth at prey to love, its bleatings and regrets.

The swords have broken, the same as in our youth,
O my belovèd! But the teeth and nails of steel
Shall soon avenge the sword and the treacherous dagger.
O furor of old hearts driven insane by love!

On into the ravine, the haunt of lynx and leopard,
Our heroes, heedless, grappling one on one, have rolled,
And their skin shall transform the briar-thorns to flowers.

This abyss, this is hell, but peopled by our friends!
There let us roll without remorse, strange Amazon,
To make everlasting the passion of our hate!

"I Give You These Verses"

I give you these verses in order that my name
Might happily make landing in some distant age,
And one evening might make some human spirit dream,
A vessel favored by a great northerly wind.

The memory of you, like some uncertain fables,
Will fatigue the reader as would a dulcimer,
And through a link both brotherly and mystical
Will rest as if suspended from my lofty rimes;

Accursèd one to whom, from the profound abyss
Up to the highest sky, nothing responds, save me!
—O you who like a shade with tracks ephemeral,

Promenade with light step and with serene regard
Over the stupid mortals who have judged you wrong,
Statue with eyes of jet, great angel with brow of brass!

"What Will You Say Tonight?"

What will you say tonight, poor solitary soul,
What will you say, my heart, heart shrivelled long ago,
To the One, very fair, very good, very dear,
Whose divine glance has all at once renewed your life?

—We shall set our pride to the singing of her praises:
Nothing can compare with her sweet authority;
Her spiritual flesh has the perfume of Angels,
And her vision invests us with a robe of light.

Whether it be at night, whether in solitude,
Whether it be in the street, or in the multitude,
Her phantom dances in the air like a flambeau.

Sometimes she speaks, and says, "I, the fair one, command
That for love of me you love only what is Beauty;
I, the guardian Angel, the Muse, and the Madonna."

The Cats

The fervent paramour, the austere scholiast,
Love equally the same, when both become mature,
The sweet and puissant cats, the pride of their own house—
Like them, they dislike cold; like them, they like to sit.

The friends of science, and of voluptuousness,
They seek the silence and the horror of the dark;
Erebus would have them for his funereal steeds,
If they could bend their pride to serve him as their lord.

They assume, when they dream, the noble attitudes
Of great Sphinxes aligned across the desert's heart,
Great beasts that seem to sleep in a dream without end;

Their fecund loins abound in thaumaturgic sparks,
And tiny specks of gold, like tiny specks of sand,
Make tiny stars appear within their mystic eyes.

The Broken Bell

Bitter and sweet it is, during the winter nights,
To listen, near the fire that palpitates and smokes,
To distant memories that slowly lift them up
At the noise of the chimes that sing out in the fog.

Thrice happy is the bell with a vigorous throat
Which, in spite of its age, yet alert, sounding far,
Still faithfully sends forth its summons of religion,
Like that old soldier keeping watch under the tent!

Me?—my soul has been cracked, and when in its ennui
It wants to fill the cold air at night with its songs,
It often will happen that its enfeebled voice

Seems the death rattle of a wounded man forgotten
Near a lake of blood, beneath a pile of the dead,
And who dies, immobile, amid colossal efforts.

Spleen

Pluvius, annoyed with the city overall,
From his urn in big waves pours a cold overcast
On the pale residents of the nearby graveyard
And on the mortals of the suburbs lost in fog.

My cat on the tiled floor, exploring for a litter,
Agitates without stop his body sparse and mangy;
The soul of an old bard wanders in the rainpipe
With the melancholy voice of some chilblained ghost.

The bell mourns to itself, and the log, wreathed in smoke,
Accompanies in falsetto the sniffling clock,
While in a pack of cards, imbued with stale perfumes,

The deadly legacy of some dropsical crone,
The handsome knave of hearts talks with the queen of spades;
They have an obscure chat about their loves defunct.

Destruction

Without stop by my side the Demon agitates;
He swims around me like an air impalpable;
I gulp him down and feel him where he burns my lungs
And fills them with desire guilty and eternal.

Sometimes he takes, knowing my great passion for Art,
The form of the greatest seductress among women,
And under the specious excuses of depression,
Accustoms my lips to the most infamous philters.

Thus he conducts me, far from the regard of God,
Panting and crushed by fatigue, on into the midst
Of the plains of Ennui, far-reaching and deserted.

And he casts before my sight, replete with confusion,
Garments that are filthy, and wounds that have gaped open,
And the apparatus, dripping blood, of Destruction.

Epigraph to a Book Condemned

Dear reader, peaceful and bucolic,
Man of good will, sober and naïf,
Cast aside this book saturnine,
Orgiastic and melancholy.

If you did not your rhetoric
Under Satan, that cunning dean,
Cast this aside! you will learn nothing,
Or you will think me hysterical.

But if you can resist enchantment,
And if your eyes can sound the gulfs,
Read me so you can learn to love me;

Inquisitive soul, who has pain
And who seeks out his paradise,
Pity me! . . . or else I curse you!

Contemplation

(Recueillement)

Do be wise, O my Grief, and keep yourself more tranquil.
You reclaimed the Evening; it descends; it is here:
A darkened atmosphere has overcast the town,
To the ones, bringing peace; to the others, concern.

All the while that the vile multitude of the mortals,
Underneath Pleasure's whip, that merciless torturer,
Goes harvesting remorse amid the servile feast,
My Dolor, give your hand to me; and come this way,

Far from them. See the years that have died, where they bend
From heavens' balconies, in garments out of fashion;
See rise up from the water's depth my smiling Regret;

The dying Sun going to sleep beneath an arch,
And like a long shroud dragging toward the Orient,
Hear, dear heart, hear sweet Night who walks with muffled step.

The Abyss

Pascal had his abyss, which he took everywhere.
—Alas! all is an abyss—action, desire, dream,
And Words! and on my hair, which will stick straight upright,
I sense the wind of Fear many times when it passes.

Above, below, depth everywhere, with distant shores,
Silence and space, with savage fright that imprisons ...
On the gulf of my nights God with His knowing index
Designs a nightmare multiform that leaves no trace.

I am afraid of sleep as of a great big hole,
Full of shapeless horror that leads one knows not where;
Through all the windows I see but the infinite,

And my spirit, always haunted by vertigo,
Envies the insensibility of the void.
—Ah! never to escape from Numbers and from Beings!

The Complaints of an Icarus

The lovers of the prostitutes
Are happy, free, and satisfied;
As for me, my arms have been broken
Because I have embraced the clouds.

I must thank the stars nonpareil,
Which flame deep in the sky's abyss,
That these eyes, consumed, cannot see
But the memories of the suns.

In vain I have tried to discover
The end of space and its midpoint;
Beneath some eye of fire or other
I can sense that my wings are breaking;

Burned by love of the beautiful,
I shall not have the sublime honor
To give my name to the abyss
Which for me will serve as a tomb.

Consolation

"I need," my friend cried out, and cried full bore,
"I need a dose, I need a great big dose
Of music, magic, mystery, and more!"
I looked him in the eye, I held him close,
I said, "I also need that great big dose
To keep me going, balanced, sane, and whole."
I stopped, while keeping him on hold up close.
"Look, my friend, when you stand upon a knoll
In triumph, do not fret about the mountain as a whole.

"Why fret about the peak? Look after your own piece of slope.
The galaxy somehow survives, just like its own black hole.
While caring for your own locale, you give yourself some hope."

I stopped again. He stared at me, and gave a great big smile.
I then smiled back. We held that grin, and for a good long while.

Nenuphar

Wherever found in Earth's wide labyrinth,
Both commonplace and rare these blossoms are,
The orchid, the rose, and the amaranth:
From this choice group we cannot yet disbar
The water lily, or the nenuphar,
Some tropic species famous for their size:
Whether we search close by, or seek afar,
Whatever the varied colors of her guise,
Purple, green, or lavender, she still remains a prize:

A prize for hue, for image, and for general shape,
Her loveliness pervades where water flows or lies,
Wherever the opened mouths of her great blossoms gape:

Thus, like the orchid, the rose, and the amaranth,
The water lily flourishes in much of Earth's wide labyrinth.

A Third Pilgrimage to Buddha-Land

*Dedicated to Supisith and the staff
of the Swan Hotel, Bangrak, Bangkok.*

The Poet, the Philosopher, and the Metaphysician,
A threesome all in one, along with the Magician,
If not perhaps a magus from the distant past:
He is the hero of our tale, the protagonist
Of this our well-versed and wide-ranging narrative,
Don or Donaldo or even Don Donaldo,
Otherwise the Elder Poet or the Scrivener.
He had returned once more to Bangrak in Bangkok,
To the Swan Hotel, to the dear old Swan Hotel,
A sweet consummation devoutly to be wished.

Though he had not thought in advance to chronicle
This tale, he found himself doing so and why not?
Write what you know, the old adage firmly advises.
This was his third sojourn-visit in Southeast Asia,
In Thailand, formerly Siam, and in Cambodia,
And all contained within that which is Greater Asia,
Or Macronesia, in the style of Micronesia,
But Macronesia is a term but seldom used,
Beyond its usage in the present narrative:
An alternative mode always makes itself welcome.

Don Donaldo had come from far-off California
For what was his third pilgrimage to Buddha-land,
On a quest once more for exotic sights and sounds,
Bangkok itself, Ayutthaya, perhaps Chiang Mai.
Meanwhile he had the best base from which to go forth,
To Koh Samui, the tourist isle far to the south,
To Cambodia, or Kampuchea, the chief sites there,
Phnom Penh, Siem Reap, Angkor above all else,
That wonder of the ancient and the modern world,
As wonderful as anything extant from Ancient Aegypt.

What a joy to find himself back in this hotel,
In this boutique hotel, with but seventy rooms,
Balconied on two sides of the great inner courtyard,
With right in the middle of the four-story building,
The immense, rectangular, blue-tiled swimming pool,
Some twenty feet by forty feet, twelve feet at the deepest.
The single story on the west possessed a roof garden
With palm trees, fountains, bushes, and little palm trees,
Some set in pots and ceramic boxes, with two
Buddha-shrines to one side in the midst of the verdure.

But the staff, the staff, yes, the quite wonderful staff—
What a joy once more to greet and see that great staff!
Supisith, the handsome, even-handed manager,
Gracious, eternally serene, and affable.
The gracious and capable Madame Lek (pronounced Lake),
Head of the service in the dining room and kitchen,
Presenter of the food, its layout and its freshness.
Noy, unique, the embodiment of enthusiasm,
The smiling ambassador of good will and good cheer,
The server-attendant in the restaurant at night.

Another server-attendant in the eatery at night,
The slender, lovely Lady Noy, also Noy Noy,
So called by Noy to distinguish between the two.
And the last but not the least of the permanent staff—
Trim, neat, well-knit, handsome, always genial and smiling,
Bunjong, thus the all-use, all-purpose handyman,
To be found anytime anywhere fixing some problem.
I speak not of the office staff—I don't know them—
But I must mention some of those at the front desk,
Such as My, Nan, Em, Nyu, of those who come to mind.

With the Swan as his base Donaldo ventures forth,
To pay his respects toward the Ambassade de France,
That odd, octagonal construction on the west—
Could it be something like an oval octahedron?—
Or when he ventures north on into Chinatown,
A vast unknown terrain, a very labyrinth
Of streets and tangled alleys, dead ends or connected:
Where the walker enters the mysterious East,
Where the random shop or eatery might stand closed,
Long abandoned with all the furniture intact.

How strange to walk the deserted streets on Sunday morning,
With little traffic to confuse the pedestrian—
Dear Arthur Machen would have enjoyed such a stroll.
As Don penetrated deeper into this maze,
He seemed to enter some forgotten twilight zone
Of what looked like abandoned shops and restaurants,
With no metal grill or roll-down to protect them.
Dark and dusty they seemed within, the plate-glass windows
That showed nothing inside, where no people were moving.
Other windows, blind with dirt, prevented any vision.

One restaurant in particular held his attention;
A large and showy structure, it stood on a corner.
At first he thought that it was open, with folk inside,
But as he approached to look in, they disappeared.
He received an electric shock! Had he been dreaming,
Or had he projected his personal fantasy
Upon external forms? As he approached, he saw
That the proprietors must have left long ago,
Even though he noted little dust or dirt inside;
He turned, and slowly made it back to his hotel.

He somehow found his way out of that labyrinth,
Out of that twilight zone that somewhere lies beyond
Our commonplace and our everyday ur-dimension.
Thoroughly affrighted, he rejoiced to come back
To the ordinary, into the light and sound
That he could share with other folk, regular people.
Several Western women sat around the pool—
Beautiful young women, bikini-clad, they seemed
Hard-edged, smart-ass women, and smoking cigarettes.
Otherwise disdained, they helped him regain his balance.

Had he somehow trespassed on into some dream-world,
The gate to which had somehow opened up for him?
Still puzzled by it all, he waited to go forth
On the next Sunday morning with the streets deserted,
To see what he could find. And he searched and researched
For several hours in the cool of the early daytime,
But search as he might, he could find nothing at all.
No special, unmarked gate could he now re-discover,
No portal that would lead on into unknown paths,
On into an unknown and quite forgotten past.

Still puzzled by it all, he yet accepted it,
A rare departure on into something unknown.
How seldom do such adventures still come to pass!
Once past his fear, his fright, Donaldo realized
How lucky he had been to have had the adventure.
Paradoxically he began to cherish it,
In memory, as a treasure of the greatest value,
Worth more than gold or silver or even orichalch,
That pale flame-gold that Plato features in his fable
Of the lost but always re-discovered island of Atlantis.

Speech of Love

Like the splash
And the flash
Of flamingoes past the sun
And their scarlet on the sky

Like the plash
And the clash
Of the waters where they run
In a fountain at Versailles—

Like the birth
In the earth
Of the nightworm stretched at length
In the grass blades on the ground—

Like the fire
In the lyre
From the fingers at full strength
On the strings of metalled sound—

Such is mine elemental prayer to Thee,
        O Thou Universe,
With the Word, with the Verb, with the one
        and only speech—in verse.

A Far-off Memory of Notre-Dame

(Un petit poème en prose à la Baudelaire.)

The Elder Poet once more found himself ensconced at the Swan Hotel in Bangkok. The hotel faces north, only a few miles southwest of the old Grand Palace, and very close to the Chao Phraya river that flows right here to the west. The Swan Hotel has remained for the Elder Scrivener a solid refuge and a secure oasis.

On the ground floor the hotel rents several shop spaces to various businesses, and behind them a corridor separates the shops from the hotel's restaurant, rather like an indoor alley. The shops look out north onto the street like the hotel, but they also look out onto or into the wide corridor between them and the restaurant. Both the eatery and the shops have inner windows, tall and wide.

One of the shops has conspicuously featured on its own large window a see-through photographic image of Notre Dame de Paris, once much loved and celebrated by Victor Hugo in the novel with the same name as the cathedral. The image offers a lateral view of the church complete with flying buttresses and an imposing rose window, this view showing to one side the altar end rather than the front with the two towers.

During the High Middle Ages the ecclesiastical authorities had the cathedral constructed on the site where the Temple of Jupiter once had stood. On one of his visits to Paris the Elder Poet had once prayed at one of the five altars at the inner end of the great interior space. Kneeling before an altar left of center, he had intoned a prayer or two, but with a difference.

As he had looked around him, the Elder Scrivener remained acutely cognizant of the soaring and inspired Gothic architecture that enclosed him, not to mention the odor of sanctity, the ghost of incense past and present.

When he knelt down inside the pew he had chosen, he had made the Sign of the Cross in the traditional manner, and he held his hands in proper prayer mode before him, in the style so eloquently depicted by Albrecht Dürer in one of his most famous black-and-white sketches.

Conceiving to himself the Temple of Jupiter that had stood there for a long time, but very long ago—during the period of the Roman Empire when Paris bore the name of Lutetia Parisiorum as one of the capitals of Gaul—the Elder Scrivener proffered his prayers not to any Christian deity such as Jesus, Joseph, or Mary, nor to any of the numerous demigods or demigoddesses known as the martyrs and/or the saints.

But instead, intoning the several Roman Catholic prayers, he directed them (with suitable adjustments) otherwise, one to Jupiter as father and king of the gods, and one to Isis, as a once popular avatar in advance of the Virgin Mary. And the Elder Poet intended these redirected prayers just as piously as if he had said them to Jesus, Joseph, and Mary. So be it, *ainsi soit-il*, amen!

On Going Past a Curio Shop Deep in Bangrak

One day, while walking in old Bangkok town,
I spied a lovely, black-skinned figurine,
Indra the god, with his high turban-crown,
And with (all over him) a glamour-sheen,
With lusters here and there, and in between,
And with his wondrous head of elephant!
His eyes betrayed a wisdom seldom seen,
No less his wondrous trunk, as was his wont,
Wisdom not often made so manifest right up in front!

Fragmentary

Full moon along the Nile, along the Pyramids,
Near ancient Memphis, where—with little now to show—
One might well ask, Where are those massive fanes and shrines?
Those giant courts and pylons, all made out of stone,
The statues made of stone and brass, of gold and silver?
The plenilune reveals the starkest emptiness,
The sterile nothingness that the desert remains.
The splendors here, of Memphis, ranked with those of Thebes,
The hundred-pyloned Thebes that stands far to the south.
The stones here have departed, rafted down the Nile,
Long ago, to form part of Cairo and Fustat,
With little or nothing for later spade or shovel.
Thus in the end Ptah had to yield before Amoun,
And then the Christian god, that uttermost eclipse.

Baan Shadis, Koh Samui

(Koh Samui, Thailand)

Two Australian investors own this compact resort, and had the seven main structures designed and built in 2001. The resort sits in the middle of a coconut plantation-forest. Baan Shadis covers about half an acre. The name translates as House or Place of Shade, a name now quite well deserved. Going from south to north, we begin with the biggest building, the large office edifice, which sits up higher than all the others (except for the water tower), and whose extended verandah in front facing north measures about thirty-four by twenty feet.

We continue through the pool area, a special and separate locale, and then reach the main space, with the five cottages or villas, three on the west, and two on the east. The main resident lives in the first cottage on the left, and a young (Russian) caretaker couple inhabit the third cottage on the same side. Almost all the structures have low hip roofs of red tile to discharge the heavy rainfall, above all in the winter, heaviest in December, gradually lessening in January and February, the months that are the main tourist season.

The owners chose to have bamboo planted abundantly, so that the mature stands furnish privacy and real shelter from the blazing summer sun, the hottest season of the year. Each cottage has its own good-sized verandah, as well as a small one in the back, largely unused. Typical of tropical architecture, all the roofs extend far out, say, about a yard from the stucco walls.

The long rectangular property, with a suitably large parking lot, faces the paved road on the west. On the north and west, the outer walls of alternating wood and stucco panels divide the resort from the road and the outside. Inner stucco walls divide the pool area from the rest of the resort. On the south and east, an unpaved road, bamboo stands, with trees and bushes, demarcate the property from the surrounding area.

In the extreme northeast corner of the resort, a strategically important structure rises up above everything else, the water tower with the roofed-over storage chamber (a permanent steel ladder climbs up to it), supported on four thick square pillars atop their square cement foundation. Two big shining stainless-steel water tanks lift up inside the storage chamber.

The chief neighbor to the north on the same road (which leads into the town of Maenam), but past some "organic" native abodes, harvests the coconuts from the ambient plantation-forest, to process them for the meat, the milk, the oil, and the fiber, a major industry in many of the tropical islands at least of the Indian and Pacific Oceans, wherever a heavy enough rainfall allows the coconut palms to produce in lavish abundance.

Baan Shadis, the Swimming Pool

The gem, the pearl, the pride, the prize of Baan, or Bahn, Shadis remains the swimming pool and its ample environment, separated by rather more attractive stucco walls than those dividing the resort from the outside. The over-all place furnishes us with a perfect example of what the British term a compound, a term deriving from the Malay *kampung*, or village.

The kidney-shaped pool measures roughly fifteen by thirty feet, and about six feet at its deepest. Emphasizing the separation from the rest of the resort, the walls around the pool area remain the most attractive, pierced as they are by pretty windows or apertures with pointed arches, rather suggestive of Indian, or Indic, architecture.

In most of these apertures variously sized jars, mostly brown, dominate the window ledges. It reminds our Elder Poet a little of the *Arabian Nights*. The stands of mature bamboo flourish on either side of the simple stucco walls. The feathery fronds at the top of the bamboo seem to mimic the more solid fronds at the top of the coconut palms.

The pool appears to invite the swimmer to step down into the cool and lovely depths of the water accented by the medium dark blue tiles. (The tiles in the big pool at the Swan Hotel contrast with these at Baan Shadis by their baby blue color.) The broad flight of outward-curving stairs on the south side—of which the steps themselves are done in baby blue tiles (with the margins in azure)—helps the swimmer to descend into those cool and inviting depths.

Quietude

When in the quiet vigils of the night,
Secure within some verdant garden-close,
And distant from all things that harbor fright,
How sweet to sit amid the world that grows,
Wrapped in the idleness that grants repose!
A peace descends that never seems to end,
One wants to hold it tight before it goes,
But care and vigilance we must expend
Unless back to the Other Side one might by chance transcend:

Transcend whenever time ordains, through fate or circumstance,
When soul must part from flesh wherein it lives
                                        while bound and penned,
Until another birth and life, then onward to advance:

Beware the hidden ecstasy that lurks in quietude,
It might prove fatal if—if too relentlessly pursued.

Geometry for Picnic Time

We often picnicked on that promontory,
That famous headland with the elder shrine,
Long since renowned in fable, song, and story,
Where it lifts up above the ocean's brine,
Where vines and broken columns intertwine,
Somehow the curving volutes yet intact,
The columns making three times three, or nine,
Three columns for three sides, per each in fact,
The shattered stones more beautiful for being prone and cracked:

The Atlanteans might have built the shrine, or so folk say—
If that is true, how long ago would they have had to act?—
Where earthquake and tsunami once long since have had their way:

Strange piety to drink and eat with ruins as the table,
Somehow that seems more appropriate for something in a fable.

On Walking All Around the Old Grand Palace in Bangkok

The king as god must always live apart
Out of sheer need. These lofty walls, these towers,
Protect his person, to protect his heart,
His status as a source of awesome powers—
Beyond mundane—here, where his godhead flowers,
In sacred circumstance and privilege,
In halls, in chambers, and in verdant bowers,
And plied with love, with food, with beverage,
Even when he would live as would a monk, close to the edge—

The edge of mere existence, in austerity,
To counterpoint his status and its leverage—
This points his self-control, his true divinity:

That latent paradox of power, exemplified long since,
The Buddha shows him how to rule . . . his person, and as prince.

Aftermath

The storm had raged all night from dusk to dawn,
And then it cleared. At low tide, at midmorn,
We walked down to the beach, to find what spawn,
What spoils, the waves had left. We spied a horn,
A narwhal's horn, a single unicorn!
But where then was the whale? There was no whale.
In wonder we picked up—and held—that horn,
Keeping it with us, while we took the trail
Down to the cave, to look for any change brought by the gale.

Unending tides and storms had carved an awesome lair
Out of that spacious cave, fit locus for some grail,
Sculpting odd forms and shapes, fantastic, foul or fair.

We found a shelf above the tides, and laid inside that nest
The single narwhal's only horn, an apt and arcane place to rest.

A Meeting with Rimbaudelaire

(During his later life.)

The Intoxicated Steamboat

As usual, the drunken steamboat plied
Between Djibouti, Africa, and Yemen,
Arabia, while it lurched from side to side,
Like seaman seeking prostitute or leman,
As any sailor worth his salt or semen.
Nor captain nor skipper, the boss man sat
In the cabin, remaining thus the key-man,
While pondering the divers cargo that
His ship transported without pity, waste, or fat.

The vessel carried guns, and slaves, and ivory,
Where those enslaved but without option also sat,
Chained, in the hold below, like breathing ebony.

Nor fabled peacocks nor yet Golden Fleece
        as worthy freight or cargo,
Just human entities for sale or trade
        in this ignoble *Argo*.

Goodbye, Brother William

Dedicated to William C. Farmer, in memoriam.

Fare-you-well, dear friend William, fare-you-well,
Back to whatever bourne you have returned,
For some celestial space in which to dwell:
Summer Nineteen Sixty, too long inurned—
Summer Twenty Fifteen, too soon inurned—
Our friendship made a far-enduring arc:
Fifty-five years the flame of friendship burned
Before you left our regions of the dark,
With light-filled space to merge, for anthem-hymns to hark:

Magus of history, theology, and poetry,
You have withdrawn where other realms will fire in you their mark,
Until you come back here in some obscure futurity:

You had me enter that Crown Court, that of the Faerie Queene,
A place to linger, to abide, in truth a matchless visne.

The Lighthouse Above the Cemetery

The lighthouse stands above the burial ground—
An odd choice, but from here the ships at sea
Perceive the beacon without bar or bound:
Despite the waves' unending monody,
Despite the storm's huge fugue and melody,
The silence forms the greater music here:
The wind's susurrus makes polyphony
From all the other sounds that tease the ear
As to their source, or whether minor, minimal, or mere:

What fuels the beacon's flame? Or coal or wood or gas or gases?
Decaying bones, decaying coffin with decaying bier?
Or from the graveyard's decomposed or decomposing masses?

Does any wisdom from the dead ascend to feed the flame?
To taint the lighthouse keeper's mind—with ill that has no name?

Undersea Tableau

(For Wade German)

The massive temple sits beneath the ocean
But not so deep that seaweed cannot grow
Like mad, away from chaos and commotion:
The currents here swim quiet, calm, and low,
While solo fish dance past, waltzlike and slow,
No sharks or other predators in view:
Sometimes a single crab will come and go,
Enter the fane, to say a prayer or two—
Its devoirs done, it ambles on, for many a pace or few:

True, Mother Nature might be red, at times, in tooth and claw,
But sometime also whimsical, with charm, as if on cue—
She runs the gamut from refined to nasty, crude, and raw:

And so the undersea parade processions on and on,
From dawn to noon, from noon to night, from midnight
                                                back to dawn.

NOTES

by Dlanod Yendis

A Spectral Realm Nearby.

Several big houses on big estates at Lake Tahoe might answer to the description of the mansion featured in this narrative poem.

Pohnpei and Kosrae, Micronesia.

This poem reflects the latter part (two weeks) of the month that the author along with a friend took, from mid-April on into early May of 2015, to visit parts of the Pacific Ocean. It was the monumental ruins at Nan Madol on Pohnpei (PON-pay), and at Insaru in the town of Leluh (LAY-luh) on Kosrae (KOSH-RYE or KOR-SHY), respectively, that led the author and his close friend to choose these especial islands to visit amid the vast stretches of water that make up most of Micronesia.

Hawaii, the Big Island.

This poem in prose reflects the first part (two weeks) of the month-long trip undertaken by author and friend to selected islands amid the Pacific Ocean in the Spring of 2015.

Pool Sweep, Hollywood Hills.

This narrative poem does actually reflect an experience that happened to a friend house-guarding an estate in the Hollywood hills (that overlook the plains of Los Angeles to the south), minus the supernatural element. He did get entangled in the extensive hose of one of the pool sweeps that service the multiple pools that lie below to the south of the house.

Nenuphar.

This poem has evident affinities with *Amaranth* that appears early in the third series of *Songs and Sonnets Atlantean*, to which it is a pendant.

Fragmentary.

This "fragment" reflects the author's not quite month-long trip in Egypt during February 2013. The itinerary included Cairo, the Pyramids, Saqqara, the Serapeum, Memphis, Thebes, Aswan, and Abu Simbel. Although technically winter, and cold or cool at night (it was almost hot at Abu Simbel), the days were comfortably warm. The author deliberately chose not to visit the antiquities above during the summer. Due to the need to return home in Westchester (Los Angeles) because of a crisis, the poet could not visit Alexandria and the half-dozen good-sized towns in the Western Desert, originally planned as part of the trip.

On Walking All Around the Old Grand Palace in Bangkok.

This piece came into existence to honor King Mongkut, who lived and studied as a monk for a long time before he assumed the throne. He counselled his people about the Europeans, "Welcome the strangers." In this and other ways he preserved the independence and autonomy of Siam. He saved his people from foreign (European) domination during the nineteenth century, a major piece of thaumaturgy at the time, not only magical but miraculous.

A Meeting with Rimbaudelaire.
The Intoxicated Steamboat.

The reference to (Jean-Nicholas-) Arthur Rimbaud (1854–1891) as Rimbaudelaire, not less than that to *Le Bâteau ivre* as *The Intoxicated Steamboat*, are merely playful and affectionate. The poem itself is a fiction, a pure fantasia, based upon aspects of Rimbaud's later life and career as an African adventurer and only incidentally based upon aspects of his earlier life and career as a poet. The references in the poem are neither geographically nor historically "correct," it should be patent. His tumultuous love affair with Paul Verlaine (1844–1896), Rimbaud left behind him when he departed for Africa at nineteen.

Anyone seriously interested in Rimbaud as person and some kind of great poet must somehow square his later life (as a slaver in Africa) with that of the idealistic and gifted youth who was the fervent enthusiast and champion of Baudelaire (1821–1867) as a major literary figure. This problem has obvious parallels with those that the earnest student might also have squaring the early and later ideal of the dandy (to which Baudelaire aspired) with the great poet that he became.

Donald Sidney-Fryer at 76.

ABOUT THE POET

Poet, performing artist, critic, and literary historian, Donald Sidney-Fryer is the last in the great line of California Romantics that reaches from Ambrose Bierce to George Sterling, from Sterling to his protégé Clark Ashton Smith, and from Smith to his disciple Sidney-Fryer.

Carrying on the tradition of "pure poetry" begun in early modern English by Edmund Spenser and revivified by the English and American Romantic poets (Samuel Taylor Coleridge, John Keats, Percy Bysshe Shelley, Alfred, Lord Tennyson, and Edgar Allan Poe), long after the mainstream poetic establishment had abandoned it, the California Romantics created two monuments in verse, Sterling with *A Wine of Wizardry* and Ashton Smith with *The Hashish-Eater*.

During his long career Sidney-Fryer has given dramatic readings from these poets and from Edmund Spenser's epic *The Faerie Queene*, across the U.S.A. and Great Britain.

Overall he has written and edited some two dozen books and booklets. He has edited four books by Smith for Arkham House and three paperbacks, also by Smith, for Pocket Books, in addition to *A Vision of Doom*, 50 best poems by Ambrose Bierce, published by Donald M. Grant, who has also brought out Sidney-Fryer's monograph *Emperor of Dreams: A Clark Ashton Smith Bibliography*.

From 1980 to 1999 Sidney-Fryer assembled *The Case of the Light Fantastic Toe* (still awaiting publication), his massive historical monograph on the Romantic Ballet. As a poet Sidney-Fryer has crafted *Songs and Sonnets Atlantean* (the first series), the final book to appear from Arkham House under the personal supervision of its founder, August Derleth; as well as the *Second Series*, published by Wildside Press; no less than the *Third Series* brought out by Phosphor Lantern Press; all these now subsumed in an omnibus edition.

That large collection of poetry, prose-poems, and curious notes, *The Atlantis Fragments*, Hippocampus Press (beginning in 2008-2009) has published along with other books whether Atlantis-themed or not, whether authored or edited by Sidney-Fryer, including these titles: *The Hashish-Eater* (narrative in blank verse), by Clark Ashton Smith; *The Outer Gate: The Collected Poems of Nora May French*; *The Golden State Phantasticks* (collected essays and reviews); *The Atlantis Fragments: The Novel*; and the present volume. These other publishers have also brought out some of the other writings by Sidney-Fryer: Black Coat Press, Centipede Press, Mirage Press, Silver Key Press, and Silver Scarab Press.

Moreover, Sidney-Fryer has accomplished his chief prosodic innovation, the creation of the Spenserian stanza-sonnet, long before the recent and welcome emergence of the group of poets known as the New Formalists, who have restored a much-needed and long overdue balance to the ongoing evolution of American poetry and poetics. As an innovative poet working in traditional forms, besides reviving the Spenserian stanza itself as a vehicle for lyric poetry, he has also created a new blank verse cast in alexandrines.

Although he has resided in both Northern and Southern California (alternately since 1955), the self-styled Last of the Courtly Poets presently lives in North Auburn, and thus northeast of the state capital Sacramento.

www.ingramcontent.com/pod-product-compliance
Lightning Source LLC
Chambersburg PA
CBHW070958160426
43193CB00012B/1829